OECD DOCUMENTS

THE CURRICULUM REDEFINED: SCHOOLING FOR THE 21st CENTURY

PUBLISHER'S NOTE

The following texts have been left in their original form to permit faster distribution at lower cost.

ORGANISATION FOR ECONOMIC CO-OPERATION AND DEVELOPMENT

ORGANISATION FOR ECONOMIC CO-OPERATION AND DEVELOPMENT

Pursuant to Article 1 of the Convention signed in Paris on 14th December 1960, and which came into force on 30th September 1961, the Organisation for Economic Co-operation and Development (OECD) shall promote policies designed:

- to achieve the highest sustainable economic growth and employment and a rising standard of living in Member countries, while maintaining financial stability, and thus to contribute to the development of the world economy;
- to contribute to sound economic expansion in Member as well as non-member countries in the process of economic development; and
- to contribute to the expansion of world trade on a multilateral, non-discriminatory basis in accordance with international obligations.

The original Member countries of the OECD are Austria, Belgium, Canada, Denmark, France, Germany, Greece, Iceland, Ireland, Italy, Luxembourg, the Netherlands, Norway, Portugal, Spain, Sweden, Switzerland, Turkey, the United Kingdom and the United States. The following countries became Members subsequently through accession at the dates indicated hereafter: Japan (28th April 1964), Finland (28th January 1969), Australia (7th June 1971), New Zealand (29th May 1973) and Mexico (18th May 1994). The Commission of the European Communities takes part in the work of the OECD (Article 13 of the OECD Convention).

The Centre for Educational Research and Innovation was created in June 1968 by the Council of the Organisation for Economic Co-operation and Development and all Member countries of the OECD are participants.

The main objectives of the Centre are as follows:

- *to promote and support the development of research activities in education and undertake such research activities where appropriate;*
- *to promote and support pilot experiments with a view to introducing and testing innovations in the educational system;*
- *to promote the development of co-operation between Member countries in the field of educational research and innovation.*

The Centre functions within the Organisation for Economic Co-operation and Development in accordance with the decisions of the Council of the Organisation, under the authority of the Secretary-General. It is supervised by a Governing Board composed of one national expert in its field of competence from each of the countries participating in its programme of work.

Publié en français sous le titre :
REDÉFINIR LE CURRICULUM :
UN ENSEIGNEMENT POUR LE XXIe SIÉCLE

Foreword

The purpose of this report is twofold. Firstly it brings together the principal results of the thoughts and action on curriculum matters in CERI during the last decade. Secondly it is a running commentary on a very broad and diverse range of topics discussed at an international Conference which was organised in order to review the CERI work and to draw upon the expertise and experience of a large and varied body of specialists from OECD countries. This breadth of interest is presented in one volume to ensure continuity and to give the reader a better flavour of the Conference deliberations. The papers presented to the Conference are retained since they add to the diversity of the debate and provide insights into particular issues and concerns.

Thus two sets of perspectives are evident in the report, that of the rapporteur, and those presented by specialists and country representatives. This combination enriches the report and enables readers both to identify the unifying ideas that were pervasive in the conference and to pick out the viewpoints of those who individually presented papers.

The major contribution in drafting this report and editing the papers is that of Phillip Hughes, Emeritus Professor of the University of Tasmania and Consultant to the OECD in 1993. Professor Hughes collaborated closely with the Secretariat in preparing the final publication.

Table of Contents

Introduction 9

Opening Address 13

I. CONTINUITY AND CHANGE 15

   1. A basis in past OECD work 15
   2. A continuing debate 15
   3. The Conference of Ministers, 1990 17
   4. Trends and issues 19

Paper 1 Curriculum Reform -- Recent Trends and Issues 20

II. CONTEXT AND GOALS 29

   1. The context of change 29
   2. Implication of commitment to quality for all 30
   3. Issues for reform 35

Paper 2 An Agenda for Reform in the U.S.A. 37

   4. Goals of education 41
   5. Curriculum goals as statements of value 45
   6. Processes of reform 47

Paper 3 Ends and Means in Curriculum Reform 49

III. PROCESS AND PARTICIPATION IN REFORM 51

   1. Curriculum reform: A major social task 51

Paper 4 Implications for the Curriculum of the OECD Activity on the Effectiveness of Schooling and of Educational Resource Management 52

   2. Centres of power and control 65

Paper 5 Curriculum Reform and its Implementation 70

Paper 6 Implementation of Curricula in a College 89

5

IV. THE CURRICULUM: MEANING AND IMPLICATIONS 93

    1. The Content, Structure and Organisation of Learning 93

Paper 7 The Core Curriculum 95

Paper 8 The Common Core 101

    2. Science, mathematics and technology 103

Paper 9 Project on Innovations in Science, Mathematics, and Technology Education 104

Paper 10 Technology in the School Curriculum 114

    3. Humanities and arts education 117

Paper 11   Project on Humanities, the Arts and Values in the Curriculum 118

Paper 12   Media Education, Trends and Experiences -- seen from a Humanistic Point of View 136

    4. Changes in teaching and learning 141

Paper 13   Implications for Curriculum Reform from OECD Associated Projects 144

    5. Pupil assessment, evaluation and system accountability 163

Paper 14   Relating Pupil Assessment and Evaluation to Teaching and Learning 165

Paper 15   Mass Evaluation Exercises in France since 1989 170

Paper 16   The Contribution of International Comparative Assessment to Curriculum Reform 173

V. THE CURRICULUM FOR THE TWENTY-FIRST CENTURY 187

Paper 17   Curriculum for the 21ST Century 192

PANEL DISCUSSIONS 198

Paper 18   The Options to Emerge: Where do We Travel From Here? 208

Paper 19   Summary Comments 212

ANNEX: LIST OF PARTICIPANTS 217

Introduction

This is a report on the Conference on The Curriculum Redefined, held in April 1993 in Paris, but covers a much wider territory. It acts as a summation of the work and thinking on the curriculum centred on OECD over the past decade. In that period, OECD and its Member countries have been active in their reflections, studies and activities on the school curriculum, taking account of the massive changes which have occurred. These changes are evident not only in technology, but in political associations and boundaries, in social mores and attitudes, in economic situations and approaches and in the outlooks and expectations of individuals for the future. In many countries this review has already led to significant changes in policy and structures yet it is clear that the most significant changes lie ahead.

The report is thus, inevitably, also a consideration of prospects and policies for the future. Our societies face the most significant educational challenge since the introduction of universal compulsory education. The challenge is to give reality to the commitment to a high quality education and training fro all, a commitment announced by the Conference of Ministers at OECD in 1990. The magnitude of that commitment, as this book emphasizes, implies not only change in the school curriculum, but concomitant changes in pedagogy, in school links, in teacher education and the involvement of all elements of society. In no sense is it a prescription for the future. That would not be realistic nor would it suit the diversity of our needs. It does identify major issues and needs which we face in common and to which all our societies will need to respond. Also indicated are some of the ways in which these responses can usefully develop.

This report is organised in five major sections.

In the first section, Continuity and Change, the background events and thinking, leading up to the current situation, are reviewed and analyzed. This analysis is brought together in the paper, Curriculum Reform -- Recent Trends and Issues, which stresses the importance of the social and cultural context of change and the need for a major social effort to build consensus if societies are to meet the changes in prospect.

The second section takes up the need for contextual analysis and identifies the major issues to which political, social and educational responses are to be made. The next two papers, though brief give significant examples of such responses. In paper 2, the now-confirmed US Under-Secretary of State for Education, Marshall Smith adumbrates the major agenda for educational reform, which faces the Federal and State governments. It is an unusual example of the use of informed thinking and research in the development of a political agenda. Of particular significance is the fact that Marshall Smith as a researcher at Stanford University had a particular interest in the study of educational change. This interest may assist in the difficult bridging needed between the time-scales of political and educational reform. In the other paper, Sir Claus Moser, recently retired Warden of Wadham College, Oxford, outlines a quite different type of initiative in educational reform. The National Commission on Education in Britain is a privately funded initiative, developed because of the perceived failure of Government to respond to the urgency for change. In future developments, both types of initiative will clearly be important.

9

The third section covers Process and Participation in Reform, looking both a the broad OECD scene and at particular national initiatives. Judith Chapman considers OECD activities and studies on the effectiveness of schooling and their implications for reform across the broad range of Member countries. Takashi Yamagiwa focuses on a particular national situation, considering how reform ideas have worked out in practice and the issues which remain for resolution. With Monique Claude's paper this focusing goes further, to the context of a particular institution. It is precisely this interaction between school initiatives, national priorities and broader social and educational concerns, which OECD is able to clarify and strengthen.

Section IV deals with Curriculum Meanings and Implications. It explores key ideas such as core curriculum in the papers of Malcolm Skilbeck and Didier Dacunha-Castelle, indicating the unavoidable issues which each society must find ways of resolving. Again, these broad but vital concerns are anchored by specific accounts of area where the concerns must find resolution. Mike Atkin deals with the area of science, mathematics and technology and the issues raised for general education. A promising initiative using case studies is explored. This is taken further in the analysis on technology by Paul Black. A more contentious area is explored by Robert Moon in humanities, the arts and values. The area of values emerges as a central issue in almost all considerations, and is still more remarkable for the questions raised than the answers available. These issues are explored further in the paper on media education by Birgitte Tufte.

Two major sets of OECD initiatives are explored next. OECD has significant activities under the headings of lifelong learning, vocational education and training, environmental education and students with special education needs. The Hughes paper explores the possibilities that these areas offer for reform, not only in the analysis of foundation ideas such as life-long learning but in the identification of new teaching and learning possibilities in the area of vocational education and environmental education. The picture which begins to emerge, and is further clarified by the issues raised for students with special educational needs, is not an enterprise with a signal, neat resolution but a highly complex inter-relationship requiring advances and initiatives of many kinds. The evaluation issues explored by John Nisbet, Claude Thélot and Tjeerd Plomp with William Loxley provide another set of challenges and opportunities. A potential clash exists between evaluation for student assessment, as a help for learning, and evaluation for monitoring, as a help for management, accountability and resource allocation. The easy solution is to concentrate on one or the other approach. The challenge her is the constructive use of data for both sets of purposes, achieving both improved learning and greater equity.

The final section, The Curriculum for the Twenty-First Century is necessarily open-ended. We are not now, and are unlikely to be in the future, in a stage where clear prescriptions for the future are possible. Yet we are at a period when, if we accept the goal of a high quality education and training fro all, we accept also the need for a reconsideration not of the curriculum alone, but of the ways schooling operates, of school and class organisation, of teaching and learning approaches, of the uses of technology and of the involvement of people and groups in decision processes. Robert Carneiro explores these broad questions, asking us to be prepared to think and act in quite new ways. The Carneiro agenda is then taken up by the Panel of John Singh, Walo Hutmacher, Chiara Croce Castelletti, Ed Bales, Robert Harris and Bi Puranen. Each was asked to concentrate on developing a signal aspect from the Carneiro analysis.

The final conference paper by Malcolm Skilbeck identifies seven major themes which might form the basis for action, by OECD or the member countries, individually and in concert. These seven themes identify areas of activity from which priorities for action will emerge. The summary comments emphasise this further, that the surprising degree of commonality on curriculum issues, and the desire to move further ahead, are to be seen not as "prescriptions or recipes but as starting points for action or further consideration." Our actions and inactions, our decisions and indecisions, will shape the curriculum in all our societies. The continuing and underlying question in this book is to ask "Can we shape the curriculum to strengthen our societies and enhance the quality of personal life?"

Opening Address

Opening remarks by Mr Pierre Vinde
Deputy Secretary-General, OECD

Ladies and gentlemen,

It gives me great pleasure to welcome you to this conference on the Curriculum Redefined -- Schooling for the 21st century. This conference represents the culmination of five years of work in which all countries here present have participated in one way or other at various stages -- either by submitting case studies and other information, by attending meetings at the OECD, or by organising national seminars. I take this opportunity to thank your authorities most warmly for the strong interest shown in this CERI activity and the long-standing support it has received. At the same time, we are convinced that all countries stand to gain from continued cooperation in the analysis of data and the discussion of issues related to school curricula. We have much to learn from one another's experience and in jointly creating ideas for the future.

The OECD/CERI curriculum activity has been based on work in five areas:

-- Learning to Think -- Thinking to Learn
-- Core curriculum
-- Pupils' assessment and evaluation
-- Science, mathematics and technology education
-- Humanities, arts and values.

Reports on all of these areas are available either in published form or as part of your dossier. But this conference attempts more than a synthesis of the results of work in these five areas, significant as that undertaking would be as an end in itself. It brings together, for the first time, the results of work on the school curriculum being carried out both within CERI and within the Education and Training Division of OECD. As you will see this body of work covers a large territory and through it we have become more conscious than ever before of the very real challenge facing all those who would re-define the curriculum.

In a sense, this conference can be seen as a continuation of the deliberations of the Education Ministers who met at OECD in 1990. Their theme was High Quality Education and Training for All. This remains the underlying theme of the present conference which is centred on the challenges posed to the school curriculum by a changing world, a world where many young people emerging from our present school systems are insufficiently prepared to meet the challenges confronting them and, therefore, see unemployment as a major threat.

We believe that the school curriculum represents the heart of the educational reform process, the place where the goals of reforms, the ideas for change are turned into the reality of the learning situation. For this reason, a conference on school curriculum is a means of bringing into focus a wide range of concerns and issues. Despite all the work that this conference brings together and the expertise and experience you as participants will bring to it, the aim is not to produce detailed prescriptions or specific solutions. They remain the responsibility of those in charge of the education systems in Member countries. However, we hope that given the prospective nature of this conference you will together be able to reach a broad set of agreements about directions to take in terms of what constitutes

13

the curriculum, how learning outcomes are assessed and what the basic definitions of High Quality Education for All involve.

Each of you brings a personal experience as well as professional knowledge and expertise to bear on these issues. One of the abiding questions in the curriculum debate is whether it is desirable, and if so in practice possible, to reach basic agreements on a common set of learning experiences, values and beliefs for schools to foster and develop. And, if we do think this is the way to go, what of the great and indeed growing diversity of countries and cultures and the individual path each student must follow. Democratic societies seek both a common base of ideas, values and beliefs and the freedom for individuals to develop and express themselves. Schooling, it seems, must endeavour to strike and to maintain a balance between the two. What that is and how it is to be expressed through the curriculum is, I hope, one of the issues that will be examined in depth as the conference proceeds. There are also other issues which you will have to address such as the balance between the arts, humanities and sciences; the changing nature of assessment; and the continuing challenge to prepare young people for the dramatically changing world of work.

The OECD commitment to education has been both long and consistent. Education is one of the great formative influences in our society quite clearly contributing to economic development but it is also an agent in enriching and broadening social development. The emphasis today is on the future, not on an unrealistic attempt to predict its outcome, but on concrete and practical ways to shape what we individually and collectively wish that future to be. Decisions we take now -- as governments and societies or as individuals -- concerning the education system and its contents will contribute to this future, either positively or negatively.

The final paragraph of the Education Ministers' Communiqué says "The challenge of the 21st century will not be met in a spirit of more of the same". It is with this idea in mind that I wish you well with your deliberations and affirm that OECD looks forward to what emerges from this conference as a crucially important contribution to its educational programmes for the years ahead.

I. CONTINUITY AND CHANGE

1. A Basis in Past OECD Work

The concerns of this report, which direct our attention firmly to the future, are strongly grounded in the thinking, initiatives and programmes of OECD relevant to education in recent years. It may be important to look back briefly at some of these, before looking ahead, for the issues identified and the problems needing resolution are still relevant and in many instances even more pressing.

The OECD Secretariat initiated in 1987 a series of projects on which Malcolm Skilbeck reported (1990) in a state-of-the-art study of trends and issues in curriculum. It involved analysis of questionnaire returns, expert colloquia and a selected literature review.

The study emphasized the domination of the context of action for schools by economic and social concerns arising from structural adjustment, employment changes, new ethnic patterns in the population and the change from prescriptive value systems into "...the relativistic and elective styles that characterise the industrial democracies". It continued by emphasizing the convergence across countries in the preoccupations of policy-makers and opinion leaders.

> "Thus, there is a widespread concern for the overall quality of learning in classrooms and the acquisition of basic skills; parents are enjoined and affirm the right to be directly involved in the schooling of their children; assessment of pupil performance is on everyone's lips; the curriculum is to become more vocational in tone and direction; learning skills are emphasized over subject content and multi-skilling is a key word for life preparation; and the need for improving the accountability of the education service is reiterated" (Skilbeck, 1990).

This convergence of thinking, from the 1987 returns and discussions, is still very evident and has been carried further in a number of instances by national initiatives, sometimes through legislation, sometimes through administrative action.

In examining specific sectors, Skilbeck concluded that in elementary schooling there was a need to reconcile individualisation of teaching and a flexible pedagogy with system requirements for age-related content and testing. He identified comprehensive approaches to reform in Italy and Japan, both well-conceived and emphasizing the importance of primary schooling yet both "illustrations of the 'top-down' approach which is now all but universal". The same tendency was observed at the secondary level, where curriculum issues were seen as central. Yet, he points out, that central concern is not reflected in wide and well-informed debate, either public or professional. The results in many countries showed a consistent move to build secondary curricula around an enlarged core of compulsory subjects. Skilbeck raised the pertinent question as to whether this was a sufficiently forward-looking response.

2. A Continuing Debate

The contention is lively and continuing. Britain's Education Secretary, John Patten, stated the government position clearly in a recent article:

15

"My over-riding aim is to improve opportunity for all children of whatever background in our state system. ...Excellence will be available for all. To do this, we need competition for excellence in schools. By 2000 I want most state schools in this country to be centrally funded and running their own affairs. Their success or failure -- the bad ones will close --will depend on how good they are, on the parents they attract and the pupils those parents send to those schools. ...We need to push on with our radical programme of giving more power to schools themselves and taking it away from bureaucrats" (Patten, 1993).

In this instance, the greater power given to schools is in the context of a national curriculum which in Patten's words "sets out what children should be taught so they all get the equal opportunity that the 1960's theorists talked about but never managed to produce". In this case, the equal opportunity comes through parents choosing schools on the basis of test results at ages 7, 11, 14 and 16. For their part, teachers, and more recently the teachers unions, have expressed deep concern at the haste with which the testing is being implemented and the possible injustice to schools if decisions are made on the basis of test scores with no reference to the nature of the population of each school. It is possible that the increase in choice for some parents may be at the cost of wider equity.

The differing views on assessment, so strongly held, confirm the need identified by Skilbeck for a vigorous and open debate, featuring all participants. Other issues, similarly, are very much alive. One is the need, at both elementary and secondary levels, to reconcile the requirements of society for responsibility, order and vocational readiness, with the freedom of the individual. Skilbeck sees this balance as having to be developed in the core curriculum, where "values education is not well focused, yet there is widespread concern about human conduct and behaviour". A further issue identified was the need for a flexible and adaptive curriculum rather than a tightly defined form. The social and technological changes prompting this need, continue at an even faster pace. For this to happen, the need was seen to involve the schools and the teaching profession in the implementation. At the same time as this local involvement was obtained, Skilbeck stressed the need for a more comprehensive approach to the curriculum, one that went beyond the curriculum design itself, to include guidelines for implementation involving adequate support services. This would confirm the need for attention to the central issue of the consideration of the values implicit in the education process.

The need to translate the many expectations, themes and issues identified in the survey constitute an agenda for new directions in schooling. That agenda relates to the whole curriculum, with the central issue being the core curriculum, those learnings essential for all students. To do this, the study states, requires that the continuing debate be on a wider base of participation and develop a clear view of the central mission of the school in contemporary society. A further issue identified is the need for schools to demonstrate clearly that standards of student performance have been maintained, even in the context of the increase in numbers and the broader spectrum of educational participation. This may well be the case but schools and systems have not been convincing in demonstrating it to be so. In the absence of such demonstration, external criticisms of the schools becomes sharper.

Skilbeck stresses that the schools' success in maintaining progress under difficult circumstances should encourage the education profession to take a leading role in the process of large-scale curriculum implementation. This is particularly necessary where there are large-scale national initiatives, as in France, Italy, Japan, America, Britain, Australia and New Zealand. The tension between vocational, utilitarian and instrumental functions, on the one hand, and liberal, humanistic and general education values on the other, can be a healthy situation. From such a tension, purposes and priorities can be clarified and effective impetus given to the change process. Again, this remains to be done.

The final tension identified is between the concept of a commonly shared set of values and beliefs which can help to shape curriculum and pedagogy, and the idea that there is no common pathway and that many routes need to be followed.

> "Perhaps the answer is that both approaches are correct. Not a single student, anywhere, should be deprived of access to fundamental forms of knowledge and ways of experience. ...But both individuals and society need the specialist skills, techniques and understandings upon which the very existence of society depends..." (Skilbeck, 1990).

The Skilbeck analysis of curriculum issues drew on the studies and discussions of 1987. Essentially, those issues remain unresolved and are part of the continuing discussion on curriculum as illustrated in the British example. They remain active focuses of concern and of policy initiatives in many Member countries and their responses and activities will be further addressed in this paper. The OECD work programme has also continued the study of key curriculum issues. One series of studies focuses on particular areas of the curriculum: e.g. science, mathematics and technology; humanities and arts education in the curriculum; vocational education; and, the effectiveness of schooling and of educational resource management. Another group of studies has identified particular curriculum themes as worthy of attention: e.g. core curriculum; pedagogy and learning with particular emphasis on thinking skills and on the implications of the current broader concepts of intelligence; the highly contested areas of assessment and evaluation and the interrelation of both with the curriculum. These work programmes of OECD report here on their findings and suggestions for further action but they already represent a substantial development, following on the Conference of Ministers.

3. The Conference of Ministers, 1990

The commitment of OECD to continue and deepen these concerns was confirmed strongly at the Conference of Education Ministers, held in Paris in November 1990, the first such meeting for six years. The task was seen as identifying the main challenges of the 1990s, setting priorities in the light of these and deciding on appropriate strategies and options. While there were differences in national approach, in institutional traditions and in stages of development, the Ministers commented on the substantial degree of common ground. This common ground was affirmed by the theme chosen for the Conference: High Quality Education and Training for All (OECD, 1992a). This issue had arisen clearly and strongly in the Skilbeck analysis for OECD. It is the issue addressed, sometimes in differing ways but with a clear recognition of the same purpose, by the activities of the Member countries. High quality for all remains the key issue and from its analysis and development will come the nature of the curriculum for the future.

The Ministers' Communiqué concluded its analysis of the challenges for the 1990s, on covering the new economic, social and cultural challenges for OECD countries:

> "These challenges and changes make learning pivotal to contemporary progress. Initial education and training systems need to be of such universally high quality that all young people secure the foundation of knowledge, skills and values to enable their full participation in meeting these different challenges. To do so, they should acquire the ability to learn and relearn. Widespread and flexible opportunities need then to be available to build on that foundation through education and training, formal and non-formal, organised recurrently in accordance with the aim of lifelong learning. These ambitious aims raise the broad issue of

17

financing of education and training, against the background of continued constraints on public budgets" (OECD, 1992*a*).

This statement, while recognising the constraints on education, identifies an agenda which is indeed ambitious but on which realistic hopes for our future depend greatly.

In developing that agenda for policy and action, the Ministers' Communiqué identified eleven goals.

"(i)   *A high quality start to lifelong learning -- the crucial role of initial education and training*. Effective schooling should lay the ground and motivation for continued learning -- in all -- settings. Effectiveness is strengthened through close partnerships.

(ii)   *Quality and access in a lifelong perspective*. Quality provision should be as much a feature of vocational programmes, higher education, enterprise training and adult education as it is of schooling.

(iii)   *Education for all implies priority for the educationally under-served* ...countries cannot afford to leave large pools of talent untapped.

(iv)   *Overcoming illiteracy* ...illiteracy in the traditional sense and in the new forms generated by ... change.

(v)   *The need for coherence and focus to avoid curriculum overload*. The widening range of tasks and clienteles call for a rich diversity of offerings and of teaching methods... Diversification of offerings thus accompanies convergence of purpose -- the aim is to develop programmes that meet the talents and interests of all. To avoid incoherence and overload, the special tasks and missions of each level should be clarified.

(vi)   *Improving the quality and attractiveness of teaching in education and training*. Expert, motivated, flexible teaching staff are the most vital components of high quality provision...

(vii)   *Information and data: preconditions for sound decision-making*. Well-developed information and guidance systems -- for pupils, students and trainees, but also for parents, the employment sector and the wider community.

(viii)   *Evaluation and assessment -- identifying progress, diagnosing problems*. Evaluation and assessment -- of students, trainees, institutions and the system as a whole -- should constitute an integral component of policy and practice.

(ix)   *Research and innovation need further development*. The potential of educational research as an integral element of improvement remains largely underdeveloped...

(x)   *Enhancing the international dimension of education and training policies*. Increasing interdependence [implies the need for] acquisition of foreign languages...mobility of skills...comparison of research findings, educational indicators and practical experience across countries...

(xi)   *Financing high-quality education and training for all.* Realising high-quality education and training for all depends on investment [for the] young and in recurrent education. New approaches to the financing of post-school education and training must be considered..." (OECD, 1992a).

In the final paragraph of the Communiqué, the Ministers emphasize that "The challenges of the 21st century will not be met in a spirit of 'more of the same'". As is evident from the variety and scope of the OECD work projects, it is in this understanding that the work has continued.

4. Trends and Issues

The continued relevance of the issues of the survey and the applicability of the Communiqué goals does not imply a lack of progress, either in the Member countries or in the general programme of OECD. Nor should that relevance and applicability be accepted too easily. The further changes of the last few years, both in social circumstances and in decisions and actions on education make it necessary to re-appraise priorities and emphases and to make further assessments on the issues to be faced and the decisions to be taken. The next section of this report will consider the changing context and the implications of that context for our redefinition of goals. In the section to follow that, we seek to consider the themes and the issues raised for the major conceptual and practical task of redefining the curriculum. In looking ahead to another century we should not be limited in aspirations or efforts by the achievements of the past. Neither should we forget the lessons which are discernible from history, particularly with respect to curriculum change. Continuity and change, vocational and general education, common values and individuality, each of these involves a constructive tension out of which new concepts and practices will arise.

The next paper considers how these issues have developed in recent years and how they relate to our present circumstances.

Paper 1

CURRICULUM REFORM -- RECENT TRENDS AND ISSUES

by Phillip Hughes and Malcolm Skilbeck

New Trends -- or a New Urgency?

The task of considering the implications of curriculum reform is not new. The curriculum is a subject of continuing concern, in most if not all Member countries and the education programmes of the OECD, which have had a significant dimension of curriculum analysis over a long period. The task we have, of identifying important issues and deciding on action has of course, been carried out before. How have the issues changed in recent years, or is it just the context which has altered?

In 1987, OECD initiated a survey amongst its Member countries, a survey of recent trends and issues in curriculum reform. There was a strong response from the Members and OECD used the analysis of these responses to publish a state-of-the-art report on curriculum reform (Skilbeck, 1990). That report played a significant role for the 1990 Conference of Ministers for OECD, setting priorities and directions for the years ahead. In October 1992, OECD convened a conference with a different membership. The Hiroshima Conference on International Education involved seven OECD Member countries and six of the Dynamic Asian Economies, (Taiwan, Hong Kong, South Korea, Thailand, Malaysia and Singapore). That conference, too, identified a number of issues common to all participants. Those issues, identified by a more diverse group, in a different setting, and some five years later were almost identical to those outlined in the report on the 1987 OECD survey.

The first issue in common was that of the major potential influence of education on broad social issues, economic development, employment, social cohesion and order, individual well-being. The requirement for high quality in education was a second issue, in particular the need to develop foundation levels of knowledge, understanding, skills, shared values for all students. The third was the importance of cultural and moral values and the need for a balance between social responsibility and individual freedom. The changing nature of work and its continuing impact on the concept and practice of vocational education, and of general education, were a fourth issue. Decision-making in education, its location and the participants was a fifth issue. The final common issue was on the management of change , and the ways in which evaluation mechanisms and processes could and should be used. In the most recent identification, managing and resourcing expansion was identified as a major issue. It had not been specifically identified in the earlier occasion.

What is the significance of this continuing interest in the same or similarly stated issues? One conclusion is that these are quite basic issues, of a general and pervasive character, fundamental to our thinking about the curriculum. Further than that, their continuation implies that they are not easily resolved, that a continuing effort is required. The Ministerial Conference pointed out in their report, significantly, that the recurrence of the same issue at different times does not necessarily imply the same response. They used the issue of "quality in education" as an example. "This combination -- growing expectations of education alongside unprecedented criticisms and the declining recognition of the professionals -- suggest that the concern for raising quality is, in important measure, an expression of malaise and confusion about the educational ends and means. A challenge for the 1990s is thus to engage in fundamental debate, positively inspired rather than defensively reactive, about the major goals to be set for education in all its different settings and the means by which they can actually be realised

20

in practice. If the 1980s debate about quality in education has been to establish the case for change, that of the 1990s may well go much more profoundly into what change should be and how it should be brought about". (OECD, 1992).

This comment on the search for quality provides a more general reminder to us. If we are now dealing with the same issues, albeit in a new context, can we now move forward? What priorities should we set? What actions need to be taken? Where do we require further study or discussion? In deciding what needs to be done, we need to look again at those issues which have shown such durability. In particular, the contentious nature of the concept of quality must be borne in mind. How will quality be defined? And by whom?

The Continuing Issues

The impact of education

In the late 1980's and early 1990's there was a dramatic change in political context. The Berlin Wall was destroyed and Germany became one country again. Changes in the Soviet Union led to the dissolution of the Union, the emergence of separate republics, the fall of Soviet communism as a dominant political power and the end of the Cold War. In Eastern Europe, once seeming indissolubly linked together, the separate countries emerged and some, like Yugoslavia, broke up in further and hostile units. The economic scene, already gloomy in 1989, became even more so, with a substantial recession, major disagreements on international trade, substantial economic restructuring and, through it all, meagre or negative employment growth and rising levels of unemployment, especially high among the young. Concurrently change of a less visible or dramatic nature, but potent for the future, continued in science, technology and culture. There was a rising tide of concern over social problems including poverty, crime, homelessness and drug abuse, with growing drains on the social services added to a sense of deep discomfiture and anxiety about the future. Throughout this period of dramatic change, political and community leaders expressed confidence in the capacity of education to be a major agent in beneficial change, if with some qualification, usually in the form of remarking on the gap between the potential and its actual performance.

In the period of growth of the 1960s optimism about the effects of education was taken for granted. The rationale for the extension of the interest of OECD into education during the 1960s was the assumption that increasing participation rates in education and increasing achievement levels were not only desirable social purposes, but were a major requirement for economic growth (OECD, 1965). In the mid seventies this belief was suspended, if not cast aside. One factor was the substantial recession following the crisis in oil supply. Another was the particular interpretation based on the Coleman and Jencks' studies on school effectiveness, which raised major questions about the value of education as a social investment. Now, we see that belief restored, not perhaps with the same easy optimism. Many of those who had accepted that investment in education would of itself yield economic benefits now had a harder edged belief, that investment in effective education would yield economic benefits, where 'effective' was defined to mean acquiring particular skills and competencies relevant to vocation. The easy optimism of the 1960s had not returned. The new feeling contained an element of mistrust. Investment in education can be worthwhile, provided there is a monitoring of outputs as well as inputs. Such investment, moreover, must be on the basis of a very broad understanding of the education process, the agents and institution responsible for it and the links it forms, especially with technological development and other research and development. That is, the very concept of education, and hence of its impact, is taking on a wider, more diverse range of meaning.

Quality in education

The title for the 1990 Ministers Conference was chosen to reflect an ambitious aim, High Quality Education and Training for All (OECD, 1992). The conference emphasised that this was not merely linked with a critical aspect, the need to improve on inadequate performance. It was a forward-looking emphasis "seeking to identify more clearly than hitherto the qualities that are most relevant for young people and adults as the twenty-first century approaches".

At the Hiroshima Conference, two years later, the emphasis remained, but now with a more specific reference. The words of the Swedish Under-Secretary of State are representative: "... our own history and wealth have proved the intimate relationship between a nation's prosperity and the qualities of its educational system. This relationship is abundantly clear. And when this relationship is proved, education policies are no longer an area to be the exclusive preserve of specialists and technicians ... The key to success lies here in building an educational sector that is cost-effective, productive and quality-oriented" (Eiken, 1992). Again, there is an emphasis here on the benefits of an education which is responsive to national needs and is required to show its efficiency in specific results. These results are to be disclosed not only in the longer term and frequently intangible, impact of education, for example the labour market, or scientific and technological development or social mores, but immediately through new means of monitoring and quality control. Some of their means are quite directly related to the curriculum and especially to ways of assessing learning.

Cultural values, moral values, individual rights

This continuing issue is strongly emphasised throughout the period, yet is more elusive and difficult to define. Spirited cries for an renewal of interest in values education are heard on all sides. But what, precisely, can schools do in societies characterised by pluralism, cultural diversity, moral relativism and the abandonment of a common foundation, either religious or secular? In the tension between continuity and change, order and individuality, there is something ambivalent about our approach to values in spite of the lasting interest and growing concern. "Values education is generally not well-focused yet there is substantial evidence of a widespread concern about human conduct and behaviour" (Skilbeck, 1990). Moral issues are highly publicised: racism, sexual harassment, violent crime, drug abuse, sexually transmitted diseases. Yet moral education is one of the least well defined areas of the curriculum. Schools alone cannot determine the cultural and ethical values that are to be taught. There is need for a community wide dialogue and debate on these difficult matters and for greater investment in research and development projects.

Vocational emphasis

Throughout the period under review, vocational education has been a continuing and indeed a strengthening emphasis. It is also an area where the conception itself is changing dramatically as the work-place needs and opportunities change. The role of general education in contributing to vocational preparation is now more clearly recognised, as is the failure of the view that vocational education is a matter of training in set skills. For the period of compulsory education, the vocational aspect is now more constructively recognised. Rather than being an inferior course for the less able, the vocational element is now seen as capable of providing a motivational aspect to general education which it has lacked for many students. Vocational education will, however, require substantial political and community support to establish it as an equal partner.

The vocational emphasis may also provide a diversity of settings which will strengthen the perceived relevance of study. This same diversity offers new opportunities in pedagogy as the implications of contextual learning are further studied and developed. For its part, vocational education will have a much stronger general element, as the much broader and more flexible skill requirements develop for work situations. An interesting further link is being pursued in some countries through the idea of generic vocational competencies, as appropriate achievements for all students by the end of their schooling. This confluence of general and vocational education may well be beneficial to both. It does, however, demand a more active co-operation from business and industry rather than a stance of criticism from outside.

Decision making

In the 1987 survey, the particular emphasis in decision making was the strong demand by parents for a general involvement in educational decisions. That issue is still alive. In some countries, such as New Zealand, England and Wales, and Sweden, governments have moved to put substantial power in the hands of parents, notably at the individual school level. This may include general education policy, such as the curriculum, staffing and financial management. On a more individual basis in these countries, parents also have the right to select the particular school for their children to attend. In England and Wales, this right is informed by published results of the achievement tests of the individual schools. Such a situation raises interesting questions of social equity, as the capacity to move children to another school is restricted by the finance available to parents. The effect on individual schools may also be a matter of concern, where results perceived to be poor could lead to the movement of many of the most able and motivated children, further reducing the capacity of the schools to perform well.

In the period since 1987, more general and far-reaching questions have arisen about decision-making. Parents, clearly, need to be given an appropriate place in educational decisions, in view of the major interest they have in the results and of the significant contribution made to the learning of their children by positive attitudes of parents, a real role for parents, as distinct from token participation, requires a substantial effort.

Increasingly, a variety of other institutions, people and groups are claiming a stake in education. The institution defining its role most strongly is central government. In many countries this has always been the case. In France, for example, it is a major tenet of French political life, frequently and consistently confirmed, that public schooling is a major concern of government. This concern quite specifically includes the curriculum. In other countries, this has not been the case. A Former British Prime Minister, Mr Callaghan identified a felt need, in speaking of what had been called "the secret garden of the curriculum", in commenting on its separateness from government influence. The garden is secret no longer! The 1988 Education Reform Act in the U.K. gave to government the power to define the curriculum and governments have moved strongly in this direction. Similar moves have followed elsewhere. At the same time, these governments have moved to increase significantly the responsibilities of schools in certain regards, notably financial management. Still other governments, like Sweden, formerly involved in central specification of the curriculum, have moved back from that direct control, but have put in place "steering mechanisms", the use of goal specification, curriculum frameworks and assessment to maintain what they see as appropriate power.

In the relationship between governments and schools there is an essential tension: the long-term time scale for educational change and the short-term requirement for political decision.

It seems likely that this issue will continue to be a lively one, not only for governments, but for other actual and potential stake-holders. What should be the involvement of students, those most centrally concerned with the processes and outcomes of education? What of business and industry? How and where can they express their involvement? What of the special interest groups? On health, the environment, on civics, on technology? The real complexity of the educational process requires a more rigorous and searching analysis of the nature of decision-making, not only with respect to the curriculum. At what levels should particular decisions be taken? Who should be involved? The simplistic distinction between centralised and decentralised decision-making is no longer adequate, if it ever was. The resolution which is required looks not only at where the decision-making occurs and who are involved in the process, but at the nature of the decisions involved. What is frequently presented as a one-dimensional problem has at least three distinct dimensions: the level of decision-making; the participants in the process; and, the nature of the process.

Evaluation and change

In both 1987 and 1992, the use made of student assessment results, and the manner of that assessment, raise some difficult questions. If there is further change in the period, it is in the direction of raising higher levels of controversy.

The concern of governments is to receive adequate information about the expenditure of money to ensure it is being spent well. Education takes such a large slice of national income, that increases in real terms are difficult to attain, particularly when there are other pressing social needs. The point is made in many countries that expenditure per capita in real terms increased substantially in the sixties and early seventies, but with no evidence of increased quality. Whether qualitative improvement of any significant degree could reasonably have been expected in a period of massive quantitative growth is open to question. However, the press for qualitative improvement in contemporary policy-making is widespread and cannot be ignored.

Parent bodies have also moved aside from their traditional alliance with teachers, to ask why it is not possible to obtain clear information on the achievement of students in key areas, in forms which permit them to assess the adequacy of the levels of performance.

Teachers point out that wherever major external tests of basic skills have been established, they have encouraged minimal levels of performance to satisfy the tests, have discouraged the high achiever and distorted the emphases of the course.

Each of these groups is presenting a valid and useful viewpoint. The conversations between them, however, are not occurring. Three separate monologues are not contributing to the general exchange that needs to occur.

Managing and resourcing expansion

Strangely, only one issue was identified specifically in 1992 which was not stressed in the responses of the 1989 survey. There is little doubt that it was an important issue at that stage, perhaps so much taken for granted that it was not mentioned. Nevertheless, the realisation of the full implications of high quality education and training for all has given further emphasis to the importance of resources. What the OECD countries embarked on with that commitment for all students involves not only a substantial increase in participation, costly in itself, but it involves much more. As the Ministers' statement stresses, more of the same will not be enough. This curriculum reform involves not only a fundamental consideration of what we teach, but how we teach it and where we teach it. This commitment represents an unprecedented task, to provide an effective and relevant education for an entire generation and not a selected minority. That massive investment in the future will carry a substantial cost with it, and challenges us to explore new ways of providing education for all in late adolescence and early adulthood and beyond.

If we take seriously the nature and durability of these issues, how can we best answer the challenges they pose? We now accept that changes are necessary. What should they be? How should and can they be brought about? Both questions are of particular importance, yet most attention has gone to what and very little to how. Change in a complex social process such as education requires careful thought. We shall raise three questions as deserving particular attention in considering the future:

a) What are the implications of high quality for all?
b) Can we reconcile the functions of evaluation in assisting learning and evaluating quality?
c) Can we cope with the scale of change required?

Fundamental Questions to Consider

What are the implications of high quality education and training for all?

Many people feel, though rather fewer express, misgivings over the concept of high quality for all. Does it imply a levelling down, a reduction of expectations to allow more to succeed? Is it a move away from the encouragement of excellence, of the very highest levels of performance for some students? Will it encourage a lowest common denominator of achievement? The folk-lore of 'payment-by-results' testing in the basic skills in the early years of compulsory education is that the imposition of standards of achievement turned these into the maximum levels, rather than the foundation for further achievement.

That levelling down was clearly not the intention of the OECD Ministers' Conference in 1990. The commitment is to the concept of a just and cohesive society which will recognise the full range of human talent and will take on the awesome task not merely of providing opportunities, but ensuring achievements. This is what is meant by 'the basic essential learning's, the democratic entitlement', the curriculum guarantee', to be discussed later under the heading "The core curriculum'.

This pathway, though intimidating in its consequences, is the alternative to a society which sentences thirty to fifty per cent of its population to low-level participation. Such a society will fail. Fail in its social purposes. Fail in its individual purposes. Fail in its vocational purposes.

The core curriculum is conceived as a foundation which provides the capability and the will to continue learning. It is a new sort of literacy, opening not only access to language and thinking, but to the wider culture. By its nature it implies not only ambitious, but high quality achievement.

Fundamental to the notion of the core curriculum is not only what it includes, but how it is presented. The genuine involvement of our society in that development is a necessity. So too, is the challenge to teachers and students in their involvement, and in the reconceptualisation of teaching and learning which is involved.

Can we reconcile contrasting roles of evaluation?

Some of the complexities of this issue have already been outlined, as has the failure to engage in a genuine conversation on means. We now have a more sophisticated understanding of evaluation than before and a more comprehensive range of evaluation techniques and approaches. In evaluation terms we are being asked to reconcile summative and formative evaluation, judgmental and diagnostic evaluation.

The issue is one of tremendous practical as well as theoretical importance. Evaluation is one of the most powerful instruments in education, in relation both to teacher and to student behaviour. In an area where there are so many difficulties in bringing about change we cannot afford to neglect this powerful influence. For many teachers and students, it is not statements of aims which define our real purposes, our real values. It is in what and how we assess that we define those values.

Currently there is an almost universal concern with standards. As one of the preludes to this conference OECD combined with the U.S. Office of Educational Research (OERI) in circulating a questionnaire on educational standards to the Member countries. The results of the analysis of the responses are available in a special paper prepared by OERI. Fourteen members of the Asia-Pacific Economic Co-operation group had previously completed the survey. All the respondents indicated the importance of standards, with almost universal support for a definition at the national level, accompanied by some form of monitoring. As we have implied earlier, some of the approaches have aroused controversy. There is nevertheless a valid and very important role for evaluation in monitoring quality in education, as well as in assisting individual students. If that monitoring is tied to the allocation of resources, if it is linked with professional development of teachers, if it feeds back for a constructive dialogue on curriculum aims, and processes, then it is beginning to fulfil a role that is desperately needed in guiding change.

Can we cope with the scale of change demanded?

We are being faced with the need for major changes in a wide variety of areas:

1) in the aims and purposes of schooling;
2) in the process of curriculum formation;
3) in the teaching-learning process;
4) in assessment and evaluation and their uses.

Can we succeed in such a task, recognising the difficulty of achieving change in education, even in the curriculum needs of a single subject?

The question is one of the genuineness of the commitment and the will to involve all those aspects of our societies with a genuine concern for and interest in education. Legislation may be a part of such a process, but not the whole. The type of effort that our societies are capable of making in war, is now required in this peaceful endeavour. The magnitude and the complexity of the effort, even in countries such as the OECD Members should not be under-rated.

There is a substantial commonality within the OECD countries which provides a basis. This includes:

1) The extension of participation in education and training progressively to all young people in the age-group 17, 18+, thus removing this age-group, gradually, completely from the labour market;

2) providing these young people with a broad general education which in some cases involves specific preparation for occupations but which is in any case, a foundation for further education whether full or part-time, work or college based;

3) a continued emphasis on quality and relevance geared to the needs of an internationally healthy economy;

4) a range of quality of life goals, including personal development and citizenship, to provide a broad developmental function in both personal and local times, linked with the declared values of democracy and human rights;

5) a common concern for accountability and good management.

Does this commonality provide a basis for practicable, large-scale government reform strategies? The analysis of the successes and failures in large-scale reforms provides some lessons. Put briefly, the greater the divergence from established practices, organisational structures and values the greater the likelihood of failure. This analysis supplements conclusions to be drawn from studies of the large projects of 1960, and 1970, namely that where large scale reforms fail or do not advance far it is because they are neither planned nor prepared for in a systematic fashion. The major effort goes in the conception and development of the project and not in obtaining the necessary involvement for its success.

Factors that need to be considered in national level curriculum reforms:

1) initial teacher education;
2) curriculum frameworks and resources;
3) professional development;
4) assessment;

In addition, the following principles apply:

-- Statements of purpose, such as goals, aims and objectives, need to be clearly stated and understood;

-- those statements need to relate to widely held values and to widely agreed needs;

-- the active interest, engagement and support of major stake-holders, including teachers particularly, are necessary for success;

-- national level, government-led reforms measures need to address a major widely perceived need and to offer benefits to large numbers or to specific groups experiencing great hardships.

The underlying issue is clear. There is a broad consensus on the need for change in education, and specifically for the extension of education to provide high quality participation for all. In societies as complex as the Member countries, where people as individuals and groups require convincing on the value of particular initiatives, this broad consensus is not enough. Great care in the planning and broad involvement in the process is needed if reform is to proceed and develop into established forms. The desired direction of change is clear: now we need the will to implement those changes as a major, planned, coherent effort by our societies.

II. CONTEXT AND GOALS

1. The Context of Change

The last decade of the century, and of the millennium, gives us special reason to look ahead. Education, in many ways such a conservative enterprise, is also inescapably forward looking. Those who enter school this year will be completing a secondary education by the end of the year 2004, and their working careers are due to continue past 2050, their life spans for a further 20 years. What we do now, and what we do not do, what we decide and what we do not decide, will all give a shape to that span of the future. Yet, as we look at the past century, it exhibits dramatic changes in political grouping, in forms of government, in productive activities, in the arts, in economic development, in the use of world resources, in communication and transport, in family and individual life -- every conceivable aspect of human thought and activity. There is a temptation to see the future as an independent entity, as something that happens beyond our control, where we are restricted to predicting the main features and reacting to the unpredictable. The future is something to which we can give some shape and direction through our choices. Education is a vital part of these processes. While our focus is on the period of compulsory schooling, we shall also need to consider that wider process, education.

The events of the past decade on the world scene illustrate vividly the unpredictability of change. We have seen the break-up of the Eastern Bloc: the USSR has become a set of independent republics; Czechoslovakia has split into two separate republics. Yugoslavia's form, torn apart by bloody conflict remains undetermined. In Western Europe, on the other hand, the European Community moved in 1993 closer to becoming a unified system. In South Africa, apartheid has been abandoned and while the political future is still uncertain, dramatic steps towards a democratic social order have been taken. In the Asia-Pacific region, many countries including USA, the People's Republic of China, Japan, Hong Kong, the Philippines, Korea, Chinese Taipei, Canada, Thailand, Australia and New Zealand are working through a new organisation, Asia-Pacific Economic Co-operation (APEC) to determine the benefits of wider co-operation between countries in areas such as economics and education.

Unpredicted as these events were, they show a general pattern. On one hand societies are recognising their interdependence and need for co-operation: this has led to groupings such as the UN, UNESCO, OECD, the European Community, APEC and the North American Free Trade Association. On the other hand societies formed by tightly-bound disparate elements are breaking up into smaller, more coherent, more homogeneous groupings, sometimes bringing about inter-group strife in that process.

In education, the events lack the obvious drama of the above, yet what is happening has profound implications for the future. The population involved in education is changing in both structure and rates of participation; the administrative and control patterns of education are changing substantially; the climate of attention to education is different, involving broader elements of the community and bringing new insights to bear.

2. Implication of Commitment to Quality for All

As was said at the Ministerial Conference, this lofty aim is no longer a utopian ambition but a social necessity.

A number of issues have emerged as countries grapple with that necessity.

Participation rates

One of the events involves increased participation. Many different societies are changing education profoundly through their participation rates. UNESCO, through its programme of Universalisation of Primary Education is seeking to provide a minimum level of basic education for all countries. In the more industrialised countries, the provision of secondary education is now rising to levels formerly found in very few countries such as Japan and the USA. This increase in participation is partly due to deliberate policy by government, and partly due to increasing demand for education from individuals.

In October 1992, OECD sponsored an International Conference in Hiroshima, Japan involving both OECD countries and the so-called Dynamic Asian Economies, DAEs. One of the striking aspects of the discussions was the similarity of the issues identified by the participating countries. The DAEs, Thailand, Korea, Hong Kong, Chinese Taipei, Malaysia, Indonesia and Singapore recognised the same needs as the OECD countries represented, as summed up by the Swedish representative who commented that the countries faced the same challenges and the same need for new insights.

> "For the majority of us, our own history and wealth have proved the intimate relationships between a nation's prosperity and the quality of its educational system. This relationship is abundantly clear. And when this relationship is proved, education policies are no longer an area to be the exclusive preserve of specialists and technicians. Educational policy has now become a central and strategically important area for the whole range of policy making. The industrialized world knows very well that our prosperity could not have been achieved, and cannot be maintained if we don't have breadth and excellence in our educational system. Sweden, like Japan, has experienced one of the most rapid growth-rates of the 20th century. And we know that this is closely connected to access to cost-free education with high quality" (Eiken, 1992).

The points made here, of this link between national prosperity and the quality of the educational system and the consequent requirement for a system of "breadth and excellence", are supported very generally. They are the basis of the increases in secondary retention which are a feature of many countries. In Australia, for example, whereas in 1986 only 48.7 per cent of secondary students were retained to year 12, by 1992 this had risen to 75 per cent, with the recommended target rates for the year 2001 set by the Finn Review at 90 per cent. These are dramatic changes and they are a part of deliberate government policy (Finn, 1991). In France, similarly, a major emphasis by government is directed towards the increase of participation, including the politically sensitive area of the *baccalauréat*. President Mitterand made education the major theme of his second term of office and set a target of 80 per cent of the age-group achieving a pass in the *baccalauréat* by the year 2000. This contrasts with the figure of 15 per cent of the age-group to achieve this goal during the 1960s (Ministère de l'Education Nationale, 1989). Such initiatives frequently relate specifically to policies designed to provide more flexible and higher level skills in the workforce.

"The demand for and appreciation of quality means a reorganised work-force where human resource management is fundamental, where decision-making occurs at the level of the individual worker, where skill is applied minute by minute, where workers are involved in management through consultation and application of their knowledge and skill, and where small highly competent teams replace the production line" (Carmichael, 1990).

While the changed situation, including unemployment, relates particularly to the post-compulsory years, its impact both on compulsory education and higher education is just as significant. The recognition of changing work prospects is a major factor in strengthening students' commitment to instrumental purposes. The government policy change in Australia followed a change in employment that was already substantial. Whereas in 1966, 60 per cent of the 15-19 age-group has full-time jobs, by 1992 that proportion has fallen to 10 per cent, a loss of 600,000 full-time jobs. The choices for young people are thus much more limited, with 90 per cent of the age-group choosing some combination of education, training and part-time work or unemployment. In one sense, then, the increase in participation is a matter of choice for students to stay longer in order to enhance employment prospects. That choice does not necessarily involve a higher commitment to education, with over half of the students in year 11 studies reporting that they would take a job as first preference over continuing at school. As will be discussed later, increased participation on such a basis is not necessarily a benefit.

High unemployment has been a continuing problem for OECD countries in the 1980s, with the figures in Europe ranging between 10 - 11 per cent in the decade 1983-1992 (OECD, 1993). Only a few countries, notably Japan 2.0 - 2.3 per cent and Germany 4.4 - 5.5 per cent performed significantly better than this. For Europe the forecasts for 1993 and 1994 remain at this level, just below 11 per cent (OECD, 1992). As part of the social context, this has a substantial effect on education particularly as the rates for 15-19 year-olds tend to be substantially higher and the periods spent by individuals in unemployment grow longer. As has been implied, growth in education participation rates which have been encouraged by the employment situation is unlikely to be an adequate response.

Administration and control

A second major education change is in respect to patterns of administration and control. It was possible in the past to speak broadly of systems being centralised or decentralised with respect to the control of issues such as curriculum, staffing and finance. Thus, countries such as USA and Britain were de-centralised while others such as Japan and Sweden were centralised. Changes over recent years have blurred these distinctions, with initiatives to centralise and decentralise both occurring, often in the same countries.

Sweden and the Netherlands have both made significant moves to implement their policies of decentralisation, while retaining significant steering mechanisms at the centre. In both countries, there was a long-standing tradition of central control but both have now analyzed more closely the implications of particular structures and have adopted greater flexibility. In the 1992 publication, *The Swedish Way Towards a Learning Society*, Sweden spells out clearly the nature of responsibility devolved to schools. This responsibility is considerable but within the clear framework of national goals and expectations as indicated in the earlier comments by Eiken (1992). Similarly in the Netherlands, as pointed out in the OECD Review (1991), national policies are defined clearly but leave a substantial choice and responsibility for the schools in their approaches and modes of action.

The recent Green Paper in Ireland, *Education for a Changing World* (Brennan, 1992) in putting forward its proposals for discussion, distinguished clearly between the role of the centre in determining

31

goals and setting standards of achievement and the role of individual schools in developing education programmes. The proposals mean fewer but better defined powers at the central level, more powers at the school level but in a clearer framework. However, the picture is more complex than recognised by an analysis in terms of centralisation-decentralisation. One pattern for the devolution of power involves moving specific responsibilities to the school level, so that the centre-school axis is the location of responsibilities as in England. Another pattern for the devolution of power is represented in France, where the national system locates different responsibilities at central, regional and local levels, but with the system remaining clearly national. In England and Wales the Education Reform Act of 1988, ERA 88, provided for a national curriculum and national assessment while moving simultaneously to Local Management of Schools, LMS, providing substantial financial and management power at the school level. This included the power for schools to 'opt out' of the control of their Local Education Authority, taking with them that part of LEA finance formerly devoted to servicing that school. Thus, both the national system and the individual schools had their powers enhanced, but in different areas. The loser was the intermediate authority. In France, on the other hand, the intermediate authorities have been substantially strengthened.

In Sweden, as in England, the schools are being given greater responsibility. There is still a concern for steering mechanisms at the national level, for both curriculum and assessment, while increasing the right of parents to choose their children's school and to be actively involved in the schools' policies and management. This includes rules to give all parents the right for equivalent financial conditions when choosing a school for their children, regardless as to whether the school is public or private.

These complex patterns repeat to some degree the two distinct patterns of movement in world events: the tendency to combine groups into larger entities to reflect a greater degree of common interest; and, the tendency for existing groups to break down into more fundamental and communally-based groups. In education, there is some basic consistency between those countries which are reinstating or strengthening central control and those where decision-making is being decentralised to local or regional authorities or schools. In both cases, however, there is a clear framework by which the curriculum is defined and there are structures for monitoring and accountability.

There is an implication in much of the effort devoted by governments to shaping the form and nature of education that this can be done through some form of central specification. There are, of course, many centres of power which influence the formulation and implementation of the curriculum. Politicians, increasingly, exercise a role either through formal legislation or through establishing conditions under which change can operate and reform can be initiated. Educational administrators in central ministries and local departments frequently establish mechanisms for reform, including curriculum guidelines and frameworks and the development of materials. Teacher educators, researchers, institutions involved in evaluation and school inspectors also make their own contributions. Teachers, of course, play a pre-eminent part, whether or not it is formally recognised, as do students and parents. Increasingly, outside bodies such as business and industry, the trade unions, professional associations and interest groups are contributing to the dialogue and the recommendations on the curriculum. However, as Skilbeck has said: it is necessary "to distinguish between public area discourse on educational policy-making and on the structure, organisation and process of education itself. Much of the national level debate seems to leave the schools, the teachers, students, parents and the local communities unaffected" (Skilbeck, 1990). This is an important point and it applies with particular force to the curriculum itself. It is easy to assume that specification of a curriculum programme or development of a curriculum package implies change in the classrooms. It is one of the hard-learned lessons of curriculum history that this is not so. The current context reinforces the need for a more sophisticated approach to curriculum, one that considers the lessons of the past.

The pattern of curriculum development has been through many stages. The early pattern depended on the development of a detailed syllabus, including recommended texts and materials, by a syllabus committee or a central authority. The use of inspections and examinations was seen as a means of ensuring implementation. The perceived weaknesses of this approach led to the professionalisation of curriculum design, culminating in the curriculum projects of the 1960s. This involved the use of subject scholars, media specialists, learning specialists working co-operatively with teachers in developing clearly specified curricula, high quality materials and teacher induction courses. While the thinking behind the projects and the materials produced made a lasting and significant change to curricula, early results did not show the expected wide impact. The next pattern to be used was school-based curriculum development, SBCD, under the assumption that any lasting and major changes in curriculum depended on the active initiation and co-operation of teachers and that the appropriate working unit was the school. Again, this has not been a complete answer. This approach placed a heavy burden on teachers, for whom preparation time became a major burden. Further, it was seen as a wasteful process where many schools worked independently on the same problems, learning little from each other's failures and successes. For SBCD, as with the curriculum projects of the 1960s, while the success in achieving change was mixed, valuable lessons for curriculum development were learned. In many schools, the involvement of staff in the process of curriculum development was seen as, and accepted as, a professional challenge. While the materials developed, and the courses produced, were in logical terms no better than before, the involvement of staff brought a greater commitment and understanding and, thus, probably better results. In many other schools, particularly those with a high mobility of teachers and/or students, the process led to abrupt and unrelated changes, and thus to discontinuity and a lack of coherence. Unfortunately this tended to occur in inner city schools, struggling often with ethnically diverse populations, and with remote rural schools where teachers often have short stays. These situations are precisely the types of disadvantage that curriculum reform should address. Can we now with the benefit of hindsight use the advantages to come from teacher involvement in curriculum design, without losing the necessary characteristics of continuity and coherence?

The climate for policy decisions in education

A third feature of much of the current education situation is the development of an active and frequently hostile climate of debate. The attention given to education by politicians, and the much more active role played by them, has already been mentioned. The reasons given include those already identified by Eiken, the cost of the enterprise and its perceived importance for national development. This perceived importance, together with individual demand, has led to increasing participation, particularly at the upper secondary and higher education levels, both of which are costly. The OECD participants in the Hiroshima Conference were interested to note that in the DAEs, the political pressures from rising aspirations for higher education were similar to those in the Member countries. In Korea, as a dramatic example, the portion of the relevant age-group engaged in higher education jumped from 3.1 per cent in 1953 to 9.7 per cent in 1970, 16.5 per cent in 1980 and 35.1 per cent by 1985. Much of this growth was fuelled by the very high rate of economic growth and the consequent heavy demand for graduates. The accompanying lift in expectation, however, has had the consequence of a large number of unsuccessful applicants for admission, growing from 70,000 in 1970 to 700,000 in 1980. This type of situation carries its own political pressures. The increased political intervention linked with such factors frequently carries with it the implication, more or less explicit, that educators had been too unworldly or too unwilling to change to meet the needs, justifying the intervention and the frequent restructurings of education systems that often results.

Business and industry. Further sustained attention to education comes from the vocational sector, including industrial and commercial management and the trade unions. While this interest has been a tradition in some countries such as Germany, for many it is a new phenomenon. Education in general, including teachers and system administrators, are frequently somewhat wary about this attention, seeing it as part of an over-emphasis on vocationalism. It is a dialogue that is destined to continue. Educators have frequently proclaimed the importance of schooling to society in general and must now expect to be taken at their word. In this instance, the importance of vocational education must be taken seriously. In many countries, vocational education has been the Cinderella of the education sector, dismissed as being involved merely with training and not education. In the vocational world of today and tomorrow, that distinction becomes increasingly irrelevant. Vocational education cannot be limited to a set of skills imparted before commencing work and used thereafter in a career. The pace of technology change means that vocations require new sets of skills continually and that the capacity to learn and to keep learning is more crucial than particular competencies. The dialogue between the business-industry sector and education is crucial if a proper understanding of the position of both is to develop. It will be crucial, too, from another viewpoint. Increasingly, much vocational education will occur on working-sites, contextual learning as many business leaders call it. With the expansion of education for those for whom school environments are not conducive to learning this is important. It is important, too, to make available to schools a wider range of situation and of technology than they will be able to provide. At the moment these links are relatively few and on a small scale. Likewise there is a lack of research and analysis on important ideas such as contextual learning or situational learning. Both these areas deserve more attention.

Interest groups. Other interest groups are making particular claims of their own for a place in education. In one sense, this is not new as there have always been contenders for a place in the curriculum. Now, and in the future, major social issues will make their claims for attention because of the perception that education is an effective agent of change, in concert with other processes such as legislation. One major area is the environment, where the issues range from the small scale, such as re-cycling and conservation to major national and global issues, such as rivers and oceans, and the green-house effect. The issues in this field are so comprehensive and so critical for the quality of life that they make a compelling claim for attention. A further area of equally broad significance is health and well-being, including a range of concerns such as road safety, drug use and sexually-transmitted diseases, notably AIDS. Again, the importance of the issues is very evident and they have already gained significant attention within education. The issue to be reckoned with for the future is how to deal with such concerns on a more considered and effective basis. At the moment, the place in education of such issues owes more to the power of advocacy than to any comprehensive consideration, either of the claims for a place or of the capacity of education to provide effective responses.

Academic commentators. Interest groups broadly within education but not in school systems make significant contributions to the climate of debate. Academic commentators have always made a significant contribution and in recent years this has increased and become sharper in tone. By the nature of such commentators the emphases and areas of concern vary widely. An aspect which is worthy of note, however, is that the comments of some academics take form in government initiatives or in social pressures or in educational programmes. One such is the substantial analysis developed by Claus Moser in his Presidential address to the British Association for the Advancement of Science. In turning his attention to education on such a significant occasion he drew substantial public interest. His analysis was severe: "despite substantial efforts and 'islands of excellence', [Britain] is now in danger of becoming one of the least adequately educated of all the advanced nations -- with serious consequences for its future socially, economically, technologically and culturally" (Moser, 1990). His analysis covered 14 points, including: the high rate of withdrawal from school at 16, dissatisfaction with vocational training, the limited offerings in upper secondary for the majority of students, wide dissatisfaction with achievements in the basic skills, excessive specialisation both in upper secondary and undergraduate courses, poor provision of education, gaps in primary school achievement, concern for the quantity and quality of the teaching profession ("central to all school problems"..."a third of the profession say they would like to leave"), limited access to higher education, need for more continuing, part-time education, tensions between government and higher education, science funding, shortage of graduates in key areas, the need for higher priority for education funding. Moser recommended to the government the formation of a Royal Commission, initiating "a review which would be visionary about the medium and long-term future facing our children and this country; clear about the goals we wish to achieve; with emphasis on ends as much as means; treating the system in all its interconnected parts; and, last but not least, considering the changes in our working and labour market scenes" (Moser, 1990). The government rejected the idea of the Royal Commission but, significantly, there was so much public support for the idea that a "non-government National Education Commission" has been established to press ahead with the concept. In other countries also there are significant examples of academic comment taking positive form. Two of America's more prominent commentators on education, Chester Finn and Diane Ravitch took up the issue of the lack of relevant historical and cultural knowledge as exhibited in tests for 17-year olds (Ravitch and Finn, 1990). This concern touched a more general chord in American thinking and had its impact on the programme America 2000, developed by the Committee of Governors under (then) Governor Clinton and accepted by (then) President Bush. Ravitch took a senior role in government in the Bush administration, with Finn as a significant advisor to government. This interplay of academic analysis and government or social initiative will continue to be influential. This has already been a pattern of action for the new U.S. administration. Before his election, Governor Clinton established the K-12 Task Force to look at the full sweep of school education, involving many academics in this transition exercise.

Need for a more comprehensive approach. This climate of debate has become a significant element for education and will become even more so. With lifelong learning becoming a reality for all rather than a slogan, the provision of education, the nature of education and access to education, all become more significant issues. The attention to education will remain for it has become the key to opportunity for individuals and society. The critical nature of much of that attention will also remain, since the defining for education of what constitutes worthwhile learning will remain a contentious issue. Educators have lost status badly where, and this is often, they have attempted to build walls and isolate themselves from criticism, sometimes under the excuse of professional privilege. No profession is now exempt from public comment, either about its purposes or its achievements. Where educators can make a significant reply to outside commentators putting their claims on education is in their knowledge of what will work. Purposes of education cannot be a professional privilege, but procedures for their achievements can be. Too often, good purposes become frustrated in their achievement by naive conceptions of how they might proceed. Schools have become too familiar with the curriculum package passed on to them for implementation, with quite unreal prospects of substantial achievement.

3. Issues for Reform

The dominating issue for the educational context is that of unemployment. That issue has been particularly powerful in changing the participation rates, in influencing changes in administration and control of education, in bringing education under a broader community scrutiny, sometimes a hostile one. Schools and teachers feel uncomfortable with many of the movements in these three broad areas and have not taken an effective role in the debate. The focuses for that debate will be on purposes and processes, on curriculum and assessment. If strong national initiatives are to be effective in implementation at the school level, the breadth and the rigour of that debate will be vital.

-- What are the major implications for the compulsory years of the changing participation rates?

-- Different countries are developing different patterns of administration to deal with the responsibilities given to different levels of education, national, regional, local, school. What are the responsibilities you feel must remain at the national level and the school level respectively?

-- Many different groups need to be involved in the continuing debate on education's purposes and priorities. How might this be best organised?

In Paper 2, Dr Marshall Smith indicates the relevance of these issues for the agenda of reform in the United States, with the Clinton Administration.

Paper 2

AN AGENDA FOR REFORM IN THE U.S.A.

a précis of the presentation by Dr Marshall Smith

A New Agenda

President Clinton's agenda for the USA is essentially a "human capital agenda", emphasising the central importance of human development in the future of the nation. Under this approach, five major national priority areas have been defined, one of these being education. The importance of education had been emphasised by President Clinton in his appointment of the former governor of South Carolina, Mr Richard Riley, as Secretary for Education. Governor Riley has a long history of involvement with education, both in his own state and nationally, as has President Clinton himself. Both men, as governors were involved in the school reform movement of the 1980s.

In their speeches and policy statements, President Clinton and Secretary Riley have defined a sense of direction for action:

i)   To stimulate state and local education authorities to up-grade the entire school system. While this would be a major departure from the past, it appeared as a necessity.

ii)   To formulate the Federal-State partnership in education in clearer terms, with well-defined categories of involvement.

iii)   To develop clear goals and directions for the system, including attention to standards. The work of the National Council of Teachers of Mathematics (NTCM) in defining content standards for their subject area was one example of the type of activity needed.

iv)   To add to and make more precise the sense of responsibility for decisions at the local level in education, increasing the flexibility of the system and providing clear authority for decision and action.

v)   To initiate a comprehensive effort to obtain an alignment of processes and patterns of activity within the framework of an agreed set of goals. It is too easy to define sets of goals which bear no operational relationship to the schooling system. That relationship must be constructed through consultation and participation at all levels to provide a coherent and meaningful framework for decisions and actions.

vi)   A commitment to equity, to fairness for all in the system. The aim is for integration rather than differentiation, for inclusion rather than separation. This is an important aim to establish as a test for the acceptability of all procedures.

vii)   The recognition that this involves a long-term commitment. Our knowledge of educational change indicates the time that will be required to achieve such substantial developments in the purposes, content and processes of schooling. On the other hand, the time-scale for political initiatives is short, with governments needing to indicate their effectiveness over the short-term in order to be able to carry a long-term agenda. Those in education and those in government both need to understand the different parameters of these fields.

The point was made persuasively that while this was an ambitious agenda, it was one that flowed from an accurate perception of needs, needs which would impact deeply on the shape and nature of democratic society. In one sense this was a re-affirmation of the viewpoint expressed by Dewey at the beginning of the century, when he outlined the ideal of democratic education as "a freeing of individual capacity in a progressive growth directed to social aims" where the programme is selected "with the intention of improving the life we live in common so that the future shall be better than the past". (Dewey, 1916). At the end of the century, the need discerned earlier by Dewey is much more urgent and will have a significant effect on the whole shape and cohesion of our society.

Research and Systematic Analysis

As indicated above, the agenda is important because of its social impact. The very urgency of the agenda makes it more important that it should be firmly based, depending not on attractive slogans but on research, on sound analysis and logical argument. In respect to research there are some broad conclusions already possible on which a sound programme can be built for curricular reform.

i) All children can learn more complex material than previously believed. It seems certain that we have set artificial limits on what can be learned by particular children. Opportunity for access, teaching styles, available materials and equipment, setting, modes of presentation, organisation of classes and school, technical support: these and other factors affect the learning of individuals.

In addition to the traditional empirical approaches which have much to contribute in these areas, intensive case studies can provide invaluable material to supplement our knowledge of how to approach this problem. Under our current procedures 30 - 50 per cent of students do not make satisfactory progress with their learning, yet given the right circumstances most of them can learn complex material.

ii) Curriculum is critical. It is vital to have alignment between goals and content, professional development, organisation and evaluation. If there are breaks in these linkages and interactions, many students will miss opportunities.

iii) Teaching can be more effective. The importance of individual teachers and their capacity to challenge students to learn has been under-rated. Particular teachers have demonstrated their capacity to obtain student engagement and learning where it had been held to be impossible (cf. Escalante). Particular approaches have shown their effectiveness in reducing failure and alienation (cf. Reading Recovery). What we know can be used more effectively, both by individuals in their own teaching approaches and by systems, in providing support in the right way at the right times.

iv) Teacher development is vital. Two aspects are relevant. One is the importance of a sense of professionalism: the other is the need to base that professionalism on a deep knowledge of teaching, of purposes, content and process. For these to develop, teachers need to have a clear sense of responsibility for key decisions but also to be part of an effective professional network.

v) Change can occur effectively only where there is commitment to change at the local level. The feasibility of exchange of ideas becomes important here because of the importance of the context of ideas. Widespread reform means developing a better understanding of the effects of context so that teachers can adapt and develop ideas in ways that are relevant to their own setting. If this process is to have a wide effect, there is a strongly implied need for a commitment to clearly understood goals, not in a casual sense, but in the sense of deep meaning. Where this understanding exists, the provision of technical support is vital to success.

vi) Assessment which is independent of the curriculum can be a distorting force. Assessment is always a powerful influence and provides significant motivation to learn. If that motivation is towards limited goals only then it distorts the learning process. Thus, an important part of curriculum reform is to link assessment to the curriculum goals, in range and in emphasis. A further requirement for assessment is to ensure that it guarantees fairness in access and performance in the curriculum. This is the most fundamental meaning of accountability, the guarantee of the learning entitlement. Both these aspects are equally vital.

These ideas, broadly based on our research studies and our shared experience are the basis on which the United States is structuring its K-12 curriculum reforms. Essentially, it is a standards-based curriculum reform. Three major ideas lie at the base of that reform. Firstly, it is a broad-based definition of curriculum: it does not try to define a detailed scope, but the outcomes sought for 2-3 year sequences.

Secondly, it recognises the interdependence of the total structure and thus the need to obtain alignment: of goals, curriculum, teacher training, in-service education, assessment and support.

Thirdly, it must provide enough freedom, responsibility and resources at the local area. Top-down and bottom-up processes, to use over-simplified terms, must be in a healthy and creative tension.

Issues We Need to Know More About

There are some issues which plague us now and that we need to know more about, as we press ahead with the unavoidable commitment to curriculum reform.

Content standards

The concept is vital but who decides on the standards? How do we obtain involvement of the public in these decisions? How broad should be the participation in setting content standards?

The nature of the standards

There are four components to standards: selection of content; theory and structure of content; theory of human learning and development; theory of pedagogy. All of these are subject to change, often rapid change, and this raises problems. What are the international bench-marks? How fast can we proceed in the introduction of content frameworks?

Assessment

Alignment of assessment with curriculum is a new idea in the United States. What does alignment mean in practice? There also would seem to be a challenge to assess in depth and not only in breadth. Moreover our procedures need to become more socially and personally relevant. Perhaps we can generalise more validly from a few in-depth probes as against a lot of shallow checks? We may have been too obsessed with reliability, at the expense of validity. While it is question of balance, validity must have the priority.

Teachers' professional development

In courses for teachers how far should the emphasis be on subject-content and how far on process? How do we prepare teachers to teach to new and challenging standards? What are the most effective partnerships between schools and universities in developing programmes? How can the benefits of professional development courses for individual teachers be spread to cover a school staff?

Technical assistance

How can we best provide technical assistance to teachers, schools and school systems? Teachers tend to work in isolation and the transfer of knowledge, skills and expertise is difficult. Is there a place for the traditional school inspector or some similar role?

Accountability and Fairness

Alignment of curriculum and assessment provides means to satisfy the requirements of accountability to parents. This is both a moral and legal problem and already there are cases under litigation. The question of "opportunity to learn" is complex. It may involve providing the means and not just access. What are the implications when teachers don't know enough to present effectively a particular curriculum, e.g. maths, science?

While this presentation concentrates essentially on the schooling system, there are equally fundamental issues arising with respect to the interfaces for schools. One critical interface is in the early childhood period, ages 3-4. Can we provide high quality here on a universal basis? Other critical interfaces are school-work and school-college. At the moment there is a multiplicity of ideas but our need is to establish some clear paths for action, using the best of our current knowledge but recognising where we need to know more. We are building through partnerships a national approach, to K-12 education, to the home-school and school-work interfaces.

As implied earlier, this is a massive agenda. It has implications that will not be worked through for decades. This makes it all the more important to make a beginning now, recognising the wide front of the necessary actions and the breadth of the effort and participation required. Our society has faced and overcome major challenges before through a mobilisation and focusing of effort. We can do so again. This is a task which will take considerable time to achieve. That is no reason for further delay, but for a sense of urgency.

4. Goals of Education

Curriculum goals: vocational, social, individual

Education is always an area of tension between the stresses given to various types of goals. In various ways, writers on curriculum goals have identified a range which may be grouped under three major headings, vocational, social and personal. Gagnon emphasizes that these three elements are not simply differences in types of goals but require different styles of pedagogy.

"...it is commonplace among French educators that schools and their three purposes are, as they say, 'by the nature of things' constrained to pursue different modes of pedagogy, aimed at different -- sometimes quite opposite -- results. Schooling for work in any society is necessarily a 'conservative' function, a disciplined study of tasks from the world of work, requiring objective testing and ranking of competence. The school has to be open to all sections of the economy as it is, respecting craftsmanship of whatever sort. Schooling for free citizenship, in contrast, is a 'radical' activity, egalitarian and sceptical in style, combining systematic study of history and ideas at home and abroad with free-swinging exchange on public questions. Here the school tries to develop the taste for teamwork and the taste for critical, thorny individualism, at once the readiness to serve and the readiness to resist. Education and personal cultivation requires still another approach. The school insulates itself, for much of the time, from the imperious fashion of pop and counter-culture. It must be 'conservative' in its demand that students confront the entire range of art and behaviour conceived in the past, but only to reach the 'liberal', liberating point at which their own choices are informed and thereby free" (Gagnon, 1982).

As we have noted, of the three major emphases identified, the current priority for economic reasons is vocational. In dealing with this area first, there is no confirmation of this area as the priority issue. It is the inter-relationship which will prove to be vital.

The vocational emphasis

The restructuring of employment and the consequent high levels of unemployment give a special emphasis in the minds of young people and of society more generally on preparation for work and this requires much more than the development of vocational skills, the more specific of which are probably best learned on the job. It requires a feeling for what it is to be a member of a working group, accepting directions and co-operating with others. It requires a broader understanding of the work-phase together with a preparedness to meet different requirements at different career stages. In spite of the broad discussion in the area, not enough well-focused research is occurring and the practical projects tend to be short-term and not systematically developed.

The concept of "a productive workforce" enabling substantial and flexible economic development is powerful, particularly in the current economic situation. That governments should support such an emphasis is not surprising, given both the pressure for increased productivity and the social concern which is linked with high unemployment levels. The latter factor is important in the thinking of families and individuals for whom unemployment is not simply an economic problem but one related to social status and personal self-esteem. In such a situation it is not surprising that young people see education as predominantly instrumental with the key purpose being preparation for employment. The emphasis for young people has been consistently instrumental but the current situation has heightened that feeling, resulting in a distortion of values.

41

As we look to a future which is likely to be under pressures at least as great as the present, it is important to emphasize that such a single-minded approach is inadequate, either as a vocational preparation or for general education. If the uncertainties on employment persist for some time, even the best vocational education cannot provide a job, merely prepare for it. Vocational education, without a job in which to exercise it, can only be a guarantee of frustration. Further, the demands which many employers emphasize as important go well beyond vocational competencies to include qualities such as flexibility, punctuality, co-operativeness, creativity. Such qualities relate to values which are part of a much wider and more general preparation. Further, the pattern of increased retention as a solution to unemployment may end up merely as ineffective child-minding. Those who are now continuing on into upper secondary education for this reason are students for whom school has not been a satisfactory experience but rather a source of frustration and failure. To develop programmes which are satisfactory for them will require a quite different type of effort from schools to what has been provided before.

The social emphasis

The insufficiency of a single emphasis to cover the goals of modern schooling is accentuated as we consider some of the needs of a democratic society and what it means to be an active, participating member of such a society. Citizenship commonly features in statements of goals yet the practice within and between countries is uneven in the development of such goal statements into teaching programmes. Yet, increasingly, there are higher expectations as to how people must act as responsible members of a democratic society and these expectations must be considered in any decisions on goals for schooling. The expectations include the following for members of a democratic society.

-- They should undertake the full responsibilities of citizenship, voting intelligently, taking an interest in political issues, understanding and supporting the legal system, taking responsibilities within the community.

-- They should respect the rights of others and seek to ensure that people are not discriminated against on the basis of gender, race, religious belief or economic status.

-- They should be aware of major world issues, such as environmental conservation, and be able to play an appropriate part in their own society on such concerns.

-- They should understand the role of the media and the way the media shape public opinion.

The list could continue. The point made here is that such issues are being considered seriously by Member countries in their own development of goals.

The Swedish Commission on the Curriculum in its recent report stated:

"Developments in society encompass increased demands for influence on the part of citizens and being able to choose between different alternatives. The school has an important role in providing education for citizenship... This implies also the habit of working in democratic ways and participating in our cultural heritage in a broad sense. Demands for increased influence and taking greater responsibility are becoming increasingly important in daily working life, where personal competence, the ability to assess competence as well as to communicate and co-operate is intensified" (Swedish Ministry, 1992).

The recent Irish Green Paper includes in its aims a similar statement.

"The school must seek to create an environment that fosters a sense of political and social awareness, of civic and social responsibility, within a caring society. In this regard, the school should involve students in an active and responsible way in decision-making in the school, commensurate with their level of maturity" (Brennan, 1992).

It is significant that here, as in the Swedish example, there is an emphasis on process as well as purpose. The implication is that it may be counter-productive to teach about democratic principles if they are not being actively applied in the school, and in the teaching process itself. To teach about responsibility must imply a willingness to give responsibility.

In Spain, the process of reform initiated by the White Paper of 1989 and confirmed by the national parliament through legislation in 1990 deliberately uses the democratic process in the sequence of curriculum reform itself. Initial statements of objectives and of required standards of achievement are developed through a process of review, of public discussions and consultations, and of trial and experiment. This is based on the view that for goals to become a reality through curriculum reform there must be public support and the direct involvement of school teachers, parents, university teachers, local authorities and community representatives (Spain, 1990).

The development of social responsibility as a goal necessarily involves critical capacities. Knowledge may be conceived in at least three ways. One is the most commonly acknowledged: the function of knowledge as an instrument or tool. The second is knowledge as contextual: in some senses knowledge is dependent on the context and it is this context which provides the basis for making it understandable. The third is the constructive aspect of knowledge: this recognizes that knowledge is not a mere reproduction of reality but a way of giving meaning, of making the world understandable. Many writers commenting on the modern media note that they provide a particularly chaotic and disconnected view of the world and that one of the tasks of education should be deliberately to counteract that view.

"Television is a curriculum that stresses instancy, not constancy; discontinuity, not coherence; immediate, not deferred, gratification; emotional, not intellectual, response. In the face of all of this, perhaps the most important contribution schools can make is to provide young people with a sense of purpose, of meaning, and of the interconnectedness of what they learn. At present, the typical school curriculum reflects far too much the fragmentation one finds in television's weekly schedule. Each subject, like each t.v. programme, has nothing whatever to do with any other -- and for reasons less justifiable than those that explain the discontinuity and incoherence of t.v. After all, the major aim of t.v. is the psychological gratification of the viewer. Schools, on the other hand, offer what they do either because they have always done so or because colleges or professional schools 'require' it. There is no longer any principle that unifies the school curriculum and furnishes it with meaning, unless it is the mission of preparing students for jobs, which is hardly a morally or intellectually worthy theme" (Postman, 1983).

This task of providing young people with a sense of purpose, of meaning, of interconnectedness lies at the centre of the social goals of education. It is of equal relevance to the vocational and personal goals because of the degree to which many young people see school learning as irrelevant to the real issues of their lives. Young people in most countries have suffered the impact of social and technological changes to an inequitable degree. As Richard Eckersley states, they are the

43

"casualties of change" (Eckersley, 1990). The indicators extend beyond high unemployment to include drug abuse, suicide and violent crime, the latter frequently exhibiting aspects of racism. There can be no doubt that our societies must confront this task. What of the schools? Can they effectively confront such issues? In what ways should we teach for good citizenship? Should values education have a specific place in the curriculum? If so, in what ways?

The individual emphasis

Some initiatives would suggest that schools must include a strong social emphasis, that in a very deep sense our education is an expression of the sort of society we want to develop. An interesting study was recently carried out in Australia for the World Education Fellowship. The researchers sent out invitations to over 500 people who had contributed substantially to Australian thinking. They included politicians, historians, industrialists, educators, scientists and journalists. Of these, 125 agreed to an extended dialogue in which they expressed their views on the social emphases of schools and then received a summary of other statements before developing a more complete statement. The researchers, Campbell and McMeniman derived from the 125 statements a set of societal goals which could be reduced to 22 goals, falling into seven major sets of goals.

The seven inclusive statements read as follows:

I.   A society which **values persons for themselves**.

II.   A society which **displays international and ecological responsibility**.

III. A society which **is committed to the development of individuals within an overarching concern with moral responsibility**.

IV.   A society **with caring processes of interaction**: harmony; collaboration.

V.   A society which **provides supportive networks**: families; neighbourhoods.

VI.   A society which **offers supportive identities**: national; regional; global.

VII. A society **with a robust economy**" (Campbell and McMeniman, 1992).

Two aspects of the process were significant. Firstly, that a diverse set of people could reach a high degree of consensus on the identification and ranking of social goals for education. Secondly, that in such a diverse list of social goals, the valuing of persons is rated so highly, receiving the top rating in well over 90 per cent of the assessments. We often speak of the difficulties in obtaining consensus on goals. Perhaps, with enough care and effort a working consensus is achievable.

An interesting example of an increased emphasis on the value of the individual occurs in the 1989 Japanese curriculum reform following the major report of the National Council on Educational Reform. This Council was established by Parliament and was in session for a number of years, producing reports which stimulated public discussion before reaching its final conclusions. There were five emphases of the Council adopted for the curriculum reform: further development of 'kokoro'; focus on the basic contents; respect for individual differences; development of lifelong learning; ability to cope with internationalism. The notion of 'kokoro' is significant. It represents the idea that education is not for skills but for the "completion of character": "Such concepts in English as heart, mind, spirit, mentality, humanity" (Okamoto, 1992).

A complete education will seek realistically to develop the balance between these three aspects, individual, social and vocational in making a significant effort to put into realisable form the high expectations that a democratic society has for all its citizens. It expects them to undertake the full responsibilities of citizenship. It expects them to take vocational responsibilities. It expects them to develop as individuals. This is a formidable range of expectations, but it is what is meant by being a responsible citizen in a democratic society.

The complexity of this task makes it important to assess how the problem might be approached. It is now more important to decide on how people can best use their own capacities as we consider the possibilities made available by technology. Information is now available from more services than the print, the teacher, the parent, and the printed papers. There is a flood of information, via radio and television and through recordings of many topics. What becomes important is the capacity to assess the value of information, to judge its relevance, to use it effectively and efficiently in making decisions. The computer opens up still further levels of possibilities: in providing access to information throughout the world, in storing and analysing information, in solving problems. In this area as in the others, a capacity for performing immense quantities of lower-level skills, places an increased value on higher-level skills and on affective, aesthetic and moral decisions which can only be made by humans. The expectations of society, the possibilities through technology -- these combine to make important for each individual the choices to be made through life: intellectual, emotional, ethical and spiritual. This constitutes the new basics: what is essential to us in being fully human in a democratic society.

As the Ministers' Conference Communiqué has said, we cannot provide for the future by "more of the same". Our current school curriculum, particularly at the secondary level, is aimed essentially to provide a high level education for a minority. The attempt to revert to that traditional structure by adding a few subjects to the traditional form will not be satisfactory if we are serious in the attempt to provide a good foundation education for all. This is the basis on which the choices for life become a possibility: socially, personally, vocationally. This will require a fundamental reconsideration of content in the common core curriculum. More, as the projects have shown, it will require a fundamentally different approach to pedagogy. This includes such approaches as those encouraged in the vocational education project: situational learning. It will include much more, however, if we consider the whole progress of children through the compulsory years.

5. Curriculum Goals as Statements of Value

The OECD studies and projects in the area of curriculum reform locate that effort in a broad social and economic context. The goals which are crucial to the nature of that curriculum reform must relate to the realities of that context: shifts in political alliances, economic restructuring, the importance of high technology and information systems, concerns over environmental preservation and the growth of urban and suburban poverty. While taking account of these factors the function to be served by the development of goals is to transcend these factors by indicating unequivocally that goals are statements of our value system. They may be challenged for their achievability. They may be criticised for inconsistencies or omissions. But they remain as an ideological basis for our efforts in curricular reform. At the base is the fundamental principle: *to provide a quality education for all pupils*. This may seem an unexceptionable statement but it is one which has a particular urgency in a time when education provides so substantially the key to opportunity. Its perfectionist nature is stressed by the fact that education has never succeeded in such a task in the past. For too many students, educational handicaps carried into the school setting have not been overcome and in many instances, in comparative terms, have become more significant and more damaging.

The goal statements developed in curriculum reform provide the more detailed formulation of that principle. They are value statements by which a nation defines its concepts of "a good school", "a good person", "a good society". As such they are living statements, subject to continued analysis and testing but emphasizing at any given time the nature of the efforts to be made. Statements from different Member countries illustrate the emphases. For Japan, the New Course of Study Interim Report pronounces the following emphasis:

> "With a view to educating Japanese citizens living in an internationalised society in the 21st century, and putting emphasis on basic and fundamental contents of education... the greatest importance should be given to an effort to evoke the education system to fully develop individual ability and aptitude of each pupil/student as well as an effort to educate a person with affluent humanity and a positive attitude to his/her life, who has enough aspirations to learn and to cope with social changes on his/her own initiative" (OECD, 1989).

This is a very deliberate statement by Japan following the substantial inquiries and findings of the National Commission mentioned earlier which was highly critical of the over-emphasis on competitiveness and materialism. This deliberate shift of cultural emphasis turns attention to humanistic dimensions such as the pursuit of truth, attachment to nature and sensibility to beauty.

In New Zealand the emphases in the thrust defined by the new Curriculum Framework included a strong statement on the need for a multi-cultural society, the importance of the recognition of distinct cultural elements within an overall cohesive society.

> "The New Zealand Curriculum reflects the multi-cultural nature of New Zealand society. The school curriculum will encourage students to understand and respect the different cultures which make up New Zealand society. It will ensure that the experiences, cultural tradition, histories, and languages of all New Zealanders are recognised and valued. It will acknowledge the place of Pacific Island communities in New Zealand society, and New Zealand's relationships with the peoples of Asia and the South Pacific" (New Zealand Ministry, 1993).

The curriculum statement is a clear acknowledgement of a new social emphasis, an emphasis on inclusiveness.

A third position is evident in the programme America 2000 (1991), developed as indicated earlier from the initiatives of the Committee of Governors and taken up by the then President to make it into a national programme. It built on the concern expressed in the earlier report of the National Commission on Excellence in Education, "A Nation at Risk". This was highly critical of student achievement levels and of a lack of force and cohesion in schooling and the new initiative developed a dual emphasis. One aspect was on moral values, in particular nurturing family and community values. Another quite contrasting aspect was the concentration on improving America's competitive position in a global economy, especially through achievement in the mathematics and science disciplines where the International Evaluation of Achievement (IEA) studies had shown American students to be performing relatively poorly. In meeting this challenge, the USA developed co-operative effort between the States and the Federal Government, as indicated earlier. The goals to be reached by the year 2000 were:

-- All American children will start school ready to learn;

-- At least 90 per cent of our students will graduate from high school;

-- Our students will demonstrate competency in challenging subject matter and will learn to use their minds well, so they may be prepared for responsible citizenship, further learning and productive employment;

-- American students will be first in the world in science and mathematics achievement;

-- Every adult will be literate and have the knowledge and skills necessary to compete in a world economy and exercise the rights and responsibilities of citizenship;

-- Every school will be safe and drug-free and offer a disciplined environment conducive to learning" (US Department of Education, 1992).

While there are many echoes here of the broader aims, there is an underlying emphasis here on high-quality academic programmes and on the definition of standards of achievement. This latter emphasis has been taken up by many OECD Member countries.

All these programmes of formal education make their own statements of values. They reflect the difficulty of societies which are attempting to respond to new situations and needs yet without losing contact with deep cultural values. There is a continual tension between the tasks of conservation and reproduction and those of criticism and creation. However, this is a healthy tension and one that needs to be acknowledged more openly. It implies a clear acknowledgement that there can be no value-free or neutral education but that we define moral stances by what we include and what we omit. This situation raises questions as to how we might pursue this task more openly and more effectively. If we examine the lessons from our social context more carefully the importance of this process becomes more apparent. The small and self-sufficient communities of the past permitted the grouping together of people with common values, applying to all or most of their lives. The abolition of these parochial societies by industrialisation, the linking together of people in interdependent networks, the vast mass-migration of people, have meant more pluralist societies, in customs and behaviour, in conceptions of the world, in the definition of personal beliefs. It is precisely at times when the commonality of values is reduced, that the processes for developing and sharing value-statements become more important.

6. Processes of Reform

The means by which societies define and develop further the values implicit in goal statements deserve particular attention. In his state-of-the-art study, Skilbeck commented on the strong pattern which had developed of 'top-down' changes in curriculum through national action or legislation. He mentions in particular the comprehensive and thoughtful processes for the reform of primary education in both Japan and Italy. In these and other cases, however, he comments:

"It is difficult to avoid the conclusion that there is a real risk, if such approaches are not complemented by equal attention to the processes of change within the schools, of a widening gap between policy directions and the classroom reality" (Skilbeck, 1990).

This comment is particularly relevant as we consider the issue of developing comprehensive goal statements in such broad fields. There is a real danger that they may become little more than slogans, statements expressing broad hopes which are not translated into reality. If this occurs, then the statements are not constructive and helpful but will be the focus of cynicism and disbelief. For this process to become more meaningful and more practical in its outcomes requires a strong commitment from within a society to involve individuals, groups, institutions at all levels up to and including government, to produce statements which have real significance. In New Zealand, for example, the long series of position papers and of community group discussions, meant that many thousands of people were involved in the process of developing agreements on aims. In Japan, some discussion was achieved through the release of interim reports by the National Commission on Educational Reform. A similar approach occurred in Korea with the Presidential Commission on Education. The nature and extent of this process will be a vital aspect of curriculum reform. What processes of goal formulation should a society initiate? How should we ensure that goal statements remain relevant and effective?

In Paper 3, the Conference Chairman, Sir Claus Moser, comments on the major issues crucial to curriculum reform and reports on an initiative in reform in the United Kingdom, the National Commission on Education.

48

Paper 3

ENDS AND MEANS IN CURRICULUM REFORM

Sir Claus Moser

There are few topics more important in education than the curriculum. At this particular stage, for reasons pointed out already, there are few more important issues for our society. The curriculum has always been an issue for schools and for education generally, what is new, is the more general realisation that it is important nationally. For some countries, that is a familiar idea. For many others it is new. But for all countries, the issue of balance needs to be resolved, the balance in decision-making. Who have the key roles in decision-making? What, for example, is the balance between the roles of governments, of teachers and of students?

As we look at the curriculum issues identified so far, I have a particular concern. Our brief is to look at the curriculum for the compulsory years and this is an appropriate and important focus. Let us be careful, however, not to do so in isolation, or with too much attention to particular sectors. Because of the particular impact of employment issues at the moment, we are paying a great deal of attention to the secondary years, and particularly upper secondary. This risks ignoring the particular role of primary education and the early secondary years. Equally, it ignores the special contribution of the early childhood years, for example in pre-schools and day-care. The progress made at this stage may well be crucial for all future development. The other interfaces for education warrant equal attention. This is the case for the school-work interface but I would encourage more attention for the school -- higher education interface. We still tend to underestimate the effects of higher education on schools. Perhaps some of the lethargy in schools, with respect to change is the fault of higher education and particularly of the tendency of so many academics to focus on individual rather than on institutional concerns. While it may be a truism, it is a meaningful one to think of education as essentially a "seamless robe". We must consider it as a whole rather than attempting to change our part in isolation.

This concept of the seamless robe is important in two distinct ways. It is important in terms of the horizontal divisions we make, between child-care, pre-schools, primary education, lower secondary, upper secondary, further and higher education. It is equally important in terms of the vertical divisions we also make. The divisions between subjects. It is, of course, essential that we consider the special nature of such areas of activity as the sciences, mathematics, technology, the arts, the humanities, and the social sciences. Again, however, their interconnections and interactions are equally important and are often the growing points of knowledge. Certainly, the problems of the day, and of tomorrow, do not come neatly packaged according to particular disciplinary lines. I hope that we can recognise both the need for specialised knowledge and that for communication and interaction between specialties.

In Britain, one of our major projects in education at the moment is the National Commission on Education, which arose following an initiative of mine when President of the British Association for the Advancement of Science. While the Government did not take up the challenge, business and industry has done so and their initiative, working through a great deal of research and discussion, will emerge in October. The Commission aims to be at once practical and visionary. It is concerned with current issues but conscious also of the context of the next 50 years. We face a number of significant changes. Let me mention only as examples, the breakdown in family structures, the domination of our society by the revolution in information technology, and the recognition of the growing internationalism of our societies. These are typical of social influences which have profound effects. One, at least, of our responses is the recognition that we must become in reality, and not in name only, a learning society, a society in which life-long learning replaces our traditional discontinuous pattern. For such a concept, we need to think in terms of learning entitlement as the alternative to our fixed institutional arrangements.

III. PROCESS AND PARTICIPATION IN REFORM

1. Curriculum Reform: A Major Social Task

Our past experience reveals the magnitude of this task. The curriculum is both a complex concept and a complex activity and it would be a major error to over-simplify either aspect. The term can be used to describe the educational plan as to what should happen in schools. It can be used to describe the syllabus, which defines the content for that plan. It can be used to describe the learning experiences which result from plan and syllabus, and the pedagogic strategies which suggest those experiences. It can be used to describe the materials and equipment required for those learning experiences and the organisation by which they are utilised. It can be used to describe the outcomes of the curriculum, desired and actual, and the procedures used for the evaluation of the whole. The most realistic use of the term encompasses all these uses. Thus, for one purpose it may be useful to consider it as what happens in schools as a result of intention. For another, it needs to be regarded as a major cultural artefact of a particular society, an embodiment of what the society values. Both aspects are of value and must be kept in mind in considering curriculum issues.

Paper 4 by Judith Chapman sets curriculum reform in the context of studies of the effectiveness of schooling, many initiated by OECD.

IMPLICATIONS FOR THE CURRICULUM OF THE OECD ACTIVITY ON THE EFFECTIVENESS OF SCHOOLING AND OF EDUCATIONAL RESOURCE MANAGEMENT

Judith Chapman

The Concept of "Effectiveness"

Across the OECD there is no uniformly agreed operating definition of "effectiveness" in schooling. Rather than offering a definition of effectiveness, therefore, for the purposes of the OECD Activity it has seemed advisable to delineate no more than a broad working framework.

This includes consideration of the following elements:

-- The nature of the goals of schooling and the achievements obtained: this relates to such values as relevance, academic standards, and desirable social effects of the achievements;

-- The means by which objectives are attained: this has to do with such matters as the economy of effort, time, and resources expended on the task; and

-- The criteria and methods employed in the measurement of the objectives attained, as regards the range, depth, comprehensiveness and totality of cover.

The Relationship Between Theory, School Effectiveness Research and Policy Development

Given the extensive range of school objectives, the difficulty of researching school effectiveness is clear. The complexity of these objectives, the range and modes of their interplay, and the ways in which they are subject to non-quantifiable pressures, are often not amenable to scientific enquiry understood in terms of the traditional empirical mode.

In many countries attention has been focused in various ways on researching the effectiveness of schools, some of the research taking account of such difficulties and complexities, some not. Much research, particularly the earlier research, tended to concentrate on a select number of objectives and only those that could be stated in measurable terms. It is now clear that across the OECD a broader understanding of the objectives or goals of schooling is preferred, together with a more wide-ranging and comprehensive method of enquiry into them.

Part of the value of the original contribution of the OECD activity, particularly its study of reports submitted by Member countries and its examination of existing literature and contributions by Experts, has been the realisation that intelligible accounts and plausible analyses of school effectiveness cannot be restricted to those only deliverable in the quantitative mode.

Recent work in the epistemology and methodology of the natural and social sciences has moved decisively away from the emphasis upon measurement and so-called "value-neutral" description, that was typical of an earlier era in research, when workers believed completely in the academic tenability of the empiricist paradigm and tended only to develop and apply research designs and instruments exclusively based upon it. Modern researchers in the social sciences have now moved much more towards an approach based on advances in epistemology and methodology that arise from post-empiricist work in the philosophy of science and the social sciences, such as that of Quine, Popper, Lakatos and Winch [1].

This work has made it possible to move beyond the hard-line demand for a so-called "value-free" objectivity, typical of former empiricist research, and beyond the untenable relativism of much writing in the social sciences that was too heavily influenced by subjectivists and ethnomethodologists of various kinds, and to articulate accounts, develop analyses, and produce tentative conclusions, that are quite as complex, heterogeneous and multiform as the corpus of material upon which they are based and towards the elucidation of which they may be applied.

Most past investigations and treatments of school effectiveness comprised such dichotomies of description-evaluation, fact-value, and quantitative-qualitative analyses as were previously thought to be mutually opposed and exclusive. There is now a need in school effectiveness enquiry to fuse description-evaluation, fact-value, quantitative-qualitative methods in new forms of enquiry, that are valuable both for the researcher and the policy-maker. Such an approach will involve both groups in a common enterprise -- what Lakatos called a "progressive research programme" -- of understanding and policy generation. Future work in the investigation of school effectiveness would be well advised to incorporate approaches of this kind.

The Context within which Effectiveness is being considered across OECD Countries

The question of how effective outcomes are to be secured and in what most cost-efficient manner, while at the same time achieving the broadest social benefit, is an issue of major concern in all OECD countries. Responses of member countries to this question reflect the commitments governments have to a fundamental set of ethical, political and social beliefs regarding the nature of human beings and the ways in which they can best arrange and institutionalise their relationships for the various purposes, individual and social, they have.

Although there is no simple and direct relationship between values, goals and administrative structures and practices it is possible to discern significant differences in approaches to the provision and administration of education across the OECD member countries. These make manifest fundamental changes in the administration of public education, reflecting a change in the very concept of public service.

Public education systems in most OECD countries have traditionally been based on the assumption that the public interest was best served when public goods such as education were provided by agencies under public control exercised through the various institutions and services of the state. The new view in some OECD countries rests on the notion that education is to be conceived of, less as a public good but rather as a commodity. The selection of this is held to be a matter of private choice and depends upon personal provision and the norms of the market place.

A crucial question, yet to be explored, is whether the approach to educational policy and administration based on the norms and values of the market place actually enhances the effectiveness of schools. Are the changes proposed in and by this model based on any solid evidence that they will in fact produce the benefits described?

Underlying the proposals for a more market- or consumer-oriented approach to education and for the privatisation of educational provision is the stark reality of restricted funding for education in many OECD countries. Even in countries which have not moved towards a market-oriented approach to education, economic forces have impacted on education in various ways. Re-assessment, rationalisation, and enhanced efficiency have increasingly been called for. The requirement of more efficient resource utilisation has inevitably brought to the fore issues relating to control of public services. In many countries this has led to decentralisation, devolution, and a new approach to control, with a movement away from regulative control to one based upon steering by goals and results.

Economic pressures and increasing international co-operation and competition are also forcing many countries to question whether they are following the right ideals and pathways in education. From an ethical point of view, they are asking, are we doing the most to contribute to the growth and development of our people? From a competitor's point of view, they are asking, how shall we be able to survive as an independent sovereign nation and an economically thriving unity, with the values that have been foremost in the past?

A problem here is that educational goals for curriculum action can realistically only be set with regard to the time and resources available for their achievement. Political time-scales, especially at ministerial level, are short; educational ones are long. Education, as Edward Bond [2] remarked, "cannot be put on like coats of paint". And, given the lifelong duration of education, there will never be a time when we can say that the evidence as to its effectiveness is all in. We may, of course, try to make intermediary assessments, and some of these will be directed at the formal stages of education, when one of the chief instruments of educative action will be that applied to the student by means of a structured curriculum.

The major questions must therefore start at this point: what shall be the educational goals of a country's education system, institutions and schools; what shall be the curriculum that is held best to conduce to those goals; and who shall decide the nature and composition of that curriculum? The answer to this last question is that the decision can only be made by a selection of judges from among a whole array of interested parties. But the question of who makes that selection, and on what basis, is crucial to this whole endeavour.

At the present time, throughout the OECD a widespread stock-taking is occurring on these and other related questions: Does it matter if, at the national level, legislation enacts requirements as to those subjects to be covered in the curriculum. How do such enactments determine delivery? Are there inflexibilities that inhibit change? If legislation sets in place the objectives and goals to be achieved in specific subjects, does this interfere with the professionals' rights in respect not merely of appropriate teaching methods and curriculum, but also their properly qualified view of what constitutes and counts as the subject itself? Is there any danger that the promulgation and imposition from the centre of national statements of goals and curriculum might overtly or covertly condition and shape the nature of curriculum subjects, in such a way that the ontology of a subject can become distorted from what the professionals believe it to be? From which dominant intellectual traditions and cultural values shall the curriculum selection be made, and on what grounds?

The question of dominant intellectual traditions and cultural values is a crucial one. However, we also need to examine the ways in which cultural values are passed on in the school as a social institution in informal or extra-curricular ways, as well as formally through the child's exposure to the curriculum and to subject learning. School is a highly effective social and socialising institution and we need to consider how it functions and affects and effects the learning and the development of the child, in all the various ways, formal, non-formal, informal and para-normal, in which these occur. This is particularly important in the case of the question of access to the curriculum. Should there, for example, be different curriculum goals for different groups in society? Is the curriculum we envisage for all students the same curriculum we have in mind when we are looking at the learning and access needs of students with disabilities?

The Design and Implementation of Reforms conceived to achieve the Goals of Schooling: Knowledge and the Curriculum

The evidence suggests that across the OECD significant differences exist between countries in their approach to the design and implementation of educational reform conceived as appropriate to address these questions. But no matter what the approach to the process of change, no-one can doubt the over-riding importance attached in all current reform efforts to three key matters:

-- the nature and purposes of the goals of schooling;
-- the body of knowledge and skills that shall be constructed to help those goals be achieved;
-- the quality of the teaching and learning processes, their impacts and outcomes.

In arranging for effective and quality teaching and learning, it is clear there will be differences and difficulties over the meaning and use of such words as "curriculum" and pedagogy". It is widely agreed, however, that the question of the goals of schooling and the curriculum to deliver them transcends the immediate and local nature of school, and that these are not merely characterised as the sum of all the activities going on within it. There is a need for a broader account of goals and curriculum, one that takes in all that involves all educational objectives, the transmission of values, attitudes and beliefs, and the educational point and purpose of all those teaching and learning activities and experiences in a school, to which value can be attached.

Conceptions of Knowledge and the Selection of Curriculum Content

It might be helpful at this point to cite instances of some goals that have been laid down for schools' activities. It is plain that a concern of very many countries is to link education to economic advance. The function of schooling is seen as providing personnel and fuel to run the economic engine of the state -- to enable a state to be, so far as possible, economically self-sufficient, and, if not, to give it a leading edge of economic competitiveness in the world economic market-place. Recent education reforms and efforts at curriculum determination in some OECD countries make it clear that the goals of education are seen primarily in these instrumental terms: education is seen less as an activity worthwhile in its own right, but more of value insofar as it leads to other, much more worthwhile, ends -- of which the chief one has, in the world today, to be that of economic power and self-sufficiency.

There is also another current of thinking which holds that the prime function of schooling is to induct the coming generation into all those traditions, experiences and cultures that constitute both the identity and value of being human in today's world. Proponents of this view [3] hold that students are "entitled" to be given access to all the great and good things that have been thought, said and done in the ascent of human-kind, and that form the starting-points for all future endeavours. These curriculum "entitlements" can be concentrated into number of areas of experience, culture and value, entry and learning which would provide the building blocks for a life in society that would enable the young person to enjoy civilisation and culture, and cope with the exigencies of the modern world.

55

Yet a third approach considers the delineation of educational goals that transcended immediate economic, political or social concerns, and stand aside from the momentary interests of particular groups or pressures. Proponents of this approach regard the central undertaking of educational endeavour as being beyond the need for vocational training, moral development and cultural awareness. For them what is important is the tenet that education is first and foremost about initiating and developing the life of the mind. A truly liberal education is one that gives a person access to and competence in all the various forms of intelligence, all the powers of rational thinking, without which any approach to questions of vocational, moral or cultural import is impossible and unintelligible. For Hirst, Gardner and others [4], what matters is that we direct our educational attention towards developing the powers of intelligence and rational mind. It is in and by those modes of experience and understanding which mankind has progressively structured, developed and made meaningful over the millennia, that people are able to make sense of their experience and communicate about it intelligibly with others of their kind. Such modes of intelligence and rationality are of a finite number, but the number of various discrete modes of understanding constitutes the totality of the rational apparatus by means of which human beings can understand and appraise the reality they share, and tackle the exigencies it brings them.

These different conceptions of knowledge and goals for schooling generate different curricula by means of which a student may start on the road to their achievement. Instrumental education, for example, will see it as a prime necessity that the curriculum concentrates on the transmission and acquisition of those selected bodies of content and forms of cognitive skill, that will be causally related to vocational competence and strong economic performance. In such a curriculum subjects such as english, mathematics, science and technology, foreign languages, and some knowledge of history, geography and economics will clearly be crucial. Competence at other skills, such as team management, the organisation of knowledge, research, and interpersonal relations will also conduce towards the end of efficient and successful commercial, industrial and business production and performance.

Those who opt for an "entitlement" curriculum will lay down as a requirement that access to a knowledge and understanding of all the various products, artifacts and advances that have marked what Bronowski called "The Ascent of Man" [5], and to all the great human traditions of critico-creative thought [6] by which these major cultural, social and intellectual accomplishments have been wrought, will form the main content of such a curriculum. Mathematics, science, technology, the arts, religion, medicine and philosophy will all be among those subjects where the store of human excellence can be concentrated and in which human potential for future development might begun to be realised.

For the third group, what matters is that, either by the skills of cognitive psychology or epistemological and philosophical enquiry, those modes of intelligence and ways of knowing that constitute the totality of human rationality, at its present stage of development, be identified and defined, and that then, in some shape or form and at some time or other, students in our educating institutions be given induction into them and practice in their application and deployment. Such ways of thinking as the mathematical, the scientific, the philosophical, the historical, the moral, the religious, the aesthetic and artistic, will all function as building blocks upon which the edifice of human intelligence and rationality can be constructed. Using these forms of intelligence and awareness students will be able to understand and address the issues and problems arising from their situation in the world and the needs and concerns they have; without them no such address or engagement would be possible.

At this point it will be clear that such positions as those delineated above have some features in common. One is that, in the quest for educational goals, there will always be some foundations that have to be provided, which function as basic building blocks for the construction of curricula and the articulation of appropriate teaching and learning activities and processes. The second is that those foundations will be separable and discrete: the central concepts, operating procedures, tests for truth claims, and criteria for evaluating success, for instance, will be different as between, say, mathematics, morals and the arts, and it is these varying characteristics that require us to provide a differentiated and heterogeneous curriculum. What is agreed among proponents of such approaches is that there are different forms of cognition and intelligence: all that has to be done, in curriculum terms, is to define what they are and, in educational terms, what they are for.

It should be pointed out, however, that these premises have been under considerable challenge for many years. It has been argued that their status is no more than that of dogmas, to the refutation of which Quine and others have devoted considerable logical power. By some modern curriculum theorists [7] Quine's arguments have been re-deployed to telling effect. There is now a substantial body of theorists who claim that the holding and promulgating of the curriculum beliefs such as those described above may be seen as little more than the promulgation of particular positions by people with strong ideological convictions, contentious theories of intelligence and meta-cognition, or controversial and out of date philosophies of knowledge.

Clearly educational epistemologies and cognitive psychologies are key areas in the planning and formulation of appropriate curricula -- but it would be a proper academic requirement that they accord with the most recent findings and advances in these subjects proper. And the fact is that recent work in epistemology and cognitive science suggests that the theories set out above have no uncontested rightness, self-evidence or plausibility about them than any other set of curriculum proposals.

Post-empiricist philosophies of knowledge suggest the giving up of the idea of foundationalist epistemology altogether. A better way forward, it has been suggested, in any cognitive enterprise is the working out of theories to apply to the issues, topics and problems of such key human activities as education, medicine, politics, and economics. Curriculum philosophy, seen in this light, is not an activity of conceptual clarification; rather it is an activity of theory construction, correction and contention. Those theories that have greatest power are those which operate to the best functional advantage. Cancer is better tackled by the medical theories of the hospital laboratory than by those of the folklore of traditional societies; it was modern applied physics that sent human beings to the moon and returned them safely; and in the Lysenko affair the genetic theories of an open scientific society enabled more grain to be grown, and more people fed, than those based upon Marxist historicism.

So it is with curriculum construction. Curriculum building and planning, from this post-empiricist "scientific" perspective, is devoted to the framing of answers to problems, the examination and criticism of the hypotheses proposed as answers to those questions, and the to tentative trying-out and application of those theories that have hitherto resisted falsification. In this way curriculum construction becomes an activity of facing problems, planning, criticising, and the tentative adoption of solutions to the problems onto which they are directed.

It is thus problems that provide a set of agenda for curriculum action: agenda that stand instead of much larger-scale "Aims of Education". To try and frame the latter is, it is argued, a mistaken undertaking. On Popper's account, the millennium will never come. What is important is that we address the problems, topics and issues that constitute the staple of the curriculum diet for a society's schooling and educating institutions -- that, in other words, we adopt pragmatic approaches to problems that press in on us today.

As examples of some of those problems we might point to the common concern of many countries to enhance the literacy of their citizens. Attention might also be drawn to the need of many countries to acquire the requisite skills and competences to enable its citizens to operate in a world where the amount of available productive work is decreasing, where service industries of all kinds are increasingly likely to provide the main means of work, where advances in knowledge and the information technology revolution will mean that a worker will have to be prepared to change jobs four or five times in a working lifetime, where working life is likely to become shorter and shorter, and where many persons will enjoy increasing longevity. There is the problem of workplace relations in such circumstances: how can people, in times of employment shortage, work together co-operatively so as to enhance productivity and a sense of workplace satisfaction and reward, instead of the industrial competitiveness and confrontation that disfigure so many of our industrial and commercial activities at the present time. There is also the problem of international relations, in a world with scarce resources, where the economic gulf between "north" and "south" nations is not likely to decrease, and where commitment to various forms of extremism, political or religious, will be a continuing cause of tension and possible conflagration. There is also the question of interpersonal relations, in a time when the incidence of phenomena such as domestic violence and child-abuse shows no sign of decreasing, when the divorce rate is already high and climbing, with all the attendant dysfunctions that brings about, and when the problems of diseases of various kinds are continuingly recalcitrant to treatment. There is the problem of food supply and world hunger; there is the problem of protection of the environment; there is the problem of the increasing demand for energy at a time when the store of fossil-fuels is declining. Above all, perhaps, is the problem of how to assist human beings to acquire and retain their values of *humanity*, of sensitivity, sympathy and compassion, at a time when the emphasis upon what Habermas [8] called technocratic rationality, upon technicisation and the dominance of particular kinds of economic interest, threatens us with the loss of a sense of individual worth and commitment to a set of values that will help define and enrich the quality of relationships between ourselves and others -- what we might call the problem of the need for the humanisation of the present-day curriculum.

There is no shortage of problems that provide a rich diet for curriculum address. For an attack upon even a few of these problems requires engagement in a number of forms of intellectual activity, so that our coming generation can not only begin to understand their difficulty, complexity and multifariousness but also start to help the present generation try to make tentative moves towards their solution.

Mary Warnock [9] suggested that the education of students as the coming generation of society was concerned with three kinds of preparation: preparation for the world of work (and, we might add, for the world of non-work and leisure); preparation for the life of virtue (what we might also associate with interpersonal relations); and preparation for the life of the imagination (the ability to understand the past, to appraise all the many facets of the present, and to plan for all the potentialities of the future). All these elements are of vital curricular importance, but much more still needs to be said. For, due to the rapidly changing nature of knowledge itself, to the means and instruments by which knowledge is both acquired and generated (not least by the information technology revolution), and to the rapid increase in the range and type of the problems we daily encounter, the curriculum must be pragmatic: dynamic, flexible, responsive to rapid changes in matters of work, morals and leisure choices. And those who come to it must do so on a pragmatic basis.

It should be pointed out, however, that there is one element in such an approach that is still needed to provide a set of guidelines for steering current curriculum planning. What is needed is a criterion of stability, consistency and coherence to guard against what could otherwise be a somewhat anarchical curriculum situation. One way that will enable curriculum planners and developers to see

58

the wood as well as the trees may be found in the pragmatism articulated and pronounced by Peirce and James [10], and espoused so firmly for education by Dewey, Popper, and their successors up to the present day (Ackerman, Mendus, Guttman and White) [11]. Such a criterion is provided by the idea of "education for democracy".

A modern curriculum, of the flexibility and dynamism described, may be constructed and continually adapted for delivery on the basis of those forms of knowledge, skill and value that future citizens of a participative democracy will need in order for them to be able, on a fully-informed and committed-for-action basis, to participate in the democratic processes of policy formulation, appraisal, criticism, application and assessment. Such participation will be required, as a matter of course, on any of the issues raised above and tackled as matters of over-riding importance by the community -- it could be workplace literacy, it could be concern for the environment, it could be for the fluoridation of the water-supply [12], or the educational imperative of inhibiting such life-threatening diseases and conditions as AIDS, drugs, crimes of violence, and nuclear accident.

To understand and plan for dealing with any of these necessitates nothing less than the highest degree of engagement in those intellectual forms of knowledge and criticism that enable students as future citizens to understand past causes, monitor and appraise the present situation, and plan, for themselves and their community, how to act in the future (an enterprise in which, incidentally, competence in harnessing the power of the Personal Computer will be an important aid in the quest for knowledge, the building of alternative worlds of possibility, and the running of simulations and thought-experiments). And this will further require that educational curricula will not be merely the setting forth of sets of facts or values, that are paraded before our students for them simply to acquire and repeat when necessary: it will also mean an introduction to the forms of engagement in the activities of action and assessment, appraisal and planning, criticism and correction, that are called for in the very conception of an education for life as a citizen in a modern democracy.

Thus, from this examination it is clear that of vital importance in the undertaking of re-defining the curriculum for the future must be the debate regarding what constitutes appropriate curriculum knowledge encompassing such questions as the following:

-- what counts as knowledge; how knowledge should be conceived; how knowledge should be established and certified;

-- how it should be acquired and employed in a society in which knowledge itself is continually changing and expanding;

-- how one can determine in such a case what knowledge is of most worth for the purposes the founders, directors and workers in public institutions have in mind and for all the citizens of a modern democracy;

-- how shall the values of breadth of knowledge, depth of understanding, and curriculum balance be best addressed and assured.

Knowledge, the Curriculum, and Values

This last question raises an issue of major concern in and to the OECD Activity on Curriculum. For it raises the question of what a "balanced" curriculum might look like and how children's learning can be judged to be appropriately "balanced". What this leads to is the fundamental underlying question: what are our children at school to become? What shall our future citizens need, in order to exercise their roles as citizens of a participative democracy -- and how can the curriculum give them the skills, knowledge and values that they need? The question of values is crucial here.

This relates to the important point that values exist, are found in and embodied across the whole curriculum. Values are not definable as though they were an autonomous element in the curriculum, as being in some way a separate subject, with its own body of theory, cognitive content, typical activities, disciplinary procedures or criteria for success. As MacIntyre [13] remarks, to speak of someone as a "ships captain" is to engage in a complicated activity of appraisal: the ship's captain's qualification to be described as such depends centrally upon his/her constantly valuing and performing certain standards of performance. In similar manner Peters remarked [14] that to be a scientist is *ipso facto* to be committed to the values implicit in the procedural principles that define the nature of the subject and prescribe its appropriate activities in it. Science is not value-free: it is shot through with value elements that help structure and define it.

Thus it is plain that questions of value in knowledge and the curriculum are not solely restricted to subjects or areas such as the humanities, the arts, and religion. Questions of value also underpin and indeed permeate the whole syllabuses of other curriculum subjects such as science and technology.

This interplay of epistemological and axiological elements and considerations, in association with reflections drawn from the psychology of learning, the sociology and anthropology of school as a social institution, and the values -- both individual and social -- attaching to and embodied in the institution of schooling by the society in which it is located, will obviously occupy a central place in discussions about the effective development of schools across the OECD in the 1990s and into the next century, and the re-defining of the curriculum, as a consequence.

Further Epistemological Questions and Issues

A number of issues come to the fore:

-- The question of adjustment to epistemic change, as against the need for cognitive stability, in selecting the content of the curriculum;

-- The concept of knowledge itself, that should underpin and be exhibited in curriculum development, and the related questions concerning the skills of knowledge-getting, research, and "learning to learn";

-- How shall the goals for education be determined, and how shall they be translated into curriculum terms?

-- What shall be the content of the curriculum and its relationship to the promotion and achievement of targeted goals and ends aimed at? Who shall determine this? How shall it be assessed?

In all this one clear point emerges: the curriculum is no longer seen as a solid, stable and immutable organisation of existing and traditional valued knowledge, but as a dynamic process involving large-scale and rapid epistemic change, planning, delivery, and assessment. We have still yet to work out what is the part that co-operative relationships between the different levels of action, sectional interests, and community concerns can and must play in the development of appropriate curricula in schools, that will help each country secure its future and make the fullest possible contribution to promoting the good of countries internationally.

Evaluation and Accountability

There is perhaps one further question to be asked: whether assessment can be used as a means of reforming the curriculum. Of course assessment is vital to the curriculum: it is part of the curriculum. However, the uses one makes of the information supplied by the assessment is different from the learnings involved in curriculum progress, even though such a use may be the formative one of re-defining and re-directing educational progress.

Stress on assessment is educationally important during the curriculum delivery phase, when it is employed for diagnostic purposes, and this adds some rationality to learning. This use is quite different from that of the publication of final examination results, which enables the public to make what they regard as summative judgements about the supposed quality, effectiveness or worth of a school overall.

The issue at stake here relates to the philosophy of the school, the curriculum and education, of progress in attaining the ends of which assessment is only an indication. Assessment will determine whether or not we have a broad curriculum in operation or whether teachers simply take up a part or even a narrow element of the curriculum, as determined by the assessors. The assessment debate in the next decade, therefore, is likely to revolve around the use made of assessment to call systems and schools into account. This is intrinsically linked to the question of what schools are about -- their underlying philosophy, theories and goals.

The Curriculum Re-defined: Concluding Questions

Some final questions and over-arching issues remain. Perhaps they may be summed up as follows:

-- Who should decide what in matters of curriculum construction? Should policy-makers be responsible for the formulation of the wider, higher-order goals, with education professionals overseeing the targeting of lower-level and/or more specific curriculum objectives?

-- Where does responsibility for defining appropriate elements of the curriculum and accountability lie?

-- How can a curriculum be created, that is easily and quickly responsive and adaptable to changes in epistemology, administration or environment, without having to have Acts and legislation changed too?

-- How does one achieve an inter-relationship between curriculum, student assessment, and teacher education?

61

-- How does one achieve curriculum reform as a piece of co-operative action among and between the different agencies and actors involved in education and its effective delivery?

-- How does one best approach the relationship between assessment and concerns for equity and the socio-economic background of students?

-- How does one ensure that the system of assessment does not dictate or dominate the educational goals; how does one develop goals that are not overly detailed, particularly in specific subject areas?

-- How does one employ computers to facilitate the establishment and development of new ways of learning and discovery?

-- As far as teachers and educational professionals are concerned, how does one maintain a progressive attitude towards the curriculum among teachers?

-- Given the extended age group beyond the age of 16 in upper secondary schools, how might one re-define syllabuses to meet their needs and the needs of the community and economy?

-- How does one re-define the curriculum in terms of the perennial questions of education's goals and objectives, and how does one relate the issue of goals to objectives, curriculum processes, implementation and evaluation?

-- How does enhancing quality relate to standards of achievement? The process of the imposition of a specific curriculum imposed by law raises the problem of fixity and ossification in curriculum knowledge and how such dysfunctional phenomena can be avoided. How can flexibility in curriculum change be ensured, so that the professionalism of teachers is not undermined?

-- When considering a re-definition of the curriculum, in whose terms is that process to be framed and in response to what pressures, values and concerns?

-- In what ways might the curriculum be most appropriately re-conceptualised: according to traditional subject distinctions, or according to new conceptions and theories of knowledge?

-- With what difficulties must re-definition of the curriculum contend: adjustment as against stability in planning curriculum content; the relationship between freedom of choice, equality and equity?

-- What implications might flow from re-defining curricula: if one redefines curriculum in terms of its goals, what are the implications for assessment? If one redefines curriculum to respond to the needs of the changed student population, what are the implications for the traditional academic curriculum and for post-compulsory and higher education? If one redefines the curriculum in terms of new conceptions of knowledge and new ways or theories of knowing, what are the implications for teacher education and in-service education and training?

-- What articulation might be necessary between the various phases and sectors of education -

- primary, secondary, post-compulsory, tertiary -- if both curriculum change and education for self and society is to be best achieved?

References

1.   Quine, W.V. "Two Dogmas of Empiricism" repr. in his *From a Logical Point of View* Cambridge Mass.(Harvard University Press) 1953;

Lakatos, I., "The Methodology of Scientific Research Programmes" in Lakatos, I., and Musgrave, A.W. (Eds.) *Criticism and the Growth of Knowledge* London (Methuen) 1966

Popper, K.R., *Objective Knowledge* Oxford, Clarendon Press, 1972; see also his *Open Society and its Enemies* London (Routledge and Kegan Paul) 1943; and his *Logic of Scientific Discovery* London (Hutchinsons) 1949

Winch, P.G. *The Idea of a Social Science* London (Routledge and Kegan Paul) 1958; see also his *Ethics and Action* London (Routledge and Kegan Paul) 1973

2.   Bond, E., "An Introduction to 'The Fool'" in *Theatre Quarterly* Spring 1976

3.   Department of Education and Science U.K. (Papers of Her Majesty's Inspectorate} *Curriculum 11-16* London (HMSO) 1977

4.   Hirst, P.H., *Knowledge and the Curriculum* London (Routledge and Kegan Paul) 1973

Gardner, H., *Frames of Mind: A Theory of Multiple Intelligences* New York (Basic Books Publ Co) 1983; also see his *The Mind's New Science* (Basic Books).1985

Sternberg, R.J., and Kolligian, J., *Competence Considered* New Haven Conn. (Yale University Press) 1990

5.   Bronowski, J., *The Ascent of Man*, London (BBC Publications) 1973

6.   Passmore, J.P., "On Teaching to Be Critical" in Peters R.S., (Ed.), *The Concept of Education* London (Routledge and Kegan Paul) 1967

7.   For criticisms of this thesis see:

Phillips, D.C., "The Distinguishing Features of Forms of Knowledge" in *Educational Philosophy and Theory* (EPAT) Vol 3 No 2 October 1971

Hindess, E., "Forms of Knowledge" in *Proceedings of the Philosophy of Education Society of Great Britain* (PESGB) Vol VI No 2 October 1972

Kleinig, J., "R S Peters' Use of Transcendental Arguments" in PESGB Vol VII No 2 October 1973

Watt, A.J., "Forms of Knowledge and Norms of Rationality" in EPAT Vol 6 No 1 March 1974; also "Education and the Development of Reason" in EPAT Vol 8 No 2 October 1976

Evers C.W., and Walker, J.C., "Knowledge, Partitioned Sets, and Extensionality: a refutation of the Forms of Knowledge thesis" in *Journal of Philosophy of Education* Vol 17 No 2 October 1983

8.   Habermas, J., *Knowledge and Human Interests* London (Heinemann) 1972

9.   Warnock, M., *Schools of Thought*, London (Methuen) 1978

10.   Peirce, C.S., *Writings of Charles S Peirce: a chronological edition* Frisch M.H., (Ed.) Bloomington (Indiana UP) 1982 ff

        James, W., *Some Problems of Philosophy* Cambridge Mass. (Harvard UP) 1979

        Dewey, J., *Democracy and Education* New York (Free Press) 1966

11.   Ackerman, B., *Social Justice in the Liberal State* New Haven Conn (Yale UP) 1980 see especially Ch 7 "Liberal Education"

        Mendus, S., *Toleration and the Limits of Liberalism* Atlantic Highlands NJ (Humanities Press International) 1989

        Guttman, A., *Democratic Education* Princeton NJ (Princeton University Press) 1987

        White, P.A., *Beyond Domination: an essay in the political philosophy of education* London (Routledge and Kegan Paul) 1983, especially Ch 3 "Democracy"; see also her "Education, Democracy and the Public Interest" in PESGB Vol VI No 2 October 1973

12.   This is the argument of Powell, J.P., "On Justifying a Broad Educational Curriculum" in *Educational Philosophy and Theory* Vol 2 No 1 March 1970. See also the case advanced in Norton, D.L., *Democracy and Moral Development* Berkeley Cal., (University of California Press) 1991

13.   MacIntyre, A., *Against the Self-Images of the Age: Essays on Ideology and Philosophy* London (Duckworth) 1971; see also his "Against Mr Hume on 'Ought'"in Hudson, W.D., (Ed.) *The Is-Ought Question* London (Macmillan) 1969

14.   Peters, R.S., *Ethics and Education* London (Allen and Unwin) 1966 Chs 1 "On Education" and 5 "Worthwhile Activities".

2. Centres of Power and Control

The government and the schools. In recent moves to redefine the curriculum, the net effect has been to strengthen or make clearer the national role in the process. In countries where there was no national control, there are distinct moves in that direction. In all countries it can be accurately stated that the curriculum is seen explicitly as a subject of national policy.

> "...the curriculum of schools is now part of the public policy agenda in this country (in Australia). In the same way that policies concerning a nation's trade, foreign affairs, industrial relations and defence are exposed to public debate, scrutiny and change, so too the curriculum has become the focus of attention for governments and all criticisms and groups who are influenced by it. Such a notion contrasts markedly with the notion that the determination of the curriculum is largely a matter of professional judgement or is best left to the school community. In the 1980s and 1990s, the curriculum has become an instrument for national development rather than a means whereby individuals can learn and grow in a personally fulfilling way" (Kennedy, 1991).

There is, of course, a danger in this process as the quotation implies. The danger is that national issues, which by their nature require broad, perhaps universal, application may overshadow the need for the curriculum to provide specifically for individual growth. This is more likely to happen when the processes of implementation ignore the need to involve teachers and students in the decision-making.

The way in which the curriculum became part of the national agenda has varied. For countries where there was no such tradition, the approach has often been through legislation, as in England where the former Chairman of the former National Curriculum Council explained the government approach as follows:

> "...until recent years we have prided ourselves on the absence of a national curriculum. We regarded a national curriculum as characteristic of foreign educational systems such as those of the Japanese, the Germans and the French but alien to our English liberal tradition. We have moved in England towards a national curriculum because we became increasingly aware of the need to set out what it was that the education system aims to provide for all children" (Watkins, 1991).

England, in its definition of what the education system "aims to provide for all children", is following a similar direction to that in New Zealand, USA and Australia, in spite of their differences in the organisation of education. In all of them a common pattern is being enacted: more responsibility is being directed to individual schools under the title of "self-management" while at the same time there is a national priority to define common elements and a common framework for the curriculum, together with more explicit ways of recording student achievement.

For England, that common agreement is expressed through the 1988 Education Reform Act, which had three emphases, of which one was the National Curriculum. This specified, in addition to the already required Religious Education, eight foundation subjects: english, mathematics, science, languages, history and geography, art and music, physical education and technology. All students were required to be assessed in these areas for achievement at ages 7, 11, 14 and 16, using ten levels of achievement for all students. As we have seen in the comments of the British Education Secretary, Mr John Patten, this process of assessment and the subsequent public reporting are seen as means of providing equality of opportunity. This is on the basis that parents can select the school to which their children will go and that these procedures provide fair bases for that selection. In contrast, France, which also has a pattern of national assessment avoids publishing the results on a school-by-school basis. The very different ways in which assessment may be used will be discussed further under that heading.

In New Zealand, which like England, introduced its national curriculum through legislation, a more elaborate effort has been made to express different elements of the curriculum, rather than confining the statement to a set of subjects. The Ministry of Education distinguishes between the New Zealand Curriculum and the school curriculum.

"The New Zealand Curriculum comprises a set of national curriculum statements which define the learning principles and achievement aims and objectives which all New Zealand schools are required to follow. The school curriculum consists of the ways in which a school puts into practice the policy set out in the national curriculum statements. It takes account of local needs, priorities, and resources, and is designed in consultation with the school's community" (New Zealand Ministry, 1993).

The New Zealand curriculum framework includes a set of working principles; the definition of seven essential learning areas comprising language and languages, mathematics, science, technology, social sciences, the arts, health and physical well-being; a detailed list of essential skills, communication skills, numeracy skills, information skills, problem-solving skills, self-management and competitive skills, social and co-operative skills, physical skills, and, work and study skills; and, a statement of attitudes and values which are seen, along with knowledge and skills as an integral part of the curriculum.

"The school curriculum, through its practices and procedures, will reinforce the commonly held values which underpin New Zealand's democratic society; for example, honesty, reliability, respect for others, individual responsibility, tolerance, fairness, caring or compassion, non-sexism, and non-racism" (New Zealand Ministry, 1993).

The New Zealand legislation, like England, also required individual schools to manage their own affairs, including finances.

Schools will also play a strong role in assessment in New Zealand, balanced against a national role, which is seen as defining overall standards. School-based assessment will play an important role at both the primary and secondary levels, contributing to teachers' knowledge of students and assisting to compile records of school achievement. At year 4 and year 8, however, there will be national monitoring, using light samples, to build up a picture of students' achievement over time on a national basis. Also, for years 7 and 9 item banks of nationally standardized assessment tasks are being developed to allow schools to assess the relative performance of their students against national standards.

Other countries have moved position also on the various dimensions for centralisation / decentralisation. The OECD Review of National Policies for Education on the Netherlands (OECD Review, 1991) makes a distinction between two major domains of control in educational institutions: control over procedures (money, personnel, curriculum, textbooks) or control over outputs (setting attainment standards, assessing schools and students). It describes France, Italy and Spain as exercising national control over both procedures and outputs while Denmark exercises control over neither. The Dutch system, on the other hand is described as moving from high procedural but low output control to one of low procedural but higher output control. The new pattern is described as "steering at a distance" under the assumption that "the dominant educational values and aims could be well served if general cognitive and societal aims of education are articulated at the centre while the means of reaching those ends, and the articulation of social and moral development goals, are largely determined at the periphery" (OECD Review, 1991). In this pattern, the Netherlands is thus making a distinction between the national role on curriculum purposes and the school role on pedagogy.

In Spain, on the other hand, the legal responsibility for the control of the curriculum is shared between the Ministry of Education and the Autonomous Regions. The Ministry prescribes 45-50 per cent of the curriculum content and the Autonomous Regions the remainder while school communities are given responsibility for supervising material resources, developing programmes to implement the defined objectives and managing the school. In revising the curriculum the Ministry first reviews curriculum objectives, with the purpose of maintaining minimum competency levels. Secondly, proposals for school improvement are drawn up by teachers, reviewed by specialists and trialled for one year in experimental schools. Currently a major initiative is to establish a common education up to 16 years of age, followed by two tracks: one in Vocational Training, the other in continuing comprehensive education leading to the Bachillerato.

Australia, in its initiative, has attempted like the USA to develop a collaborative approach between the Federal Government and the state governments. They began with a Declaration (AEC, 1989) specifying ten common and agreed goals for schooling and establishing a process of annual national reporting. To implement the agreed framework, involving eight major areas, they established a collaborative body, the Curriculum Corporation. The Corporation's work involves six phases: mapping curriculum documents in each area throughout the country; developing a brief for a national statement and profile on each area; preparing the national statements; publishing the statements; developing national profiles of student achievement in each area; producing curriculum support materials.

Almost independently three reports on post-compulsory education appeared. These reports, Finn (1991), Carmichael (1992) and Mayer (1992) had a strong emphasis on employment links of education. Finn and Carmichael emphasized the concept of generic skills which all students should have as the basis for employment, the Key Competencies. Mayer developed this into a statement of Key Competencies required for effective participation in the emerging patterns of work and work organisation. Very briefly, these were Collecting, Analysing and Organising Information; Communicating Ideas and Information; Planning and Organising Activities; Working with Others and in Teams; Using Mathematical Ideas and Techniques; Solving Problems; Using Technology. The implementation of these ideas still has to occur. In the meantime there is a range of reactions, some welcoming, some hostile. The links of this approach with the profiles approach of the curriculum framework still are not clear. More fundamentally, the idea of content-free competencies remains to be demonstrated. What is certain is that the approach is a strong indication to schools that the business community, and very probably other sections, looks for knowledge that can be applied in practical circumstances and is not merely an examination skill.

While these approaches have many different aspects, they have four in common:

-- a democratic right of access to a common core curriculum;
-- systematically developed across the years of compulsory attendance;
-- would embody monitoring processes and remedial action;
-- [to] ensure the students' own progressive access to further learning.

It is, then, a curriculum entitlement, specifying achievement and not merely coverage of the curriculum.

Efforts with respect to the core curriculum, if sufficiently broadly-based, could help to eliminate the traditional and harmful divide between vocational and general education. Changing vocational demands requiring higher levels of general education will reduce or eliminate the elements of vocational training. Those aspects of vocational education, however, with a more general application will become part of the general curriculum. Hopefully, this will help to improve the standing of vocational education, which has been seen as the path for those unable to cope with academic studies. The links with business and industry are developing and these will provide educational opportunities outside the school, opportunities of a diverse nature and links between practical and theoretical knowledge.

The national approach, as with the national curriculum in countries such as France, Italy, Spain and England, or with 'curriculum steering' as in Sweden, the Netherlands and Australia, is not, of course, the only possibility. In Germany, considering for the moment the former West Germany, the original eleven lander have their own *Kulturhoheit* (cultural and educational autonomy). Each lander has its own Ministry of Education and its own structures, including provisions for curriculum and for assessment. There are thus eleven distinct curriculum patterns, not one, and with the former East Germany this could become sixteen. The situation is not unlike Canada where each of the provinces has moved to a pattern of central curriculum goals and assessment, and where there is no Federal power aiming to seek a common pattern. In both Germany and Canada, the conference of Ministers of Education is a powerful body. In Germany, this body has developed agreements which have subsequently been enacted in the individual lander, this being most binding at the *Abitur* level at the end of full secondary schooling, where common conditions apply in the structure, the conditions and the subject of the final examination. Within the Lander themselves, the minimum specification formerly quite detached now provides broad frameworks statements, with aims, content, teaching methods and assessment procedures specified so as to leave some flexibility. In Germany, as in Austria and Switzerland, there has been an absence of major strategical and structural reforms such as those described for the United Kingdom, USA and New Zealand. The process has rather been one of gradual change, in areas such as curriculum content, the further development of testing and the introduction of new syllabi in vocational education. This indicates a substantial acceptance of the capacity of teachers to implement change, as well as strong support for the public system of education. Some pressures exist for more dramatic change. These include the concerns expressed by parents on standards, the heavy pressure for university places, and substantial social issues such as environmental concerns and violence in society.

It is too much to expect, however, that the massive challenge of "a quality education for all students" can be met by attention solely, or even mainly, at the upper secondary level. We have perhaps become too familiar with claims that the early childhood years are the most important for such key aspects of learning as language development and general intellectual and emotional development. Our familiarity may have robbed us of a sense of urgency. The same holds, if less dramatically, for the primary years. These are the schooling periods of most significant change and growth for individuals and thus are the periods most open to educational influence. For example, the work of Jeanne Chall (Chall et al., 1982) indicates that at age six, the technical reading skills of disadvantaged children are on a par with those of children from literate families. After another year, those skills diverge by much more than a year, with the significant advance going to children of literate families. This disparity increases with time in school. Chall stresses the importance of the mechanism by which we move from short-term memory with limited range to a capacity to retain much longer and more complex material such as books and conversation. We retain our memory for meaning but not for the detailed form of communication because we are able to link meaning with past knowledge already stored in the mind. Thus, the skills of reading are not enough without a framework of knowledge that provide meaning to the communication. Chall calls that framework "world knowledge" claiming that it is something conveyed to children of literate families by their home experience and that those who miss that experience lack the framework in which their technical skills can work effectively. This would stress the importance of the early years, particularly to ensure that children did not suffer a growing handicap. The figures for illiteracy in the early secondary years indicate that this is a current problem and will grow more acute with the increasing retention. Work on literacy programmes such as that by Professor Marie Clay of Auckland University, resulting in the Reading Recovery Programme, indicates that this problem can be very substantially reduced. In the effort going towards post-compulsory education, the most cost-effective means and the most humane means will include substantial efforts in the early childhood and primary years.

Paper 5 by Takashi Yamagiwa takes us through the steps involved in the curriculum process in Japan.

Paper 5

CURRICULUM REFORM AND ITS IMPLEMENTATION

Takashi Yamagiwa

NEW TRENDS IN THE REVISED CURRICULA IN JAPAN

1. Outline of Policies

Elementary and secondary education in Japan has gained an international reputation for both its level of quantitative expansion and its high quality, but it is often pointed out that certain educational systems and practices have tended to be excessively uniform and inflexible. It is necessary to improve and update the existing systems in the coming years with a view to helping children develop individuality and foster diverse abilities and talents.

With this in view, the Ministry of Education, Science and Culture carries out policies and measures for the improvement and enrichment of the school curriculum, for the reform of upper secondary school education, for the improvement of the quality of teachers and for the improvement and enrichment of educational conditions.

2. An Outline of the Revision of the National Standards for School Curricula (Course of Study) in Japan

In Japan, in respect of elementary and secondary education, the Minister of Education, Science and Culture, acting in compliance with the provisions of the relevant laws and regulations, issues the Course of Study, comprising "the national standards for school curricula" which are to be prepared by schools. The aim of this is to maintain a uniform standard of education throughout the country and to ensure equal opportunity of education as guaranteed under the constitution of Japan. The Course of Study set out the main elements of national standards with regard to objectives, contents, etc., for each of the various school subjects, and schools prepare their own school curricula for implantation in concrete form in accordance with the prescribed main elements.

The Course of Study was first prescribed in 1947. Since then, revisions have been carried out at about 10-year intervals, taking into account the progress of the times. The revisions of the Course of Study are based on recommendations of the "Curriculum Council", which is an advisory body to the Minister of Education, Science and Culture.

In March 1989, looking ahead to the demands of the 21st century, the Ministry of Education, Science and Culture (*Monbusho*) revised the Course of Study for elementary, lower secondary and upper secondary schools. Following a period of preparation, the revised Courses of Study began to be implemented from 1992.

3. Basic Principles of the Current Revision

The basic aim of the current revision of the Course of Study is to ensure the realisation of education which will cultivate the qualities required of students in coping with future social changes.

In other words, the progress of science and technology and economic development in present-day Japan have brought about material abundance as well as various social changes, including the spread of information-oriented devices and thinking, internationalization, a diversification of value systems, an increase in nuclear families and extension of the normal life span, and it is expected that processes of change of this kind will increase and accelerate in future. Under these circumstances and with a view to cultivating a foundation of lifelong learning in the light of such changes and the changes in life-styles and consciousness that they will bring about, and with the basic aim of bringing up citizens with a broad humanitarian vision and capable of coping with social changes by themselves, the revision has been made on the basis of the following principles. These require:

i) to attempt to develop young people who have rich and strong hearts and minds, through the whole educational activities of the school, while taking account of children' levels of development, as well as of the characteristics of respective subjects;

ii) to place more emphasis on basic and essential knowledge and skills required of every citizen of our country, and to enhance such educational programmes as will enable each child to give full play to his or her individuality. A consistency in the curriculum for each subject area should be secured among different school levels from kindergarten to upper secondary school;

iii) to attach more importance to the nurture of children's capacity to cope positively with changes in society, as well as to the provision of a sound base for fostering children's creativity. Children's willingness to learn how to learn is also to be stimulated;

iv) to put more value on developing in children an attitude of respecting Japanese culture and traditions, as well as an increased understanding of the cultures and histories of other countries in the world. Thus children should be helped to develop the qualities required of a Japanese living in the international community.

The revised Course of Study was put into effect in 1990 for kindergartens, and in 1992 for all grades of elementary school. The revised Course of Study for Lower Secondary Schools was put into practice in 1993 for all grades of lower secondary school. The revised Course of Study for Upper Secondary Schools will become effective progressively from 1994. (Specifically, it will become effective in 1994 for the 10th grade, in 1995 for the 11th grade, and in 1996 for the 12th grade.)

In accordance with the provisions of the School Education Law, all elementary and secondary schools in Japan are required to use textbooks in the classroom teaching of each subject. Textbooks to be used in schools must be either those authorised by the *Monbusho*, or those compiled by the *Monbusho* itself.

The "authorization" of textbooks means that, after examining draft textbooks written and compiled by private authors, the Minister approves those which he deems suitable as textbooks to be used in schools.

The writing and compilation of textbooks are left to the initiative of the private sector with a view to ensuring that creative and innovative approaches by private authors are utilised in the development of textbooks. The authorization of textbooks is aimed at ensuring that only appropriate textbooks are published.

The *Monbusho* carries out its function of textbook authorization in accordance with the *Monbusho's* guidelines for textbook authorization and on the basis of the deliberations of the Textbook Authorization Council. It is intended to ensure that the authorization is carried out objectively and impartially and that all textbooks meet relevant requirements with regard to their contents.

In the light of a recommendation offered by the National Council on Educational Reform in 1987, the *Monbusho* has amended its regulations on textbook authorization so as to simplify their provisions and concentrate them on some essential points. The amendment was aimed to reform the system so that, in textbook examination, emphasis may be placed on judging whether proposed books are appropriate or not as textbooks to be used in schools.

The power of adopting particular textbooks from among the authorised textbooks rests with the local board of education maintaining public schools.

With a view to realising to a greater extent the spirit of the provisions in the Constitution that "compulsory education shall be free," the national government has been supplying textbooks free of charge to all children enrolled in compulsory schools (i.e., elementary and lower secondary schools, including elementary and lower secondary departments of special schools for the handicapped), national, local public and private.

4. Meaning and Role of Elementary and Secondary Education

i) *Significance and role of elementary education*

Japanese elementary education is intended to cultivate the knowledge, skills, attitudes and an awareness of being Japanese which children commonly require as members of society in the future. The Japanese primary school has a long history as the organ for the provision of elementary education. In terms of mental development, children at the stage of elementary education gradually evolve from thinking using concrete objects to abstract thinking. They have a flourishing desire for learning and other activities.

They are comparatively stable in terms of their emotional state. In terms of morality, they develop from having heteronomous to autonomous morality. In terms of physical development, they are characterised by agility, co-ordination and sustaining power. Accordingly it is necessary to arouse their desire for learning, to ensure they are provided with the basic knowledge to be able to read, write and calculate, to have them form acceptable habits, to acquire sensitivity and good morals, and to build up strong bodies.

Kindergarten education is intended to cultivate the basis for the future formation of the man. This should be carried out not only at kindergartens but also through the experience of living and playing at home and in the community.

With the recent changes in the home and social environment, however, the role of kindergarten education must be studied with particular reference to home education and elementary school education.

ii) *Significance and role of secondary education*

In terms of mental and physical development, pupils up to secondary school level are characterised by the awakening of self consciousness, diversification of interests in school subjects and the attainment of puberty accompanied by unrest.

Students at the completion of secondary education tend to be introspective, have social interests and be independent. At the same time, they are faced with the problems of entrance exams for higher education, employment, acquaintance with the opposite sex, increased emotional unrest and psychological complications. Thus, secondary education is an important period, during which pupils and students are required to cultivate the character they require as members of society, acquire knowledge and skills according to their ability and aptitude, have self-confidence, form an independent sense of values. Importance should be attached in particular to their diversification and individuality.

Partly because of the fact that the former half of secondary education is the province of compulsory education in Japan, consideration diversification and individuality has not been adequate, with the result that the education of young men with marked individuality tended to be lacking. It is necessary in the future to provide diversified education responding to the individuality of pupils and students and produce young men who can survive changes in society and who have the power to continue to learn.

5. Secondary Education

i) *Structure of curriculum in secondary education*

(a) Structure of curriculum in lower secondary schools

In considering the ideal education content of lower secondary schools, it is necessary to attach importance to the idea of positioning lower secondary education within the overall framework of secondary education. For this reason, the structure of the curriculum and educational content in lower secondary schools should be restructured, so that they may be more closely related to those of elementary and upper secondary education in terms of both relevance and system. At the same time, the educational content of lower secondary education should be studied so that it can be improved and the subjects more carefully selected. The required subjects taught and the number of period must be reviewed. In addition, it is necessary to reconsider the optional subjects of the lower secondary school curricula as a whole, and to study increasing the number of optional subjects available and the number of periods allocated, in order to offer an education which responds to the diversified abilities and aptitudes of students in lower secondary schools.

With regards to the respective domains of subjects, moral education and special activities, it is recommended that their relevance, time allocation and content should be considered.

(b) Structure of curriculum in upper secondary schools

Under the generalised, flexible standards of the new course of study for upper secondary education, diversification in teaching and in the formation of curricula including a large increase in the number of optional subjects and the execution of ability grouping is under way. If the number of optional subjects in lower secondary schools is increased to some extent, it will be necessary to further advance the diversification of upper secondary school education.

For this reason, it is necessary to consider the diversification of general subjects, as well as the methodology enabling students to diversify their selection of subjects including specialised subjects. With respect to specialised subjects, measures are being taken to diversify at the discretion of the schools themselves. However, it is necessary also to study ways to provide general subject, which students can select according to their abilities, aptitudes and interest. It is also necessary to provide adequate guidance to students so that they can make an appropriate selection of subjects. It is urged that schools co-operate so that credit obtained by students at one school may be valid at another.

What must be considered in reference to the diversification of upper secondary school curricula is how to maintain and enhance the level of upper secondary school education, while ensuring compatibility with individual school subjects. Careful consideration must be given from the viewpoint of relating upper secondary education to higher education.

ii) Role of teaching in secondary education

Particular attention must be paid so that teaching in secondary education may be conducted in an appropriate manner to meet the abilities and aptitudes of respective students. A diversified method of teaching, that responds to the actual state of students, must be devised in order to stimulate the students' will to learn, and to ensure they acquire a sound knowledge of the educational content of their subjects. Special guidance such as supplementary lessons should be provided for slow learners.

At the level of lower secondary education also, a flexible, diversified method of teaching responding to the achievements of individual students must be provided depending on school subjects. In providing special lessons that match the abilities of students, careful attention must be paid to the nature of the subjects, time allocation and teaching method.

The evaluation of students' achievements must be such as to stimulate the initiative-led learning activities of students in accordance with the characteristics of individual school subjects.

MAIN POINTS OF NEWLY REVISED CURRICULA IN EACH SCHOOL LEVEL

1. Elementary School

i) Creation of "Life environment studies" for Grades I and II, and improvement in the number of teaching hours

(a) In consideration of the stage of development of children, a new subject called "*Seikatsu-ka*" (Life environment studies) is created for Grades I and II. The objective of this subject is to foster fundamental ability and an attitude of living and learning through concrete activities and experiences by children themselves so as to cultivate foundations of self-reliance. Incidentally, "social studies" and "science" was abrogated for Grades I and II.

(b) In order to improve the capability in the Japanese language, the number of teaching hours of the Japanese language was increased for Grades I and II.

(c) Yearly total numbers of teaching hours at elementary school was revised as indicated below.

ii) Japanese language

(a) With importance being attached to the fostering of ability of expressing and thinking, the number of teaching hours were increased for the teaching of composition for the purpose of substantializing the teaching of composition.

(b) In order to foster the ability of writing letters and characters correctly, the number of teaching hours for hand-writing were increased.

(c) With regard to textbooks and other teaching materials, the viewpoints for choosing such materials were indicated so that appropriate topics and themes may be taken up. For example:

-- to be of service to the fostering of understanding of and affection to the culture and tradition of Japan.

-- to be of service to the deepening of understanding of natural features, cultures, etc. of the world, and to the cultivation of the spirit of international co-operation.

iii) Social studies

(a) In consideration of the changes in industrial structures etc., the tertiary industries such as transportation and communication were added in addition to the primary and the secondary industries that exist.

(b) For the betterment of international understanding, content was enriched concerning contact between foreign countries and Japan and international exchanges.

iv) Arithmetic

(a) With a view to fostering capability and attitude to consider and treat things in a mathematical fashion, importance was attached to activities including practising of manipulation, and the degree and scope of treatment of the content was clarified so that basic content may be acquired securely.

(b) Importance will be attached to the deepening of understanding of quantity and geometrical figures, and to be enabling to utilise basic knowledge and skill.

v) Science

(a) Importance was attached to direct experiencing such as observation and experimentation, and further careful selection and concentration of content was made so that problem-solving activities may be fully developed.

(b) Such content as the human body, atmospheric phenomena and production of tools was added so that relations with daily life may be realised.

vi) Music

(a) Teaching was oriented towards fostering fertile sensibility to music.

(b) Importance was attached to the teaching of traditional music of Japan.

vii) *Arts and handicrafts*

(a) Teaching of handicrafts devised through full use of hands was increased.

(b) Teaching for appreciation of works of art of Japan and of other countries was made substantial.

viii) *Homemaking*

(a) Further careful selection was made of the basis and essential content concerning food, clothing and shelter, and enrichment of practical and experiencing learning was be ensured.

(b) Content having to do with the consumer was enriched in order to enable to live self-reliantly in correspondence to change etc. in consuming life.

ix) *Physical education*

(a) Importance was attached to the improvement of physical strength, and physical exercises to advance bodily flexibility was enriched.

(b) Teaching concerning mental health was increased.

x) *Moral education*

(a) Attaching importance to the spirit of respect for human beings and to the feeling of awe to life, improvement was made so as to foster morality lying deep in the inside of children.

(b) Content was reorganised so as to clarify the viewpoints in teaching, and concentration of teaching was ensured so that effective teaching may be made to fit to the development of morality of children.

xi) *Special activities*

(a) More importance was attached to experiencing activities concerning the adaptation to living in a group, the contact with nature and the cultivation of the spirit of service and labour.

2. Lower Secondary School

i) *Widening of the range of elective subjects, and improvement in the number of teaching hours*

    (a) In order to enrich further the education for vivifying individuality of pupils, the number of kind of elective subjects were increased, with effect that "Music", "Fine arts", "Health and physical education" and "industrial arts and homemaking" were added for the second grade, and all of these subjects may be established also as elective subjects for the third grade. Further, teaching hours devotable to elective subjects for the third grade. Further, teaching hours devotable to elective subjects at each of grades were made increasable.

    (b) Yearly total of the number of teaching hours at lower secondary school was revised as indicated below.

ii) *Japanese language*

    (a) In order to emphasise the teaching of composition, with importance being attached to the fostering of ability of expressing and of thinking, the number of teaching hours were increased for the teaching of composition.

    (b) In order to foster the ability of writing letters and characters correctly, the number of teaching hours for handwriting were increased.

iii) *Social studies*

    (a) In order to enable to cope with the progress of information-orientedness and with the change in consumption life, the content was enriched concerning such matters as the relationship between information and human life as well as consumer problems.

iv) *Mathematics*

    (a) In order to attach more importance to the fostering of ability to consider and treat mathematically, content was carefully selected and concentrated so that teaching may be made with latitude.

    (b) Importance was attached to the enabling to acquire mathematical way of viewing and thinking and to utilise such a way in a positive manner at actual scenes.

    (c) Effective use of computer etc. was promoted.

v) *Science*

    (a) In order to ensure active investigation activities such as observation and experimentation, further careful selection and concentration was made of the content.

(b) In order to arouse increasing interest of pupils in "science", importance was attached to the content concerning light, sound, heat, etc., and to the familiar natural things and phenomena and their relationship with daily life, including meteorological observations.

(c) Effective use of computer etc. was promoted.

vi) Music

(a) With importance being attached to the fostering of positive attitude of learning, teaching for fostering rich sensibility to music was promoted.

vii) Fine arts

(a) With importance being attached to the fostering of ability of expressing creatively, teaching for raising sensibility was promoted.

viii) Health and physical education

(a) Pupils were enabled to choose and learn any type of physical exercises in accordance with their own particular characteristics.

(b) A type of exercise now called "*Kakugi*" (combat sport) will be renamed as "*Budo*" in Japanese, of which teaching will be conducted by making the most of its peculiar character as a native culture of Japan. This exercise was open to both sexes.

(c) Content was enriched concerning mental health.

ix) Industrial arts and homemaking

(a) The current practice of providing different scope of learning to boys and girls was discontinued so that both sexes may cover the whole of the subject.

(b) Corresponding to the progress of information-orientedness, the change in the functions of home, and so on, new content was added concerning "computer education" and family life.

x) Foreign languages

(a) With importance being attached to the fostering of communicating ability, teaching in hearing and speaking was increased in time allocation.

(b) With a view to activating communicating activities, designation by grade of sentence patterns, grammatical matters, etc. was removed.

(c) With regard to teaching materials, the viewpoints for choosing them were indicated so that appropriate topics and themes may be taken up. For example:

-- To be of service to the betterment of international understanding on a wide field of vision, to the raising of self-consciousness as a Japanese living in the international community, and to the cultivation of the spirit of international co-operation.

-- To be of service to the betterment of understanding of life and culture of the world and of Japan, to the widening of the field of vision to an international one, and to the cultivation of fair judgement.

xi) *Moral education*

(a) With importance being attached to the spirit of respect for human beings and to the feeling of awe for life, improvement was made so that morality lying deep in the inside of pupils may be fostered.

(b) Content will be reorganised so that viewpoints of teaching may be clarified, and concentration of content was ensured so that effective teaching may be made to fit to the development of morality of pupils. In particular, teaching on self-consciousness of the way of living as a human being was substantialized.

xii) *Special activities*

(a) As in the case of elementary school, more importance was attached to experiencing activities.

3. Upper Secondary School

i) *Creation of geography and history and civics as subject-areas*

With a view to cultivating international-mindedness which enables to see Japan in a relative way from the viewpoint of comparative culture, to fostering Japanese people who live independently and actively in the international community, and to cultivating quality required of able members of a democratic and peace-loving state and community, the existing subject-area social studies was reorganised into geography and history and civics.

ii) *Diversification of subject-areas/subjects*

In order to enrich education for vivifying individuality corresponding to diversified characters etc. of students, multifarious subject-areas/subject were prepared. (For general education: from 8 subject-areas/43 subjects to 9 subject-areas/60 subjects. For vocational education: from 157 subjects to 184 subjects.)

iii) *Improvement in compulsory subject-areas/subjects*

Special consideration will be given, among other things, to the needs of cultivating the quality required of students at upper secondary school level in association with social changes. In this regard, for example in the subject-area of geography and history, world history was made a required subject. Also, home economics will be required for both sexes.

iv) ***Improvement in different subject-areas/subjects***

(a) Japanese language

-- Ability of expressing appropriately was emphasised, and in particular, composition teaching was strengthened with a view to cultivating logicality.

-- In order to deepen the understanding of culture and tradition of Japan, subjects including "Reading of classic literature" was created so that teaching on classic literature may be substantialized.

(b) Mathematics

-- Teaching of basic and essential content was increased, and subjects were reorganised so as to meet the needs of diversified pupils.

-- In regard to mathematics A, mathematics B and mathematics C, content was created which was studied by using computers.

(c) Science

-- To enable students to make diversified elective study in accordance with their characteristics etc., this subject-area was composed of "integrated science subjects", subjects with emphasis on the relationship with technology daily life, "environment" and "subjects with emphasis on the foundation and basis of science".

-- In order to foster ability of scientific thinking while attaching importance to observation and experimentation, investigation activities and project-oriented study was given their places in the content.

-- In order to correspond to the information-orientedness, use of computer etc. was promoted in relation to investigation activities and project-oriented study in each subject.

(d) Health and physical education

Physical education

-- Students were enabled to choose and learn any type of physical exercises in accordance with their own capability and aptitude.

-- As to "*Kakugi*" (combat sport), improvement was made for the purpose similar to that in the case of lower secondary school.

-- The required number of credits for physical education, which is not the same for boys and girls under the existing system, were revised so that the same number of credits may be required of both sexes.

Health

-- Improvement was made of the content regarding mental health, traffic safety, family and social life and health, first aid, etc.

(e) Art

-- Improvement was made of the content, attaching importance to the raising of sensibility to beauty and to the fostering of art-loving sentiment throughout the lifetime.

(f) Foreign languages

-- With importance being attached to the fostering of communicating capability, three new subjects, i.e. "Oral communication A" (centring on daily conversation capability) and "Oral communication B" (centring on hearing capability) and "Oral communication C (centring on debating and interlocution capability), was established in regard to "english", at least one of which will have to be taken in the course of three years.

-- With a view to activating communicating activities, designation of sentence patterns, grammatical matters, etc. for respective subjects were removed.

-- With regard to teaching materials, the viewpoints in choosing them were indicated so that appropriate topics and themes may be taken up.

(g) Home Economics

-- Content was improved so as to foster practical attitude to endeavour for the enrichment and improvement of family life built up through co-operation of both sexes.

-- Three subjects, i.e. "general home economics", "techniques for living" and "general living", were established, one of which will have to be chosen by all the students as an elective subject.

(h) Vocational subject-areas/subjects

-- With a view to coping appropriately with the rapid progress of technological innovation in different fields of industries and with the changes in industrial structures and employment structures, the composition of subjects as well as that of standard courses were reorganised.

(i) Special activities

-- Mainly at homeroom activities, teaching was substantialized concerning the way of being and way of life as a human being.

-- As in the case of elementary and lower secondary schools, more importance was attached to experiencing activities.

IMPLEMENTATION OF NATIONAL STANDARDS FOR SCHOOL BASED CURRICULA

The Ministry of Education, Science and Culture (the *Monbusho*) lays down national standards for curriculum for all school levels, from kindergarten to upper secondary, so as to secure an optimum national level of education based on the principle of equal educational opportunity for all.

A *Monbusho* order entitled "Enforcement Regulations for the School Education Law" provides for the minimum number of school weeks per year for kindergartens and the names of subjects to be offered in elementary, lower secondary and upper secondary schools.

Broad guidelines for the objectives and standard content of each school subject are specified in the "Course of Study" for each of four school levels; kindergarten, elementary, lower secondary and upper secondary. The Course of Study is prepared by the *Monbusho*, the recommendation of the "Curriculum Council", an advisory body to the Minister of Education, and promulgated by the Minister.

In accordance with the provisions of the School Education Law, Enforcement Regulations for this law, and the Course of Study, individual schools organise their own curriculum, taking account of the real circumstances of each school and each community, and the stage of mental and physical development of children enrolled, as well as their characteristics.

The Ministry of Education, Science and Culture may offer necessary guidance, advice and assistance to local boards of education and local educational personnel on curriculum standards, methods and techniques of instruction, guidance and school management, through direct or indirect methods as follows:

1) Official notification to prefectural or municipal boards of education;

2) Supervision of local boards of education and, through local boards, supervision of public elementary and secondary schools;

3) Conduct of conferences and workshops on a nation-wide scale for principals, supervisors and teachers;

4) Publications of guides, manuals and handbooks for teachers.

A number of school inspectors and senior specialists for curriculum are employed in the Ministry.

School inspectors of the Ministry provide guidance on elementary and secondary education.

Senior specialists for curriculum serve full-time and their function is to conduct research and study on the standards of curriculum for the school level and subject area to which they are assigned, and to give prefectural boards of education advice and assistance on the curriculum.

Direct guidance and advice to elementary and lower secondary school teachers are given by the prefectural and municipal boards of education.

The supervision sections in prefectural boards of education give guidance and advice to municipal boards of education, conduct conferences and workshops for principals and teachers and publish guides, manuals or handbooks for teachers, based upon the central policy for supervision, and taking into consideration the specific situations of the prefectures concerned. The principal supervisory personnel of prefectural boards of education are supervisors, who are assigned for guidance on curriculum, teaching, and other professional matters related to school education within their prefecture. School supervision is the primary function of supervisors.

Supervisors must be experienced professional educators with thorough understanding of the curriculum, teaching methods and objectives and other professional matters related to school education.

The Ministry of Education, Science and Culture, prefectural boards of education, and prefectural educational centres provide opportunities for systematic in-service training for public school teachers, principals and supervisors. Some of the larger municipalities and educational study groups also hold workshops and study meetings for in-service training.

The Ministry annually holds the Central Workshops for intensive in-service training of principals, vice-principals and experienced teachers (e.g. curriculum co-ordinators, heads of teachers' groups teaching the same grade or the same subject in a school), who are selected and sent by every prefectural boards of education. Tsukuba Annex of the National Education Center is specially facilitated and equipped for the Workshops, which are usually composed of lectures of high quality and seminars related to school administration, curriculum theory, instructional method, etc.

Prefectural boards of education also make programmes for in-service training and carry them out. Prefectural education centres, which have lodging facilities, educational equipment and apparatus, and professional staff, take an important role in in-service training. Recently, the Ministry and prefectural boards of education have been concerned in providing in-service training with newly recruited teachers and younger teachers with some five years' teaching experience as well as with those being in charge of managerial affairs.

CURRICULUM EVALUATION AT NATIONAL LEVEL

To prepare for the improvement of the new curricula and teaching methods which may become necessary in the future, the Ministry of Education specifies that Curriculum Evaluation at elementary schools and lower secondary schools be made by basic scholastic achievement tests.

The research presently being conducted is intended to grasp the actual conditions in which new curricula, based on the new Courses of Study, are implemented to determine the scholastic levels achieved by pupils and students in their respective subjects, to ascertain the extent to which the content of the new Courses of Study is understood by pupils and students, to clarify the problems involved in teaching pupils and students according to the new curricula and eventually to make use of any findings, which may be obtained, in improving the curricula and teaching methods in the future.

A survey is undertaken through the administration of achievement test in order to evaluate the expected achievement level. It made use of a paper test. However, in subjects which are difficult to measure through the paper test the evaluation using practical classroom activity technique was undertaken. Co-operating schools were selected from various parts of the country.

1. Curriculum Evaluation through Paper Test

In finding the degree of achievement, those items specified by the Course of Study, which can be surveyed by paper test, should be surveyed with respect to Japanese language, social studies, arithmetic and science for the 5th and 6th grades of elementary schools, and with respect to Japanese language, social studies, science, mathematics and foreign languages for all the grades of lower secondary schools in accordance with the purport outlined above.

A. *Survey in 1993 School Year*

a) Subjects surveyed: Japanese language and arithmetic (at elementary schools)

b) Pupils covered: 32,000 elementary school pupils of the 5th and 6th grades (16,000 pupils for each grade)

c) Time of survey: The 3rd term (February 1994)

B. *Survey in 1994 School Year*

Elementary schools

a) Subjects surveyed: social studies and science

b) Pupils covered: 32,000 pupils of the 5th and 6th grades (16,000 pupils for each grade)

c) Time of survey: The 3rd term (February 1995)

Lower secondary schools

a) Subjects surveyed: Japanese language, mathematics and foreign languages

b) Students covered: 48,000 1st, 2nd and 3rd year students (16,000 students for each grade)

c) Time of survey: The 3rd term (February 1995 for the 1st and 2nd grades and January 1995 for the 3rd grade)

C. Survey in 1995 School Year

Lower secondary schools

a) Subjects surveyed: social studies, science

b) Students covered: 48,000 1st, 2nd and 3rd year students (16,000 students for each grade)

c) Time of survey: The 3rd term (February 1996 for the 1st and 2nd grades and January 1996 for the 3rd grade)

2. Curriculum Evaluation through Schools assisting with Research and Survey

Co-operating schools survey basic scholastic achievement with respect to the contents of teaching and subjects for which it is difficult to ascertain the degree of achievement by a paper test.

A. *Number of co-operating schools:*   Five schools for each subject

a) Elementary schools: A total of forty-five elementary schools for nine subjects

b) Lower secondary schools: Forty-five lower secondary schools for nine subjects

B. *Period of survey:*   Two years

a) Elementary schools: 1993 and 1994 school years

b) Lower secondary schools: 1994 and 1995 school years

C. *Subjects surveyed:*

a) Music and drawing and handicrafts (art), sewing and cooking (technical skills), gymnastics (health and hygiene), life environment studies.

b) Japanese language, arithmetic (mathematics), social studies, science, and foreign languages (with respect to these subjects, the survey covers those aspects not surveyed by the paper test).

3. Procedures and Outcomes

From the examples here, it is clear that the process of curriculum reform is under way in many countries, in apparently contrasting ways. The patterns followed in the Netherlands are distinct from those in Spain and both are different from France. It is over-simplistic to define these differences in terms of centralisation and decentralisation, as is so often attempted. The starting-points of different countries may be so distinct that moves towards decentralisation in one may actually bring it closer to the other country, involved in centralisation. Further, it is important to ask what is being centralised and what is being decentralised. To use the terms of the Netherlands Review, we might ask what is being centralised or decentralised with respect to procedures, and what with respect to outcomes. In broad terms, managerial and financial responsibility are being devolved to schools in many countries, placing much more of the administration of education at the school level. This is often accompanied by restructuring of central administration in education, reducing the former hierarchical pyramid to a much flatter structure. On the other hand, much of curriculum planning and development is being centralised, if this is not already the case. The rather simplistic approach originally taken in school-based curriculum development is now being substantially altered. Whether this is by the specification of national legislation or by what the Netherlands Review calls "steering at a distance" the broad parameters are laid down centrally and the detailed development into educational programmes occurs in the individual institutions. Further control over the whole process is now exercised through assessment procedures, again in varying ways but with a clear intent to be more specific about the achievements of students and to achieve a "curriculum guarantee", a minimum set of levels of achievement suitable for vocational and social participation, but a vital part also of equity for individuals.

Other partners in the process

In addition to these vertical movements of power and control there are significant horizontal movements. Business and industry now are playing a much more significant and constructive role and this will certainly continue and grow. In the past, the association has tended to be intermittent and critical, often centred on criticism of the basic skills achievement in schools. For their part, schools rejected the criticism but failed to develop significant evidence to rebut the claims. In many countries, more constructive approaches are leading to a form of partnership, acknowledging that public education is a concern of the whole community and not merely of the public sector. The CERI publication, *Schools and Business: A New Partnership* (CERI, 1992) discusses a number of these initiatives. In the Netherlands, a combined initiative was developed between the Ministries of Education, Economic Affairs and Social Affairs with business, industry, the trade unions and educational institutions, called the Rawenhof process. The intention of this major project is to improve the quality of vocational schools. A necessary characteristic of such partnerships is the development of mutual trust, rather than a fear on the part of educators of being dominated. For the business side, the requirement is for a long-term commitment, not a single effort, and one that is seen to benefit the schools and society generally, rather than business interests.

A further potentially powerful player in educational reform is the broader social community, and particularly parents. Initiatives in New Zealand, England and Wales, Sweden and Spain all illustrate the new role given by governments to parent choice. As for business, the relationship between teachers and parents has frequently not been easy. Yet, the research studies (Abbott-Chapman et al., 1991) have shown with unfailing consistency, a rare quality in educational research, the importance of home background and of parental attitudes in the educational achievement of students. Any reforms which do not build on this partnership will ignore the largest single factor in educational achievement. If there is to be a substantial improvement in the quality of education, a major aspect will need to be the involvement of the broader community and, in particular, of parents. This will not be easy. A major reason for strengthening the partnership is to assist educationally disadvantaged students. For the parents of these students to have a stronger role in the schools will require careful planning. Many such parents have heavy work commitments and will not find it easy to give time to schools. Frequently, too, their own school careers will not have been happy experiences and they may feel considerable hesitation to play an active role.

The role of teachers

One of the major changes to curriculum reform in recent years has been the increased involvement of teachers in different aspects of the process. This involvement is a necessary aspect of effective change. There is a danger that this involvement should be oversimplified, in particular by assuming that an involvement in all parts of curriculum design is a necessary part of teacher professionalism. This view limits both curriculum development and teacher professionalism. Of necessity, teachers play a key role in curriculum development, regardless of what is decided elsewhere and who else is involved in making decisions. The teachers' responsibility for teaching strategies and the organisation of learning means that that role is second only to that of the student in the final formation of the curriculum.

Teaching is a key role but not an exclusive one, for clearly the student role is even more decisive. Also, the teacher never operates in isolation from other teachers, those who precede and follow, those who work in parallel. Interrelation is vital both to coherence and continuity in learning. As we have indicated, many others are also involved -- politicians, business and industry, the trade unions, the broader community. Decisions on intentions and decisions on priorities must necessarily involve these. Decisions on content involve the teacher, but they also involve others, including subject specialists. It is in the areas of teaching and learning that the teachers' role is predominant. Here the parallel is with a general practitioner in medicine, whose special task is diagnosis and treatment, and who depends heavily on the research and specialist knowledge of others. The doctor also depends on the general assent of the community on the ways in which medicine is to be practised. Finally, in evaluation and reporting, the teacher plays an important but not a lone role. If evaluation is to be reported in comparable ways, co-operation is necessary and, sometimes, common assessment tasks. In reporting, the form will be dependent on the audience rather than the teacher. The initiatives in teacher preparation courses and in professional development will need to reflect the more complex and comprehensive role of teachers, and particularly their need to plan and work in co-operation with other teachers, and to be associated closely with all the other players in curriculum reform.

One feature of concern is the increasingly common expression of public investment of teachers. This is frequently an explicit part of a political emphasis on the need for reform, as in England. It may be expressed more broadly as in the comment, on Sweden by Eiken, that education is now so important nationally that others besides educators must be involved in the key decisions. It remains certain, however, that if real reform is needed, as seems very clear, that it can be effective only with the willing co-operation of teachers.

Pupils and students as centres of power and control

It has been stressed earlier that, finally, the key agents with respect to curriculum are the pupils and students themselves. This is so obvious that it tends not to get the special treatment it deserves for children and young people in their actions, thoughts and attitudes make the key choices about learning. This is true from the moment of entry into school and only becomes more apparent as the progress continues. For some this is a progress of continued success, building self-confidence as their knowledge and understanding develop. For others, this is a story of growing frustration and failure, as early weaknesses and gaps in learning compound their effect. For still others, the story is intermediate to those other two groups. To engage the whole group in learning effectively and progressively is a task which has not yet been achieved. To do so, will require an effort to obtain genuine involvement in the process of learning from the students. It will involve a recognition by schools of a wider range of achievements than has traditionally been the case. It will require a new pedagogy.

In considering the various elements of this major task, developed differently in different countries, two major controlling processes emerge: the development of statements of purpose into working objectives and the specification of the nature, extent and means of evaluation. Countries vary to some degree in the amount of specification in these areas but the dominant pattern reveals attention to both at the national level. With respect to purposes, there is general acceptance of broad purposes for the period of universal education and a recognition of the need to specify these purposes more closely in objectives which can guide choices in content, materials, organisation and pedagogy. With respect to evaluation, the significance of the process is emerging more strongly but there are substantial differences in the value stances taken. This will be considered in more detail since it is a critical issue. We shall consider a number of areas where such issues arise.

In Paper 6, the impact of curriculum change is considered by Mme Monique Claude in a particular setting, her own college in Paris.

Paper 6

IMPLEMENTATION OF CURRICULA IN A COLLEGE

Mme Monique Claude

The value of what I have to say can only be relative and the principal of a college in a priority educational area or a rural area would no doubt take a different view.

I shall briefly describe the college in which I work, since in France schools are often the reflection of their environment.

The college is in Paris on the border of the 5th and 13th Arrondissements and the pupils come from the 5th -- a district dominated by universities, the museum and libraries -- and from the 13th -- a district now changing very rapidly.

The area thus contains different lifestyles, sometimes completely opposite ones, and the lives of the pupils thus vary enormously.

My school, which originally gave supplementary teaching to boys, then became a college of secondary education and finally a college, has had to create an image and reputation in a district where prestigious "*lycées*" still give first-cycle instruction. At present, the standard of pupils may be seen as high: few pupils change school at the end of the fifth grade; 60 per cent of age groups move on to the long-term cycle at the end of the third grade; there are no school leavers at the end of the third grade or during the year.

The 560 pupils of the college, divided into 20 classes, are taught by a stable body of teachers with many years experience.

As far as I can judge, from careful reading of pupils' work and meetings with teachers, present curricula seem well accepted and applied, with interdisciplinary experiments in some cases. This compliance with curricula does not prevent the school from being open to the world, nor work and reflection being given to pupils with difficulties.

This picture, which may seem idyllic, must be qualified in a number of ways. Teachers of so-called "basic" subjects, i.e. French, mathematics, modern languages, complain about the reduction in hours at a time when classes are becoming more and more varied (15 to 20 per cent of pupils with problems as from the sixth grade) and pupil numbers are increasing (29 to 30 pupils per class) even though, to date, we have been able to maintain more than just the "core hours" and to provide for years to be repeated.

Teachers of modern languages complain of discrepancies in the initial introduction to modern languages: from zero to three years depending on the school of origin, in one or sometimes two modern languages.

Biology and physics teachers complain of having to confine themselves to theoretical instruction, without real experimentation by pupils, owing to the failure to constitute small groups.

Lastly, everyone is aware that some pupils (15 to 20 per cent of age groups) do not master course content.

Irrespective of subject, teachers are making increasing use of available audio-visual equipment. Conversely, with very few exceptions, the use of data processing remains confined to technology teachers.

Pupil assessment is still too traditional in spite of the introduction of common testing as from the third grade and the use of assessment tests in some subjects (mathematics, english).

If teachers do not appear to challenge curricula, it is because most of them want instruction to remain the primary function of schools.

Teachers are very much in favour of opening the school to society and actively participating in pupil orientation and guidance, and organise numerous activities (museums, theatre, conferences, film-making, travel in France and abroad, participation in radio and television programmes, in-firm training courses for pupils in the third grade, etc.). But they are concerned by the number of tasks they have to carry out (from road safety to information about social problems) and the many demands made on them in the course of the year (conferences of various kinds, competitive examinations, forums, etc.). Indeed, although education and socialisation of pupils form an important part of their activity, they still need a considerable proportion of school time for transmitting knowledge and know-how.

Neither do parents challenge curricula since they are very much attached to general education and against specialisation at too early an age.

Extremely concerned about the future of their children, they are becoming "consumers of education" who expect their children to be looked after in an increasingly broad and efficient manner.

Their expectations are often contradictory. For example, a parent who, in decision-making or analytical bodies, is concerned about pupils with difficulties is often the one who deals most easily with the complexity of the educational system, and knows how to choose the most exclusive establishments and courses.

Likewise, parents who expect the school to be more open to the world are also those most concerned with scrupulous compliance with curricula and with the school's success rate.

Lastly, all parents expect the school to give their children what they need to find their place in the community.

My conclusion is that our efforts should concentrate on three main points.

1) How to help pupils with difficulties?
    -- Should remedial action not be taken as from the elementary school?
    -- Should the few hours of additional teaching given to pupils who are already saturated, be replaced by real team work with reduced numbers?
    -- Should technology courses and learning not be upgraded so that they are no longer seen as systems of exclusion?

2) How can we modernise the assessment system which usually involves ranking pupils against each other rather than actually assessing skills acquired? How can assessment be made into a tool of learning?

3) How can the constitution of genuine teaching teams be made the concern of all rather than just of some teachers?

IV. THE CURRICULUM: MEANING AND IMPLICATIONS

1. The Content, Structure and Organisation of Learning

A perennial question in education is "What knowledge is of most worth?" The answers to that question are always changing. The hunter in the small tribe has one set of answers, the farmer in the small rural village another and the factory worker in the industrial town yet another. The setting which we now examine in considering such a question is fundamentally different. We no longer live in close-knit, self-reliant communities with clear-cut needs. Our communities are interdependent. The person in the French provincial town, the person in the Japanese industrial city, the person in the Canadian farm town now live in a world where their daily existences are interdependent: where their economic prospects are determined by the same world issues; where their environments react to the same global circumstances; where their prospects for peace and war relate to the same events and movements; where their health is at risk from the same global diseases. So much of the needs of the person, as worker, as citizen, as individual have a common base that a primary answer to our question is with a further query: what should be taught in common to all students?

Core curriculum. OECD has had a concern for some years with the same question which it has handled under the heading of *core curriculum*. Malcolm Skilbeck considers various alternative approaches to the idea of core curriculum and advocates a particular interpretation:

> "This third meaning of core has as its central reference point those basic and essential learnings which are deemed to be necessary or, at all events, highly desirable for all students. They are for living in society now and in the future, and of a kind which schools might be fitted to handle. The structure and organisation of student learning, together with a map of contemporary culture, occupy the central place in this conception of core. The learnings are *common* and for this reason I have related this approach to that advanced by some advocates of the common curriculum. They are also *required* of all students and it is therefore reasonable to describe them as *compulsory*. But the point of calling them core learnings is that they are designed and selected through processes of cultural analysis which aim to get students into the realities of contemporary life" (Skilbeck, 1982).

And, further,

> "I have described these learnings as basic and essential. They are basic in that they are intended to provide a foundation or base on which subsequent or related learnings may be built. They should provide learners with conceptual and methodological tools to continue their own learning. They are essential in the sense that they are intended to equip learners for a satisfying and effective participation in social and cultural life. This reminds us that core curriculum theory has strong affinities with democratic ideology, and starts from the assumption that constructive and varied participation in social and cultural life is the right and responsibility of everybody" (Skilbeck, 1982).

Such a concept provides a strong and more inclusive base to the efforts of the many countries now involved in a significant effort to develop a national curriculum framework. This is by no means an easy task, requiring as it does not only an extension beyond the vocational but also the development of a broad social agreement.

Jean Blackburn, in her analysis of the idea of democratic entitlement, emphasizes the substantial task involved in establishing agreement.

"It seems to me that establishing publicly known and acknowledged agreements about the substance of compulsory schooling is now imperative as part of the democratic condition. Participatory processes in the governance of schooling are fine, but they need an agreed substance which has wide legitimacy. From this perspective, I find it impossible to accept that individual school communities have an independent right to determine curriculum policies in the core learning areas. All children, in my view, have a democratic right of access to a commonly-agreed core curriculum, systematically developed across the years of compulsory attendance to increasingly sophisticated levels. The curriculum would embody monitoring processes and remedial action which would ensure the students' own progressive access to further learning. The participatory working of the democratic society depends on a high degree of shared knowledge, meanings and frames of reference. It also depends on some commitment to an idea of the common good beyond self and group interest". (Blackburn, 1991).

It is interesting that these emphases -- a commonly agreed core curriculum, monitoring processes and remedial action -- are advocated not just as vocational needs but as part of the "imperative of the democratic condition".

In the National Curriculum developed in England and Wales, as we have seen, the basis of the curriculum is the specification of a number of subject areas. For those concerned with the idea of core curriculum, a number of subject areas defined in the traditional way may be a good starting-point but is an inadequate expression of the idea of "basic and essential learnings". In the New Zealand instance, the problem is approached by a multi-dimensional specification: principles, learning areas, essential skills, attitudes and values, and, assessment procedures. It represents an attempt to bridge the gap identified so often for students, where they can indicate through traditional examinations that they possess a great deal of knowledge yet prove unable to apply it in new and unfamiliar situations.

Studies of the meaning of core curriculum were carried out in Austria, the Netherlands, Spain, Sweden and the United States. Taken together with the information on other Member countries, much of which is referred to here, they reflect the variety of conceptions and the variety of practice. Significantly, however, the core curriculum concept is a lively topic in almost all countries, reflecting the general concern for developing a sound basis for further learning during the compulsory years. As we have seen, in some countries such as the USA and Britain, the emphasis has gone towards specifying core curriculum in terms of particular subjects, in those cases the traditional academic subjects. This comes from a strong feeling that past curriculum reforms emphasizing the importance of process, have underplayed the role of content. There is some justice in this claim for an emphasis solely on process has not proved an adequate basis on its own. It is in the linking of content and process that a substantial basis for further learning develops. In the approach specifying only the traditional subjects, however, there is a danger that content alone will be the emphasis as has happened in the past, with harmful effects. Further, this approach neglects the possibilities of inter-disciplinary studies, or multi-disciplinary studies, needed to deal with major problems such as the environment where not only physical science disciplines are relevant but economics, the social science, the arts and politics play a part. A major concern in developing the idea of the core curriculum, as 'essential learnings', is not merely basic knowledge, but essential ways of thinking, of solving problems, of relating knowledge to everyday life.

Papers 7 and 8 by Malcolm Skilbeck and Didier Dacunha-Castelle analyze further this concept of core curriculum.

THE CORE CURRICULUM

Malcolm Skilbeck

Why a Core Curriculum?

The idea of a core curriculum is not new and the term itself is loosely used. It was implicit in the work of Herbart and his followers in the latter part of the 19th century. It is much more explicit in the writings and the practice of John Dewey and was taken further by his colleagues and followers at Columbia and Illinois Universities in this century. The essence of the arguments put forward by Dewey is still relevant, linking as it does the nature of schooling and of the curriculum, with the concept of a democratic society and of the role of the individual. "The scheme of a curriculum ...... must select with the intention of improving the life we live *in common* so that the future shall be better than the past". (Dewey 1916, page 125)*

It is this emphasis on the life we live in common and the purpose of that life, which is so relevant today and takes on a new and greater urgency.

We have moved from the close community of Dewey's younger days where needs were specific to the environment and where survival, social cohesion and personal adequacy and development were shaped by and for that local environment. We now live in a situation where peace, economic prosperity, cultural survival, the environment all depend on national and international sources. We are members by necessity of a global society and must prepare for that situation.

However, the unity of that "common life" in our society is threatened by many circumstances, most obviously at present the occurrence of high unemployment. It poses a particular problem for many people, not only because of its magnitude -- in some cases rates of 25 per cent or more -- but because of the debilitating effects on motivation. In the long term it threatens to open a continuing division in our society, between those who regularly have work and those who do not.

In this situation our countries have accepted the need to educate all students to a foundation level of capability needed to sustain the motivation to continue learning. It is in that context of a society which requires life-long learning that the core curriculum is required as a guarantee of capacity to participate. The current emphasis on re-training, re-skilling, a flexible, well motivated and trained workforce is part of the story but only a part. For personal fulfilment, effective social participation, the enhancement of human powers and the maintenance of a high quality of life for all, we must ensure the relevance and adequacy of these foundation learnings.

The Core Curriculum

Core curriculum a multidimensional experience -- Not just what, but, How? Where? What? ..... be addressed.

There are many approaches to defining core curriculum:

a) A set of required learnings for all students within a single institution;

b) That part of the whole curriculum prescribed by central government;

c) That part of the whole curriculum which in broad outline is common to all schools, defined in *partnership* by central and local bodies and interpreted by schools (based on analyses of contemporary culture).

The core curriculum under this latter concept is *common*: there are: common features for all learners, it is common in: context; presentation; circumstance.

The core curriculum is *required* -- This extends an obligation upon the schools to provide certain types of learning and a requirement upon all students to encounter those learnings.

The core curriculum involves *partnership* in:

-- defining the essential learnings;
-- analysing contemporary culture;
-- interpreting essential learnings at school level.

It thus involves a social contract -- involving many levels:

-- a professional endeavour;
-- analysing contemporary culture;
-- interpretation by schools.

The socio-cultural dimension of core curriculum is brought out by American theorists:

".. the concept of core curriculum is grounded in a critique of contemporary culture and recommendations about internal values and meanings which it is the responsibility of the school to advance in a coherent, balanced and integrated curriculum for all students" (Smith, Stanley and Shores).

This emphasis on the need for some core of common experiences must not be taken to deny the importance of individuality and the need to take account of individual differences. The core curriculum is to be developed and structured in such a way as to provide a foundation for individual development, not only in the sense of educational and vocational choices, but also as a means of enriching individuality.

What the Core Curriculum is Not:

The core curriculum is not exclusively a *child centred* curriculum.

Froebel and Montessori showed the need to take account of individual needs and interests. They have sometimes been misinterpreted to mean that children's interests are the only criterion.

The core curriculum is not exclusively a *subject centred* curriculum, even though persuasive arguments have been put forward about the importance of the 'structure of the disciplines' e.g. Phoenix.

"The curriculum should consist entirely of knowledge which comes from the disciplines......
Education should be conceived as a guided recapitulation of the procedure of inquiry which gave rise
to the fruitful bodies of organised knowledge comprising the established disciplines" (Phenix, 1964, p.
64) and John Dewey, while noting the individuality of the child, also stressed the importance of that
individuality developing and growing in the light of other studies which he conceived, as part of a
collective race experience. For Dewey the disciplines ".... embody the cumulative outcomes of the
efforts, the striving and the successes of the human race, generation after generation". (Dewey, 1902,
Page 12). This is a much broader concept than that of Phenix and of greater relevance to an age of
universal schooling where the core curriculum has to offer something of value to every student.

The Core in Perspective

In thinking about the curriculum as a whole and the core as fundamental learnings in particular,
we must avoid the temptation to anchor it exclusively in subject disciplines, children's interests and
needs, social expectations or the values and meanings of the culture. All of these are indeed to be
drawn upon. "The curriculum is both a sharply focused representation of the values, meanings and ways
of life of the society and a source of knowledge, understanding, techniques, skills and strategies for
social as well as personal development". (Skilbeck, 1985, page 24).

It is this other dimension, this representation of "the values, meaning and way of life" which
enriches the concept of the core curriculum as something beyond the acquiring of knowledge,
understanding and competences from the disciplines. It means that the process as well as the content
is important if qualities so significant, but so subtle, are to be a part of students' experience. The way
the school is organised, its ceremonies and rituals, its discipline, its relationships -- the culture of the
school -- these must express these valued common qualities, equally with the teaching process and the
content.

The multidimensional view of the core curriculum was well defined by the Australian
Curriculum Development Centre in its 1980 statement (CDC, 1980). This publication identified three
distinct dimensions for core curriculum, for use in curriculum planning and design, implementation,
reviews, evaluation and reconstruction.

The dimensions were:

-- nine areas of knowledge and experience;
-- selected learning process;
-- learning situations or environments.

The description will be taken further under the consideration of how we might proceed. It is
the necessity of combination that we stress here.

For the moment however, there is a further distinction we must make as to what the core
curriculum is not.

The core curriculum is neither a centrally-prescribed curriculum nor the result of an entirely
school based curriculum development. The advantages of central prescription are clear. A concise and
coherent statement of purposes and content can be developed and embodied in legislation or a formal
statement. It can be supported by materials production, by assessment procedures and by teacher

development. Nevertheless, our experience shows all too clearly that this is not enough. The carefully developed RD&D approach of the 1960s projects in maths and science, well-conceived and generously funded, nevertheless failed to make the expected impact on schools. This idea of the curriculum as a product, conceived at one level and, even though with careful planning, implemented at another level, has proved to be insufficient as a means of bringing about effective change. It is to be hoped that we can now show how we have learned from the lessons of the past.

Equally, however, curriculum developed within the limits of individual schools cannot meet the requirements of the core curriculum for basic and essential learning as a common entitlement. The movement to school-based curriculum development of the 1970s was a deliberate attempt to meet the problems which arose through the large-scale curriculum projects. Like those projects, the concept has valuable contributions. The idea of the teacher as researcher and curriculum developer embodies a valuable truth. So, too, does the concept of a school, as an entire school, planning its educational programme. Yet individual schools do not have the time and the resources for a task of this magnitude of core curriculum development. Furthermore, the concept is at odds with the idea of a common curriculum representing the values and meanings of a society and culture. The school ultimately shapes and delivers the curriculum and this is not merely a matter of transmission, but it needs to work within the wider framework of well defined basic and essential learnings.

Thus, the development of the curriculum itself, from plan to practice must combine the strengths of central decision making and of local management. This is the practical meaning of the phrase "defined in partnership by central and local bodies and interpreted by schools". The reality of the core curriculum is that it can exist only as a co-operative effort. Government, the social partners, teachers, parents, students, specialist contributors, interest groups will all have appropriate parts to play. The success of the concept depends on the effective co-ordination of this partnership.

In summary then, the core curriculum consists of those learnings judged to be basic and essential for all students: basic in that they provide both a foundation on which subsequent learning may be built and also the conceptual and methodological tools to continue their own learning. They are essential through their intention to equip students for a satisfying and effective participation in social and cultural life. A vital aspect of the core curriculum is its affinities with democratic ideology, its assumption that constructive and active participation is the right and responsibility of every person.

How Should the Core Curriculum Develop

We have stressed above the multidimensional nature of the core curriculum.

The dimension, areas of knowledge and experience, involves:

-- Arts and crafts;
-- Environmental studies;
-- Mathematical skills and reasoning and their application;
-- Social, cultural and civic studies;
-- Health education;
-- Scientific and technological ways of knowing and their social application;
-- Communication;
-- Moral reasoning and action, value and belief systems;
-- Work, leisure and life-style.

The second dimension, learning processes and experiences, includes but is not restricted to:

-- Learning and thinking techniques such as the systematic recording of information, organised study habits, problem solving, decision making and memorisation;

-- ways of organising and systematising knowledge as through themes, topics, models, formulae, tables, diagrams, and key concepts;

-- specific skills as in reading, speech, experimental work, the use of tools and collaborative or group learning;

-- varied forms of expression as in story writing, oral performances and graphic communication.

The third dimension comprises learning situations or environment, the spaces and places where core learnings are to be provided, not only the classroom but a much wider range of situations given the breadth of the other two dimensions. The concept of learning environments may be thought of as a continuation extending from micro-learning situations in classrooms, laboratories, workshops, libraries, field trips etc. to the macro-learning situation, the over-all pattern of the school system. The idea of a common culture core curriculum for divided and unequal school systems may well be contradictory.

The concept of core curriculum in the form we have defined implies the nature of the way in which it needs to develop. We have stressed the need for a partnership not beginning in consensus for that is unlikely to exist but working towards consensus. What this requires is a mechanism by which the central and local authorities, the profession and representative public interests can work together to agree on a broad outline core curriculum. If this is carried out solely by national government, without properly involving the other interests, it risks raising considerable hostility and resistance from the field. It is also subject to those major difficulties of diffusion and implementation already mentioned, so fatal to the very strongly based and well conceived curriculum projects of the 1960s (See for example OECD/CERI 1993, Chapters II (viii and ix) OECD/CERI 1973. Case Studies of Educational Innovation. IV. Strategies for Innovation in Education, Paris, OECD).

The essence of this approach is the belief that there can be no effective structure for curriculum decisions at the national level that does not command general assent particularly from teachers and parents, but also involving the other key interest groups.

"The issue therefore, in respect of core curriculum as with other kinds of curriculum proposals, is how far the aspirations, values and assumptions behind the change are shared and whether the construction of the new curriculum is to be genuinely a joint undertaking" (Skilbeck, 1984, p.160).

Equally, for an effective process, there must be constructive action at the school level, presupposing that schools are not only familiar with the proposals but that their assent is a part of the process. It is schools, as collective entities, which need to be involved, rather than teachers as individuals. This again is not a simple process, given the complex organisation within a school and the multiplicity of its links with parents and the local community for example. Decisions about the core curriculum must be collective, for it is essential to develop both the horizontal relationships which provide coherence for study at a particular time and also the vertical relationships which are necessary to provide continuity. A major effort is required by the school to act not merely as an effective organisation but as a community. Within this community not only teachers but parents and students have a role. In many countries progress is being made in developing this broadly defined partnership approach to core curriculum. On a national scale and in larger countries, especially, it is difficult to achieve the integration of the various interests, local, regional, national, public and private. Democratic processes are complex, time-consuming and costly. There are questions, too, to resolve, concerning the organisation of core studies in terms of individual student interests and capabilities. These become more difficult issues once adolescence is reached and clearly differentiated pathways emerge in the educational system. Finally, the fundamental ideas and ideals of shared experience, shared knowledge, shared values are challenged by the very heterogeneity of our societies and the vigorous ideological debates that take place within them. These and other issues require educators at all levels, whether teachers, researchers, policy makers or administrators, to approach the question of core curriculum not merely as the design and delivery of a set of centrally presented school subjects to be taught and examined, but as one of the critically important social, cultural and educational projects of our time.

Bibliography

Dewey, John (1902) *The Child and the Curriculum*, Chicago, University of Chicago.

Dewey, John (1916) *Democracy and Education*, New York, Macmillan Publishing Co.

Phenix Phillip (1962) A Harry Passow (Ed) 1962. *Curriculum Crossroads*, New York, Teachers College Press.

Skilbeck, M. (1984) *School Based Curriculum Development*. London, Harper and Row.

Skilbeck, Malcolm (1985) *A Core Curriculum for the Common School*, London, University of London, Institute of Education.

Skilbeck, M. (1992) Curriculum Implementation: Conflicts or Consensus, *Educational Research and Perspectives*. Volume No. 19.

(*)   I am grateful to Professor Phillip Hughes for his advice in the preparation of this paper.

Paper 8

THE COMMON CORE

Didier Dacunha-Castelle

In all European countries, and France is no exception, the concept of a core curriculum for lower secondary education, i.e. children aged 11 to 16, is the subject of heated debate and much questioning, and it is on this aspect I shall be concentrating in addressing the issues raised by the OECD.

The key date in France was 1975 when the then conservative government, motivated by social concerns, set up the "college unique" (non-streamed, general and technical lower secondary education). This "college" system is now 20 years old and it has had to weather many difficulties, criticisms and overhauls in its endeavour to establish itself on a firm basis while at the same time taking into account the needs of all or virtually all children.

The main considerations in 1993 are the following:

-- Any move to create separate institutions or any challenge to the French "single college" system by streaming pupils carries with it a very serious risk of segregation, albeit for sociological rather than strictly educational reasons.

-- Our country's history shows that, whenever the entire school population is concerned, putting children in different categories of educational establishment leads to exclusion, as does the streaming system.

-- Although the "single college" system is thus seen as a necessity, there are a number of inherent values, difficulties and contradictions that have to be acknowledged.

2.1.   The college's prime role is to enable each child to develop his potential by giving him the instruments (particularly the ability to think) which will not only promote his independence but also develop his manual, artistic, physical and, of course, intellectual skills.

2.2.   Thereafter, but only thereafter, the aim is to help each pupil at the end of his college years to choose a course of study in keeping with his abilities and inclinations as regards a career, and thus help him to assess himself.

2.3.   It must be acknowledged that both teaching approaches and content have to be diversified to some extent, that is to say the necessary balance must be struck between a programme of instruction for all pupils, which is vital for national unity and an understanding of the rights and responsibilities of every citizen, and different courses of study that develop individual abilities and help to attenuate social, intellectual and psychological difficulties, whenever these are discernible; in other words a college must educate as well as instruct its pupils.

-- On the basis of this analysis of the situation, there are a number of practical policies that can be suggested for the coming years.

3.1.   To focus on the acquisition of language skills, by promoting improvements in teaching methods in order to enhance pupils' ability to express themselves in writing and orally and to prevent shortcomings in this respect from handicapping them in all their other activities. It is of prime importance that these basic problems should be resolved.

3.2.   To treat mathematics as a subject that is accessible to all and one which can be taught largely on an experimental and operational basis, the main aim being to encourage pupils to discover things for themselves.

3.3.   At present, science and technology education is far too compartmentalised during the early years; the various subjects need to be interrelated to a greater extent and the divisions that are meaningless for children at this age avoided. Pupils must take part in activities in which they are called on to observe, assemble and construct small things themselves, nothing too ambitious but with the clear aim of instilling an interest in science and technical subjects, and without neglecting the "hands-on" aspect.

3.4.   Any technicalities and any drift towards economics must be avoided in the teaching of the humanities, meaning history and geography in the case of children in this age group. The teaching of these subjects should be geared to instilling values and providing explanations in response not only to the search for national or regional identities, but also to the need to learn respect for other individuals in one's everyday life, for other races and for other civilisations, and solidarity with those less fortunate than ourselves. geography, in combination with science and technology, should serve as the basis for environmental education.

3.5.   More specific areas such as modern languages and, of course, physical and artistic education, must be open to all pupils and form an integral part of the core curriculum.

Two other tasks which partly conflict with the existence of the core curriculum must then be assumed: the task of diversification centred on the pupil, and the task of preparing pupils for a study option that is sadly still all too often irreversible.

Diversification should be achieved by providing set times for a range of activities that can be modified from one year to another depending on the teachers' advice and pupils' preferences. One possibility would be to organise projects combining various subjects. It was once fashionable to make fun of so-called general cultural activities, which were often of poor quality because of the lack of resources and experience.

Pupils must, however, be allowed to develop their abilities, including their manual skills, in a fairly individual way, by bringing home to them the many situations in which persons with a practical, intellectual or artistic bent, for example, can work together on an equal footing. In this respect, the new form of technology workshops based on a technology core curriculum are one of the best ways of breaking down the barriers and improving the image of the pre-professional streams to which a social stigma is at present attached.

This diversification calls for curricula that are defined on a top-down basis, not overly ambitious, and which are the subject of very wide discussion both within the teaching profession as a whole as well as outside it. And if we are to cater for the needs of those pupils who are in serious difficulty, there will also need to be variants, particularly in the form of highly specialised support and certain types of pre-professional, technical -- and general technological -- training which, as we know, can have remedial effects and enable pupils to rejoin the normal school system.

The measures to be taken and the ideas to be kept in mind therefore are:

-- a reform of subject matters and structures to be determined on a top-down basis, getting down to essentials, varied enough to activate the pupil, and making meaningful certain subject areas which need not be explored in detail until absolutely necessary (particularly in the case of science and technology);

-- a rethink of the teaching and learning of language skills,

-- the provision of periods for a variety of other activities, with strong emphasis on the career-guidance aspect;

-- more resources for those in need of them and, for those with serious problems, flexible arrangements including, if necessary, pre-professional training, primarily as a means of re-integrating pupils in the school system.

2. Science, Mathematics and Technology.

Two projects have been developed to consider broad areas of knowledge, the science, mathematics and technology for all project, and the humanities and arts in the curriculum. Background papers on both these projects will be presented. Both raise important issues.

This project covers a very broad and diverse area, with mathematics as one of the oldest studies in the curriculum, and technology one of the newest, in many countries not rating an inclusion as a separate subject. The whole area is one of some complexity, too, when considered as a study for all. The whole field of science, and the ways of applying it, clearly constitute a major part of our culture and thus merits inclusion. It poses, however, substantial pedagogic problems. After initial enthusiasm and interest, both science and mathematics do not prove to be popular subjects. Where choice is permitted they are frequently left to those students who need them for vocational purposes. This has often meant that they are then developed and taught specifically for such audiences which adds to the difficulties for others. If subjects are judged partly on the enthusiasm they develop for further learning, both these areas tend to perform poorly. In contrast, the area of technology is so new and so variously defined that it requires considerable further study, even though it is the subject of much attention and experiment. The project group plan a series of case studies to identify the nature of innovations in the SMT field and to determine the conceptual framework behind the innovation (Atkin, 1993).

Paper 9

PROJECT ON INNOVATIONS IN SCIENCE, MATHEMATICS, AND TECHNOLOGY EDUCATION

Myron Atkin

The improvement of education in science, mathematics, and technology (SMT) has been identified as a priority in virtually all countries. New programmes are being developed and attempts are being made to improve the existing ones virtually everywhere. While there are important differences in the nature of SMT reform in various countries, there are also some striking similarities, both with respect to the forces that seem to be at work in stimulating innovation and in the shapes taken by the new programmes themselves.

The CERI/OECD SMT project was initiated in response to growing demand for more information and analysis about the nature of these changes, cross-nationally. The project will provide detailed material about current developments and an examination of selected features of the innovations that seem similar, unique, conflicting, problematic, and suggestive. By understanding innovations elsewhere, it may be possible to provide useful perspective on efforts to improve SMT education within one's own country.

Since many of the innovations selected for the study are in developmental stages and not yet widely in use, the most effective method for obtaining the information needed at this stage is to investigate the innovations in depth by observing what actually is happening on site, collecting relevant documents, and interviewing participants and others who seem to influence the new developments. Thus, carefully chosen *case studies* will be prepared within each of the participating countries to describe the nature of certain SMT innovations.

The cases to be developed were identified initially by professionals and officials in each of the countries interested in participating. Brief case summaries were prepared. An International Steering Committee constituted by CERI/OECD then reviewed the innovations nominated for intensive examination. Those chosen for the study provide uncommon potential for producing useful data for cross-national analysis.

Conceptual Framework for the Case Studies

The case studies are intended to provide data in several dimensions that the International Steering Group for the project has considered particularly important: (1) the impetus and context for the proposed change(s); (2) the conception of educational change that seems to be embedded in the innovation; (3) the goals and content of the new programme(s); (4) the view of and by the students that seems to characterise the new programme; (5) the methods, materials, equipment, and setting that are envisioned; (6) the role of teachers and how they are to be prepared for the innovation; and (7) the assessment, accountability, and evaluation that is planned or in progress.

Clearly, the seven issues interweave and are not mutually independent. Certain issues (like assessment and the role of the teacher) are pervasive and arise persistently under every heading. Even so, the enumerated issues possess an integrity that, together, enables them to provide valuable perspective about SMT for purposes of cross-national analysis.

International SMT conferences sponsored by CERI in 1991 and 1992 have confirmed the viability and saliency of this framework for highlighting key elements of reform. The categories also provide a functional guide for data collection and analysis. Now, by obtaining information about each of these characteristics -- in part, by means of common research questions -- it will be possible to make more-pointed comparisons across projects and across countries.

The conceptual framework and other elements of the SMT project are elaborated in other CERI documents (CERI/SMT 90.01, 91.1, 92.2). A few of the major points are highlighted here to provide a general indication of the scope and focus of the SMT project.

Impetus and Context

It is noteworthy that, in contrast to the curriculum reforms of the 1960s when specific initiatives were strongly influenced by academicians from the science and mathematics communities, factors external to the subjects (and even the educational system) are more dominant in the 1980s and 1990s. For example, innovations intended to make SMT education serve the needs of the economy more effectively (perhaps the central theme of SMT reform today in many countries), have their origins most frequently at national and governmental level. Governmental officials in many countries, supported by many business leaders and the press, speak forcefully and regularly about the need to improve the quality of a nation's "human resources."

High-quality education is essential to fill the ranks of advanced specialists in SMT, the public is told. Additionally, technological changes, especially in the means of production and communication, have raised the skill levels needed for even entry-level employment and have transformed the structure and management of organisations. The emphasis for a broad segment of the student population has moved toward educational outcomes such as "transferable" skills, adaptability, positive attitudes to change, the ability to communicate, desirable personal and interpersonal qualities, and problem-solving capabilities.

One consequence is that science and mathematics curricula are increasingly incorporating practical applications and implications. There is also a new receptivity for cross-curricular links that relate science, mathematics, and technology to each other, and also with other subjects. Vocational education, likewise, can no longer be conceived in terms of a narrow occupationalism but as developing general work-related skills.

Another contextual influence of increasing importance in setting the direction of change in SMT education arises from social concerns about environmental quality. In a few countries, a new subject, environmental studies, has been created. In many places, the better-established subjects have been modified to incorporate environmental issues. Almost always, this development entails probing connections between scientific and technical fields, on the one hand, and political/social/economic considerations, on the other.

Finally, in terms of these illustrations of the varied stimuli for reform of SMT education, periodic national comparisons of student achievement highlight sometimes sharply drawn distinctions between the apparent quality of instruction in SMT in various countries. Those nations whose students do relatively poorly in these comparisons often point to the test scores to justify priority for reform of SMT education.

One element of the project, then, is to use the case studies to illuminate the various pressures and opportunities that stimulate and shape SMT education reform. The purpose is to outline the dynamic quality of educational innovations and the nature of the complex interactions among different groups with a stake in the results.

Conceptions of Educational Change

Different viewpoints about the process of school reform seem to characterise innovations in SMT. In some places the teacher is viewed as the central figure in reform. The assumption seems to be that unless teachers are fully engaged at all levels of the innovation, it is unlikely that deep change will occur. Thus, priority is placed on teacher "ownership" of the change, often with mechanisms to establish support networks wherein teachers can exchange ideas. In at least one instance, this conviction is carried so far as to eschew a primary focus on new schemes, syllabuses, resources, organisational structures, or adoption of a particular teaching style, in favour of placing greater authority in the hands of groups of teachers to design whatever new approaches seem important to them. In at least one country, a major, national teachers' professional association has been pivotal in initiating a major innovation.

To draw a contrast somewhat more sharply than is warranted by the preliminary data collected in the SMT project, the teacher seems to play a somewhat more passive role in educational change in other places. It is difficult to draw inferences with confidence on the basis of the brief case summaries submitted so far, but the rhetoric of teacher participation in innovation (collaboration, empowerment, autonomy, school-based change) seems to mean different things in different contexts. The operational connotation in some places is to hand implementation of an innovation to teachers -- but only after other groups have decided on the goals and the topics to be included in the curriculum. Teachers in these projects presumably have latitude to figure out how best to make goals and topics work best in the lives of students. A distinction is not drawn between initiation of the innovation by the teacher and trying to assure that teachers take possession of the innovation once it is launched by someone else.

There are several sets of overlapping tensions in conceptualising plans for SMT reform. In addition to bottom-up as against top-down initiatives, there are governmental priorities as contrasted with professional ones, the relationship between standards and standardisation, engineered change as contrasted with evolutionary imagery, and applying resources to remedying weakness as against directing primary efforts toward building on strength.

It is probably unproductive in developing the case studies and trying to analyze them to accent these polarities. Rather, there will be an attempt to document and understand the dynamic quality of the resulting tensions, possibly leading to a useful synthesis.

Increasingly, however, change is viewed as "systemic." Nothing can be changed without changing everything, it is believed. Consequently, there is a growing view that responsibility for improving education should be broadly shared among both people and organisations: teachers, teacher educators, professors, industrial scientists, political figures, curriculum developers, and producers of instructional materials, for example. There is growing interest in fostering inter-institutional partnerships or alliances. Incentives are created in some places for schools to work more closely with industry, universities, museums, and other agencies that help connect school with the broader community.

The viewpoint about educational change that has evolved in the SMT project so far is one in which change is viewed as both fluid and multi-faceted. Therefore, there is a drift away from collecting case data in the various countries that illuminate *models* that might underlie the process of change (and the rigidity that their use sometimes implies) toward thinking about change using the more ambiguous notion of *images*. When contemplating deep change in education, it may be less useful to construct a flow chart than to evoke a provocative metaphor. Educational change itself, for example, might be likened to evolution, with its concepts of natural variation, adaptation, and survival. Similarly, the image of a school "culture" suggests the depth and power of existing structures and values. Changing a culture is a qualitatively different enterprise from engineering a new system. Cultures do change, of course, but slowly -- and the signs are often difficult to detect because they are embedded deeply in the system.

Goals and Content

Questions of purpose are central, of course, to any examination of issues in SMT education: Why are these subjects to be taught and what should be emphasised for different students? Among the aims mentioned most often for the teaching of science and mathematics are the following:

-- To teach the "structure" of the subject (an ambiguous term, perhaps usefully so, usually taken to mean some of the key concepts and processes of science);

-- To teach about "scientific methods" (like hypothesis formation and subsequent testing);

-- To help students learn to use scientific methods themselves;

-- To teach about applications of science and mathematics in one's personal life (like the scientific basis for disease prevention or the mathematical ideas that underlie the premiums structure for automobile insurance);

-- To make students scientifically "literate" (another term of uncertain meaning);

-- To foster "numeracy";

-- To demonstrate that science is a product of human thought and culture;

-- To teach how mathematical ideas apply to common and complex problems (such as using statistical methods to describe, analyze, evaluate, and make decisions);

-- To help students communicate mathematically;

-- To help students develop scientific attitudes (like curiosity about the natural world and the conviction that they have a role in controlling their own fate);

-- To teach how science can and should inform social policy (like preservation of the environment or the handling of hazardous materials);

-- To teach the content necessary for scientific and technical specialisation in college;

-- To develop "higher-order" thinking and problem-solving skills;

-- To help students solve unconventional problems;

-- To teach students to perceive patterns;

-- To teach children to estimate and measure;

-- To understand quantitative aspects of public policy;

-- To help students, especially those who do not seem bound for college, develop entry-level technical skills for employment;

-- To illustrate how science relates to an understanding of other school subjects (like teaching about the role of quantitative thinking across all curriculum fields);

-- To prepare students for professional careers in science;

-- To convey to students an appreciation of the aesthetic dimensions of science and mathematics (like their stress on parsimony and elegance, their attraction to equilibrium and symmetry);

-- To demystify scientific and technical fields, thus empowering students to participate in public-policy decisions that must be made in an industrialised society.

Each of these goals (and this list is far from complete) has different implications for the curriculum, though they are seldom discussed explicitly. Only occasionally, it seems, are curriculum choices made on the basis of careful consideration of the options. When a new, attractive-sounding objective is suggested for the science or mathematics curriculum, such as the development of "scientific literacy" or "numeracy," it is added to the existing list with little understanding of its meaning or the implications for schools. One focus of the case studies will be on the specific content that is emphasised in the various innovations and the reasons for those choices.

One of the clearest developments in SMT that has become apparent in the initial stages of the CERI/OECD project is the drift toward more practical work in the classroom. A dramatic manifestation of this trend in many countries is the rapid expansion of a new subject, technology education. Details are discussed in other CERI/OECD SMT documents, but technology has come to be viewed in SMT conferences so far as a "special case," to be monitored with particular care because of it's unique features and the varied ways the subject is being treated in different countries.

Various motives for establishing technology education can be found: (a) helping pupils to live in and cope with a technological environment, (b) helping pupils to have control over this environment, (c) stimulating pupils to contribute to a technological society, both as citizens and as part of a future work force -- with industry particularly concerned about the latter and expressing concerns about pupils' innovative and creative thinking, both in design and production.

To reach the general aims above, several features seem to be a part of technology education: (a) learning technological concepts and principles, (b) acquiring practical skills in designing, making, and using technical products, (c) acquiring a balanced view of technology as a whole, (d) developing a positive-critical attitude towards technology.

A comparison between the goals and content of school technology in various countries and situations yields a number of different types of technology education, each with its own emphases and biases. Some of these types are:

-- a craft oriented version, in which the making of work pieces is the main aim;

-- an engineering-concepts version, in which theoretical analyses of matter and energy information flows in systems play a vital role;

-- an applied science version, in which technology is taught in the context of applications of knowledge that is taught in science lessons;

-- an industrial-production oriented version, that focuses on contributing to the economic production system;

-- a high tech version, in which pupils are confronted with the advanced types of technology, like CAD/CAM, robotics, telematics, etc.

It seems clear that the emergence of technology as a component of general education is a major, potentially radical, and unquestionably challenging innovation with important implications for both science and mathematics education. There is need to monitor systematic developments in different countries and to establish networks for the exchange of information.

Finally, with respect to content in this brief and selective overview of developments in the SMT project, there is the matter of links among science, mathematics, technology -- and also consideration of how these fields are related to other school subjects. Expanding cross-curricular links are a notable feature of current innovations. A primary reason for this development, though not the only one, is the increasing and significant attention in schools to applications of science and mathematics. Students are expected to understand and utilise relationships between the science and mathematics disciplines, on the one hand, and decisions people must make in their personal lives and in the development of their communities, on the other. However, the individual disciplines have been defined and delineated by internal criteria, not necessarily by their impact on human activities. They have evolved as attempts to understand the universe, not necessarily to alter it. Thus, today's tendency to ask how science relates to everyday life tends to blur traditional subject boundaries.

The Students

There is often a lack of clarity about the students to be served by SMT reform. Who is to benefit from the publicly supported educational system? While "everyone" is the ready and official response in all industrialised countries, it is not clear that school-science curricula are designed or taught with a clear, operational view of that intention. By both formal and informal means, tracking is extensive in secondary schools, for example.

For the academically oriented and able who seem headed for higher education with specialities in science, the prevailing pattern is anticipatory college-level work. In most countries, the mathematics, for example, consists of the topics thought necessary to master the calculus: algebra, analytic geometry, trigonometry. In science, the subjects taught in college guide the high-school curriculum: biology, chemistry, physics, and, sometimes, earth sciences. In the United States, it has become increasingly common for college-bound, high-school youth actually to complete college-level courses (advanced placement) for the purpose of avoiding enrolment in the introductory courses when college work begins.

What about students bound for college but who will not major in technical fields? Usually these students take the same secondary-school courses as those who will specialise later in science. Rarely are special provisions being made for them.

Then there are the students unlikely to attend an institution of higher education, in most countries the majority. Does their SMT education usually consist of a selection of the topics taught to the college-bound, except at a "simpler" level? To what extent are SMT programmes for such student emphasising something else, like entry-level job skills, or the scientific basis for various personal and social questions confronted by all people, like environmental protection, disease control, and sexuality?

The ambiguous slogan, "science for all," thus masks differences in programmes that range from those designed to help all people cope with their responsibilities as citizens to those that seem targeted to increase the pool from which specialists might be chosen. Should there be a broad, common curriculum that all students experience, or should the curriculum be highly differentiated to match the abilities and aspirations of different groups of people? Should SMT be contextualised in ways that relate to personal and societal issues, or should the emphasis be on systematic, discipline-based knowledge?

During the collection of case studies in the SMT project, it will be a priority to identify and highlight perspectives of and by students -- and not solely in dimensions associated with specialisation versus general education, discipline-based versus integrated curriculum, and secondary schooling as terminal, formal education versus preparation for college and university. There are serious attempts virtually everywhere to deal with more diverse student populations, culturally and ethnically. There is also increased sensitivity to the fact that school programmes in SMT by-pass many girls.

There will be a special effort in the project to identify elements of SMT innovation wherein attempts are being made to address these issues of greater inclusiveness. They will be documented and analyzed. Cases that address constructive ways of increasing student accessibility to SMT and its benefits, without incurring unacceptable costs in terms of differentiation, will receive priority. Particular attention will be paid to the latitude and constraints operating on schools that are attempting to deviate from deeply ingrained patterns with respect to their conceptions of serving a broader group of students.

Methods, Materials, Setting

Efforts to reform SMT education sometimes consist essentially of the preparation of new instructional materials, like a textbook. In other cases, there is special attention to small group work, simulation, and/or laboratory and field work. Scheduling, as by use of "double periods," is another element in some innovations. Computers and other sophisticated instructional technologies, like television and videodiscs, figure in some of the projects.

With respect to out-of-school settings, museums are giving increased attention to their educational roles, directing an increasing proportion of their exhibits toward young people, often with considerable flair and sophistication. Interactive displays have become more prevalent, and some museums invest heavily in teacher education and school outreach programmes (as by travelling vans), as well as on-site exhibitory.

Industrial corporations and universities have long played roles in many countries in providing out-of-school learning opportunities for students and teachers. In some cases, there are personnel exchanges and involvement in curriculum development. An industrial scientist, for example, might go on leave to teach or to help a school improve its SMT programmes.

Many of the SMT innovations incorporate project work to a significant degree. Such activity opens up new possibilities for independent student investigations and, depending on the project, opportunities for relating work in school to salient issues in the community. Indeed, that feature of project work is receiving special emphasis in some countries and will be a focus in some of the case studies because it relates strongly to attempts to make the curriculum more practical.

Changes in the methods, materials, and settings for SMT could signal a transformation of the roles of students in the learning process, from being essentially passive and detached to being active and responsible. Of course, changes of this type have implications for the role of the teacher, and information will be collected in the course of the study about how their responsibilities are changing.

It seems clear that non-conventional instructional methods, materials, settings, and even school organisation figure in SMT reform in some places. The project will highlight such innovations where they seem to have unusual potential or where they seem to be particularly suggestive.

Teachers

Prevailing views of the conditions necessary for deep educational change often place the teacher at the centre of the process. Many believe that unless the person who provides educational services directly to children is trying to make modifications of school programmes that she or he understands and supports, changes are unlikely to be significant or lasting. Furthermore, to effect significant change, the teacher needs considerable latitude in day-by-day classroom activities if the educational changes are to be geared to the capabilities and needs of the particular children for whom that teacher bears educational responsibility. This conviction seems to underlie much of the rhetoric about educational reform.

One important element of the case studies will be an attempt to document and analyze the role of the teacher in the innovations that will be studied. Much of the activity of a teacher stems from practical knowledge gained through experience. Yet many approaches to teacher education accord primary weight not to the insights gained from analyzed experience, but to knowledge derived from the social and behavioural sciences. These disciplines, however, are usually employed more to illuminate and influence classroom techniques than to highlight questions of worth. They address such matters as learning strategies and methods of grouping children. Teachers want such information. But deciding on the amount of time to spend on a certain topic, for example, is as important an issue for many teachers as how the topic can be taught most effectively.

Action research by teachers, in which they collaboratively analyze changes that they are trying to make in the curriculum and the reasons for them, is receiving renewed attention. This approach is based on the assumption that unique knowledge is possessed by those who work within a system and try to change it, and that this knowledge importantly supplements the information obtained through more-conventional modes of educational inquiry. In a growing number of innovations, the teacher is identified as the key figure in conducting research with respect to the new programme. In one instance noted during the preliminary phases of the SMT project, the new programme was conceived as building on the expertise of 40 teachers recruited for the project as they worked together to share experience and ideas. Priority was placed on "ownership" of the project by the participants. This concept, with the idea of "collaborative networks" of teachers is prominent in several of the innovations examined so far.

Thus, there is a growing "knowledge of the practical" that is beginning to gain status and influence teacher education as plans are developed for SMT reform. There are also significant professional initiatives, developed by teachers or teacher organisations, that hold promise for significant improvement. Attempts will be made to identify these varying approaches and try to comprehend their workings and impact.

At the same time that the importance of classroom- and school-based change -- a bottom-up strategy -- is being recognised, governmental authorities have become more assertive about the mechanisms for educational change and how it will be assessed. This new assertiveness extends in many countries to programmes of teacher education; there are increasing pressures to regulate teacher education more closely. Sometimes colleges and universities are monitored more assiduously; sometimes teacher education responsibility is assigned to local educational authorities and taken away from universities. Tensions between professional and political prerogatives are being worked out in different ways in different places, and, to the degree that these pressures affect SMT reform, information about the dynamics of these relationships will be collected during development of the case studies.

Assessment, Accountability, and Evaluation

In the area of assessment, accountability, and evaluation, there are similar and apparently polar pressures. On the one hand, there is renewed focus on standards of performance. What does the public have a right to expect from its investments in education? In several countries wherein local prerogatives were only recently near-sacrosanct, specific project-based innovations are taking shape within a national framework in which expected levels of achievement are being stipulated by regional or national authorities. This quest for dedication to specific results has taken the form a national curriculum and national examinations in at least one country where no such uniformity existed before. The development of achievement standards is being stimulated by governmental authorities in several places. There is also talk of a "voluntary" national curriculum where no such curriculum has existed in the past. In other countries, however, teachers are trusted to do their own assessments and produce reports for parents and employers, and the number of nationally mandated examinations required of a single student throughout the period of formal schooling can be counted on the fingers of one hand.

The fields of evaluation, assessment, and feedback are in considerable flux. Yet, in the preliminary examination of innovations in the SMT project, it appears that assessment of pupils receives very little attention. When the subject is mentioned, it is often not clear whether the assessment discussed is for day-to-day use in classroom formative assessment or for terminal use in summative, even external, assessment.

While one reads in the professional literature about experimental forms of assessment like portfolios and "performance" testing, little of it has been noted so far in the project. Nor is there much attention to enhancement of the role that pupils themselves might play in their own assessment. Overall, then, this key area receives far less attention in SMT reform than one might expect in an era when standards and assessment seem so prominent in the public press and the professional literature. Conceivably, developments in student assessment reflect initiatives primarily outside of SMT proper, and so receive little notice by innovators, even if they will have a strong influence at some point. It will be necessary to examine this apparent contradiction with some care as the project unfolds.

Likewise, accountability is not a prominent theme in most of the innovations. Issues of public accountability have surfaced in few of the preliminary reports of SMT innovations, and there is very little mention of the dilemmas that arise as a result of internal as against external control. Nevertheless, it is well known that education is characterised by pressure, often by politicians, for cheap and fast external methods of accountability. Such methods sometimes seem reliable and free from the idiosyncrasies and biases of individual teachers and schools. However, the price paid, in terms of results with serious deficiencies in both reliability and validity, is not recognised by the public and too little understood. Perhaps this is one reason the topic tends to be avoided by SMT innovators. Regardless, public interest in educational innovation is obvious and unassailable. The matter deserves attention in the development of the case studies.

In addition to assessment of students and expectations for public accountability, there is the matter of evaluation of the innovations themselves. Programme evaluation is a complex and expensive endeavour. It involves judgements about worth and saliency, as well as assessments of student attainment. There are evaluation activities associated with many of the innovations to be studied in the project, but, in general, as with student assessment, they are seldom prominent or novel. It may be that the innovator enjoys the process of creating something new and important, at the expense of being hard-headed about the product. It also may be that innovators keep well away from assessment experts because they believe that these specialists usually impose their own constraints rather than try to reflect what the innovators want to do.

Perhaps these areas -- assessment, accountability, and programme evaluation -- are ones that will begin to manifest themselves more prominently during intensive data-collection phases of the study than has been apparent in the preliminary work. Since the topic is a priority in the SMT project, attempts will be made to document any developments along these lines that seem influential or suggestive.

A Concluding Comment

The overall SMT project reflects a renewed interest in comparisons and exchange of information across nations. But it is easy to confuse form with substance: this period of SMT education is unusually fluid. It is also one in which many apparent similarities across countries are illusory once the details and the context are understood. One virtue of case studies is that they can counter otherwise glib and simplistic comparisons. Rich understanding of particulars can blunt the impulse to try to imitate hastily what one sees elsewhere, thereby avoiding potential mistakes. (If comparisons seem easy, they are probably wrong.) Cases illuminate important diversity as well as similarity. The SMT project offers the opportunity to generate substantive conversations about the meaning and context of reform, better to get the details right as one tries to benefit in one's own setting from appealing and provocative ideas generated elsewhere.

113

Paper 10

TECHNOLOGY IN THE SCHOOL CURRICULUM

Paul Black

Technology is a subject of great importance in its own right. Given the subjects importance for any economy, all countries look for effective education in technology. This alone would make it interesting. However, I focus on it within this theme because it is also interesting as a case in which issues which are latent for other well-established aspects of the curriculum come into sharper focus when this particular area is considered. In my discussion, I want to introduce some alternative perspectives for school technology, to draw out some general issues that these throw up, and to raise leading questions which ensue.

Five Perspectives

The position of technology as a school subject is peculiar, if not unique, because there is very wide variation between -- and sometimes within -- countries about its definition and its educational purposes. Within the OECD's SMT project, the misunderstanding and controversy about technology has marked it out as a very different case from either mathematics or science. Indeed, I would wish at the start of this presentation to ask you all to forget any meaning that you give to technology in your own countries and to be prepared to re-consider its definition *de novo*. I shall not attempt a definition, but rather present a set of five different perspectives.

The **first** of these treats technology as craft skills. Pupils are to be taught woodwork or metalwork, perhaps also about forming plastics. This prepares them for the industries of the 19th and early 20th centuries, or for cottage industry of today. The skill training might go further into high-tech. machinery, so there is preparation for the workshops of the late 20th century. If it goes on to computer driven machine tools then it is up to date and may be of some use in the 21st century -- but the skills are then very different. This concept matches the narrowly vocational purpose of education. Other crafts can be considered here -- notably those of cooking and making of clothes: these two can be taught in the perspective of domestic or cottage industry, but could be designed to relate to the major industries of production, processing and marketing of foodstuffs, fibres and textiles.

My **second** perspective is an expanded version of the first, in which design is added to the crafts, so that instead of making artifacts to a prescription, pupils have to learn, through their own application, about the concepts and techniques of design. This is more broadly vocational, in giving a wider perspective to manufacture, but also introduces concepts of aesthetics and of fitness for purpose which serve wider educational purposes than the vocational. Such titles as 'craft and design' or 'craft, design and technology' also serve to raise the status of craft teachers, who are often low in the order of esteem within many school systems.

'Engineering science' is better still but that demands more and so leads to my **third** perspective, which is represented by the phrase 'science and technology'. The pairing with science arises naturally in public discussion and represents a view that technology is mainly, for some no more than, applied science. However unjustified this may be historically, it is taken by many in science education to justify a claim to ownership of this curriculum territory, so giving it a status and a practice

114

quite different from that of its craft entailment. In some countries, there is a movement for science technology and Society to replace Science in the school curriculum, a marriage in which the role of each has tended to be constrained by that of the partner. The status is raised, but the science teacher now takes on a very wide responsibility. However, there are still problems within this approach. The applied science reduces all too often to applied physics -- the basis for civil, electrical and mechanical engineering. But then what about chemical engineering, pharmaceuticals, bio-technology and genetic engineering, the technologies of fibres and foods and so on? This approach is vocational in a very different way from the first two, but if it encompasses the whole range of applications across the sciences, it moves towards the purpose of general education for the future citizen of a technological society -- a purpose which can hardly be ignored.

The **fourth** perspective is broader and amalgamates the second and third. It thereby becomes a more thorough-going model for education of the future citizen. Here, skills of design and manufacture are taught in a context of the application of principles of mathematics and science wherever appropriate, but questions of purpose and value are also introduced. Thus the first step in a technology exercise would be to question the need being served, to seek alternative solutions, and to debate the values implied by the choice between them. So problems of political and social pressures, and of unintended consequences, may arise. It is then natural to include some historical cases, and contemporary examples far outside the range of the school workshops. It also becomes necessary for teachers who have never before handled discussions of values and of social and political purposes to accept a change of role which many find uncomfortable.

My **fifth** and final perspective is composed by adding a further dimension to the fourth -- that of practical capability of the pupil. By engaging in the task of working, often co-operatively, to define needs, design solutions, implement them and evaluate their efficacy and effects, the pupil can develop that synthesis of the powers of analysis, decision, manual and aesthetic skill, evaluation and collaboration which constitute practical capability. The case here is that the practical world, in which one has to take initiative in deciding and doing, is hardly represented at all in traditional education with its emphasis on the receptive, the passive and the critical. So, to add to the purposes set out above, there is a purpose of adding, for personal development and for vocational fitness, an important feature which education has neglected badly in the past.

Implications

All of these perspectives are in play in one country or another, sometimes several in the same country. Each competing perspective differs from the others in its particular priority of aims, and also in justifying a particular group of teachers and often threatening other groups. So the debate about purposes is tied up with the careers prospects of many teachers.

In deciding to develop or change to any of these perspectives, a school or region would have to consider the traditions and teaching competences of those in whose hands any change would have to be implemented. Thus some aspects of technology have a basis in current courses owned by craft teachers, others in the courses owned by home economics (cookery and dressmaking) teachers. How far can such teachers be expected to move from their accustomed practice? The english curriculum in technology is very ambitious in going for the fifth and broadest of the above perspectives -- but in so doing it has gone well beyond the skills and understandings of most of those who have to teach it, and the first evaluations have already shown up bad effects arising from these inadequacies.

The aims, whether of vocational preparation or of practical capability, cannot be achieved without a high standard of resources in schools -- so can governments who profess these aims be convinced of the need to fight for more of their national budgets? There is also, in most foreseeable initiatives, a need for extensive, and therefore expensive, in-service-training.

In many countries, there is an awareness of the need to invent a new school subject, or to radically re-define an existing one, if the national need for technology education is to be met. To wait for natural evolution to meet the national need is not acceptable given the perception of urgency of that need. Nor, given the fractured nature of developments of technology in the past, is it credible to claim that evolution will resolve the problems.

Moreover, at least in some definitions, technology ought by its nature to develop through close links between several school subjects. This can lead to creative curriculum planning in a school. However, in the absence of any such planning, and indeed in default of any rationale for the curriculum as a whole, it could degenerate into trench warfare between the subject empires along their disputed boundaries. This can leave the pupils to wander as bewildered refugees.

Questions

I suggest three:

-- how do we reconcile the perceived tension between the vocational and the general educational aims in this area?

-- given the economic and social importance, what is an appropriate response to the choices opened up by the different perspectives?

-- in particular, how do countries reconcile the desirable aims with the constraints of resources, above all of the capacity of teachers to respond to role changes?

These questions are not unique to technology. If we set ourselves to re-invent all school subjects, or the curriculum as a whole, would we have a more relevant debate?

This is not just an internal debate for schools or for the education system as a whole. If future societies cannot understand and control its technological developments, then we may not be able to survive.

116

3. Humanities and Arts Education

One problem faced in the project is that the role of values in the curriculum is so pervasive, applying as much to science, mathematics and technology as to the humanities and the arts. Indeed, as has been stressed throughout, values are a part of every teaching activity, either explicitly or implicitly. This project, again, is conceived within the framework of the core curriculum, that is in terms of the interests and requirements of all students. Again, as with the SMT area, it is not merely the knowledge base that is central but the ways of developing and testing knowledge, the way of creating and expressing. Thus, the area makes a fundamental contribution to the core. This area, and particularly the arts element, tends to suffer in terms of economic stringency. This is an unfortunate response for it contributes substantially in all areas of emphasis, personal, social and vocational and provides an essential broadening of the curriculum. Paper 11 presents an analysis and raises important questions. In addition, as well as dealing with the teaching of the humanities, and with the arts in the humanities curriculum it addresses the important question of the place of values by considering alternative approaches to the teaching of values. Two distinct approaches are considered: values education in terms of the concept and teaching of citizenship; values education as a specific field of enquiry within the curriculum. As with the SMT paper, possibilities for further enquiry are identified. These possibilities provide the conference with opportunities for further discussion and for recommendations for action.

Paper 12, by Birgitte Tufte, follows up some of these implications in the particular context of media education.

117

PROJECT ON HUMANITIES, THE ARTS AND VALUES IN THE CURRICULUM

Robert Moon

I. Introduction

The importance of the humanities in the school curriculum and the significance of the school in developing social and personal values is universally acknowledged. In all cultures the intellectual history of the humanities is shaping the form and style of curriculum organisation, as have the ongoing debate about the relative values of mathematics, science, technology and the humanities. In the evolution of humanities education many detect a sense of crisis, of the humanities in peril. The literature is replete with titles; *The Embattled Humanities* (Goombrich, 1985), *What Hope for the Humanities?* (Williams, 1987), that embody this concern. In the USA a number of authors have tapped into a broad public concern about the humanities, and humanities education in particular. Allan Bloom's *The Closing of the American Mind* and William Kirsch's *Cultural Literacy: What Every American Needs to Know*, have attracted widespread international interest. In part the criticism and concern is directed at the very diversity that is represented by the contemporary humanities curriculum. Whilst the evolution of mathematics, science and technology has progressively worked towards a common curriculum focus, including of late a growing acceptance of a core of knowledge appropriate to the school curriculum, developments in the humanities have moved in a different direction.

The tradition of the humanities has splintered into a myriad of forms of enquiry and disciplines representing contested territory philosophically, pedagogically and, more recently, politically. In some measure difficulties of definition, even terminology, fuel this contestation. The humanities also have to serve multiple, perhaps ultimately irreconcilable goals. There is the expectation that the humanities can help explain and improve the human capacity to organise, interpret and give value to experience. On the other hand the humanities are also seen as developing creative, imaginative perhaps irrational modes of thought. This dual, contradictory, purpose is expressed through the school curriculum. The humanities, for example, are expected to describe and explain the history of human behaviour and values but that process inevitably brings into question those very same behaviours and values, many of which are clearly held by majorities or minorities in national and local communities. The humanities, are challenged to define a place and role within the school curriculum and humanities educators compete with each other, amongst alternative visions of the form and structure of their subject. This diversity, sometimes division, in the field, is one reason for the limited record of international co-operation in the teaching of the humanities. Over the last thirty years world wide congresses such as the four yearly International Congress of Mathematics Educators (first meeting in 1968 in Lyon and growing from OECD initiatives in the previous decade) have done a great deal to promote developments in science and technology and mathematics. Work in the humanities has been more fragmented with co-operation on specific issues such as human rights education or the arts but with few if any initiatives to bring the different interest groups together.

This very diversity also presents terminological and conceptual problems in defining the field and in establishing an international community of interest. Can the term humanities take in the social studies curriculum of the USA, the teaching of history/geography in France, as well as the separate subject structure of the National Curriculum of England and Wales? At the level of the school curriculum does the humanities embrace literature and the arts? Is it appropriate as in the classical tradition, to associate values education specifically with the humanities? How can the role of religious educators manifest in so many disparate ways, be acknowledged in any discussion of values or humanities teaching?

It is also significant that the word humanities has different meanings between and within educational systems. In the United Kingdom, for example, in Universities, humanities has a narrower (arts, philosophy, literature) connotation than in the school curriculum (where social science, history and geography would be included). This school perception, however, has been subject to recent change, with the legislative intervention of a prescribed National Curriculum bringing more traditional subject titles centrally into the professional arena at the expense of inter-disciplinary or integrated approaches. These issues in turn can be related to the ongoing political and academic concerns about the form and structure of the school curriculum. Is a common or core curriculum in the humanities desirable? If so, how is this to be defined and by whom? Can the rationale for common experience be established across national systems of education?

The justification, however, for a programme in humanities and values education goes beyond the need to promote discourse amongst humanities educators. Over the last decade many countries have witnessed an increased commitment to the aims of reinforcing national cultures. As Myron Atkin (1988) has put it:

"underlying national worries about economic competitiveness there are concerns about national pride and prestige, even confusion and anxiety about nationhood"

and there follows, therefore a

"persistent interest in improving educational quality, with its focus on values."

Paradoxically, however, the resurrection of interest in cultural heritage is paralleled by a unique and increasingly significant commitment to international as well as national perspectives. The revolution in communications technology, world trading developments and the prospect of lasting changes in the international political order have all contributed to the promotion of global understanding, and solidarity. The humanities is uniquely placed to respond to such social, political and economic imperatives.

Schools in all countries are also seen to have a central role in establishing understanding about civic and human rights and responsibilities and the workings of democracies. There are large variations in the way this is achieved but a large measure of consensus that study of the humanities provide a significant means for promoting such aims. In a number of areas this requires the most sensitive of pedagogies. Striking the balance between developing commitment to certain norms and values, whilst also offering opportunities for critical and reflective thinking, represents one of the major debating points in this area of curriculum. Controversy can arise when the perspectives of young people themselves (youth culture) become the substance of teaching programmes. There is widespread acceptance that the contemporary concerns of youth constitute a focus for curriculum activity although there is less agreement about how the response should be made.

There is also the need to consider the spiritual dimension in human affairs. Many have pointed to the decline of religious observance as a reason for increased school involvement in issues of morality and values. Such an observation would be more true of some countries than others. There is evidence however and, for a variety of reasons (not least the increased interest in global and intercultural understanding already mentioned) that an awakened, or reawakened interest in the religious and spiritual dimension of the humanities can be discerned in a number of countries. It is a further challenge to which the humanities curriculum will be responding.

The humanities is central to the concerns of the curriculum redefined and to contemporary ideas about the nature of intelligence and the growth of the intellect. There is increasing recognition that a broader concept and understanding of human capabilities should inform schooling in the 1990s and beyond. The humanities allow recognition for achievement across a rich variety of forms and expressions. Self esteem and personal confidence can be boosted in ways that narrower visions of curriculum fail to achieve. The foundations can also be laid for learning that extends into adulthood. Changes in demographic structures are likely to make this an increasingly important part of the rationale for growth and development in the humanities curriculum.

Amongst many competing definitions of purpose, participants in a preliminary meeting on the humanities and values programme identified five that could provide the basis for further debate about the position and role of the humanities in the curriculum:

i)   establishing personal meaning amongst the complexity of societal relations;

ii) developing interpersonal relations and moving beyond the egocentricity that can inhibit personal and communal lives;

iii) helping promote an understanding of social structures and systems; providing a sense of participation;

iv) developing a harmonious and mutually aware appreciation of intercultural relations;

v)   stimulating consciousness of the environmental and ecological challenges facing society; a challenge that will qualitatively change over the next decade.

This summary paper considers three aspects of the humanities curriculum, each of which provided the focus for one of the international workshops:

-- the teaching of the humanities through social studies, history and political education;
-- the place of the arts in the humanities curriculum;
-- alternative approaches to the teaching of values.

II. The Teaching of the Humanities through Social Studies, History and Political Education

The humanities are represented in the school curriculum in all Member countries. The forms and styles of curriculum, however, vary markedly. These variations exist within and between countries, within a contemporary perspective and historically. Differences also exist across the different age phases of the compulsory school curriculum. In most countries, for example, the teaching of the humanities within the primary/elementary years has traditionally been through a form of subject/discipline integration, at the secondary level significant differences between Member countries appear.

In the USA there has been a burst of activity and interest around the social studies. Numerous federal and state documents have been produced, advocating, analysing and prescribing the form that a social studies curriculum should take. *Charting a Course: Social Studies for the 21st Century,* published by the Curriculum Task Force of the National Commission on Social Studies in Schools suggests:

A well-developed social studies curriculum must instil a clear understanding of the roles of citizens in a democracy and provide opportunities for active, engaged participation in civic, cultural and volunteer activities designed to enhance the quality of life in the community and in the nation.

The Task Force report goes on to outline a number of goals.

The Social Studies Curriculum should enable students to develop:

i) civic responsibility and active civic participation;

ii) perspectives on their own life experiences so they see themselves as part of the larger human adventure in time and place;

iii) a critical understanding of the history, geography, economic, political and social institutions, traditions, and values of the United States as expressed in both their unity and diversity;

iv) an understanding of other peoples and the unity and diversity of world history, geography, institutions, traditions and values;

v) critical attitudes and analytical perspectives appropriate to analysis of the human condition;

and particular interest has focused around the environment, ecological and global development of the curriculum with Lee Anderson providing an influential schema against which the development of social studies curriculum can be analyzed.

Moving from a curriculum that is:	Toward one that is:
Euro-centred	world centred
region centred	global system centred
group centred	species centred
nations state centred	planet centred
anthropo centred	ecosystem centred
past centred	past, present, future centred
information centred	problems centred
spectator centred	participants centred

In Japan in the post war period reform of curriculum, the social studies curriculum, initially followed the tradition of the USA, integrating subjects such as history or geography within the overall framework of syllabus construction. The values dimension to the curriculum however, was also prescribed in a set of twenty-eight more general criteria that have to be met through a moral education programme with specific time set aside in both elementary and secondary schooling. Recent reforms at the Senior High School level, have emphasised a subject orientation within the time allocated, previously given to the social studies curriculum. Geography and history are now specified although an integrated social studies has been retained for the Lower Secondary and Elementary schools.

Although in the first three grades a new subject *seikatusa-ka*, translated as life environment studies, has been created which aims to promote self reliance through a range of practical activities.

In the Netherlands a strong tradition of humanities education exists through the teaching of history, geography and the arts, especially music. In the 1960s this was challenged by educationalists who argued that insufficient attention was given to social and political issues. In 1968, following the implementation of the Secondary Education Act of 1963, a new subject, *maatschappijleer*, was introduced into the secondary curriculum. In the early years little indication was given as to the precise aims of a subject that had been vaguely defined as the:

"discussion of current issues, giving knowledge of and insight into relations between individuals and groups" (Hooghoff, 1987, p.3).

Inevitably as Hooghoff showed:

"topics varied widely, depending on what teachers and pupils were interested in, what the pupils future tasks and responsibilities were, and the extent to which values and students were involved." (p.3)

Over the last decade there had been a number of attempts to review and revise *maatschappijleer* although without great success in achieving status and legitimacy within the secondary school curriculum. The debate, however, influenced proposals for a national curriculum framework intended as the corner-stone of the Basisvorming Bill first proposed in 1987. In the autumn of 1989, for example, a working party on history and civics, after much controversy, set out specific proposals (Bogaerts, 1992):

It was stressed that Basisvorming-history and civics should be taught in such a way that the subject would primarily contribute to the development of the children as members of social communities, as consumers and producers, and as citizens of their national and of the world community as it was literally put in the opening paragraph of a still later version of these targets. In order to achieve these ambitions a lot of emphasis was (like in other Basisvorming-subjects) put upon the development of:

-- general and also more subject-specific skills and abilities;

-- the ability to recognise and evaluate values and value-judgements;

-- the ability to develop and formulate ideas and values concerning their role and position in society and the aptitude to put these plans and projects into some real, tangible practice.

As compromising part of the proposal it was surmised that this educational and pedagogical orientation into the social-economic, cultural and political aspects of modern social life coincided by and large with the accepted orientations of mainstream modern academic historiography: social and economic, political and cultural history thus making common ground for the more academically minded historians and those among the working party that had a more educational and pedagogical turn of mind.

Subsequently these elements were subdivided into the following sub-categories in which the eventual attainment targets were organised:

-- livelihood and environment, social relations, family relationships;

-- inner political relations in developments, international political relations and developments;

-- material culture, religion and philosophy of life.

To this a separate subset of targets regarding skills and abilities was added, as well as a set dealing exclusively with civics.

Civics became defined as a subject being as well entwined with history as also something separate: its object being the organisation and actual functioning of the political system in society.

In England and Wales after a period in the 1970s and early 1980s when advocacy for the teaching of the humanities as an integrated, interdisciplinary programme was strong, the introduction of a National Curriculum in 1988 reasserted the importance of traditional subjects. History and geography are now separately prescribed and assessed. In the formulation of the National Curriculum the emphasis in subjects such as history was shifted significantly. The significance previously accounted to developing skills of historical enquiry diminished and greater importance given to chronology and to an assertion of the age at which it was appropriate to consider different historical periods. The statutory legislated curriculum did not extend to defining personal and social curricular frameworks such as those in the USA, Japan and the Netherlands although all subjects were expected to contribute to developing a number of cross-curricular themes such as economic and industrial awareness or citizenship (NCC 1990a). The articulation of the links between subjects and the defined cross curricular themes is left with the schools although subject to guidance in a series of pamphlets produced by the National Curriculum Council.

All Member countries can report parallel types of innovation and development. There has, however, been little systematic work describing and analysing the different forms of humanities provision across different Member countries and what exists is now outdated. Preliminary findings from this initial study indicate that, within the different forms of subject and curriculum organisation, it is possible to identify issues of common concern to humanities educators. The teaching of controversial issues, the significance of national and world history, the relationship of subjects to each other (civics and history) and the different form of pedagogy appropriate to exploitation by humanities educators, all represent significant contemporary challenges for policy and practice in curriculum development.

III. The Arts in the Humanities Curriculum

The broad definition of humanities adopted in this programme embraces the arts in the wide range of forms existing in schools. There is a strong consensus now that the arts have fundamental contributions to make to the education of all young people. Education in the arts is important in itself, for the intellectual and practical abilities it develops and for the sensibilities it promotes. A balanced arts education can also help to fulfil some of the most pressing objectives of contemporary education as a whole. All OECD Member countries are working to develop policies and programmes in education that are relevant to the rapidly changing economic, political and cultural circumstances of our times. The development of an arts curriculum is seen as relevant to each of these concerns. In particular:

Economic. The structural changes in the industrial economies have long term implications for the balance and organisation of the workforce. More people will be expected to change profession and occupations during their working lives; there will be increased mobility between countries and places of work; for many people there will be a new balance between work and leisure. The arts in education can help to promote important abilities and qualities in all young people in facing these challenges. The arts also relate to the significant economic expansion in many countries of the cultural industries.

Political.   New political relationships are being forged which recognise the complex interdependence of nations, and the need for new levels of co-operation in international affairs. The arts can provide unique forms of communication and understanding across national boundaries.

Cultural. The technologies of mass communications have resulted in wholly new forms of interaction between different cultural groups, both internationally and within national boundaries. Patterns of migration have generated new cultural groupings within many countries.   The commercialisation of popular culture has a potent influence on the sense of identity of many young people and on the cultural relationships between generations. The arts in all their forms are dynamically enmeshed in the far reaching redefinitions of cultural identities.

The importance of the arts in schools

How can the significance of the arts in schools be defined? Two broad groups of arguments for the arts in education were identified by experts from Member countries. The first concerns the fuller development of individual capabilities and sensibilities; the second, the knowledge and understanding of national and other cultures and values.

Individual and intellectual development. All young people have a wider range of intellectual and other abilities than is touched by conventional academic or technological education. These include abilities that are most fully developed by education through the arts. There is a growing recognition -- in philosophy, physiology and psychology, for example, that human intelligence is multi-faceted. Conventional academic education focuses on particular intellectual abilities. Philosophers in a strong tradition have argued that there are other equally important modes of intelligence according to the nature of the experience and the forms of understanding at hand. The deductive and propositional modes of academic discourse are appropriate in some areas of experience, not in others. Just as some ideas can only be expressed in technical language or in mathematics, others can only be fully expressed in music, in poetry, or in visual imagery.

The education of feeling. For the most part, young people's feelings and the role of feelings in intellectual, personal and social development are not taken into account in education. All curriculum work affects the pupil's view of the world and his/her life of feeling. Work in the arts has a role in giving status to personal feelings and values; enabling a direct consideration of values and of the feelings to which they relate; and in giving forms to such feeling.

Aesthetic development. Aesthetic perception is a response to the formal qualities of objects and events. Although aesthetic experience is possible in all areas of the curriculum, it is a central and characteristic element of the arts. In the arts these qualities are controlled and refined to create forms of expression which embody the artist's ideas and perceptions and which engage the observer's aesthetic sensibilities.   arts education is concerned with deepening young people's sensitivities to the formal qualities -- and therefore the pleasures and meanings -- of the arts, and through this process with extending the range and depth of their aesthetic sensibilities and judgement.

The exploration of values. The arts are deeply concerned with questions of value. This is the case in two main senses: in general, with social and moral values, and in particular with aesthetic and artistic values. No teacher can go far into the education of feelings therefore without encountering questions of social morality and of moral education. The arts offer positive and immediate ways of raising questions of value and of exploring the cultural perceptions to which they relate.

Cultural education. The arts are among the keenest processes by which individuals and communities forge and express their identities, and shape their ways of being together. In this respect, the study and practice of the arts can be central strategies in helping young people to understand, interpret and question the values and conventions of their own and other cultures.

How well are the arts provided for in contemporary education systems? There are many examples throughout OECD countries of excellent arts teaching. Some countries and many schools have explicit and detailed policies for the arts in education. There are examples of well planned initial and post experience training programmes for teachers of the arts and for practising artists interested in working in education. But such provision is very uneven in Member countries and in some cases it is deteriorating. It is still an unusual school or education system that provides adequately for the arts in all the ways described. Often only two or three art forms are provided for, and often with too little time available for these benefits to be realised.

Provision for the arts education in Germany is typical in some respects. Responsibility for education and culture lies with the seventeen *Bundeslander*. Music and the visual arts are included in the curriculum of most schools. Drama and theatre are less commonly taught within the curriculum and dance is seldom included. On average the arts may be given one or two hours per week, but there is a danger of further reductions. There is no official policy on the involvement of artists in schools, but there is occasional involvement of professional artists and companies, and an increasing recognition in schools of the value and importance of such initiatives. The range of existing provision includes:

Visual arts
-- usually taught within the curriculum with some provision for extra curricular activities;
-- *Jugendkunstschulen* (fine art schools for young people -- in the afternoon);
-- some activities in youth clubs;
-- well established patterns of teacher education in universities and *Hochschulen*;
-- well established teacher organisations.

Music
-- usually taught within the curriculum with some provision for extra curricular activities (choirs, orchestras, singing groups);
-- *Volksmusikschulen, Jugendmusikschulen* (music schools for young people in the afternoon, for all instruments);
-- private lessons by *Privatmusiklehrer*, paid for by parents;
-- well established teacher education and teacher organisations.

Drama
-- only exceptionally taught within the curriculum as a practical activity, although reading and analysis of drama texts is included in language and literature teaching;
-- extra curricula activities in many schools;
-- no *Jugentheaterschulen*, some *Jugendkunstschueln/Musikschulen* include theatre activities;

-- no established teacher education, training mostly by workshops;

-- some professional organisations;

-- two major youth theatre festivals and a lot of regional amateur and school festivals.

A comparative analysis (SLO, 1985) of the core curricula in OECD countries showed that nearly twenty OECD countries included an expressive arts component. This provision takes various forms. In **Japan**, music provides the compulsory core experience in elementary, junior and senior high schools. In the **Netherlands**, primary schools must cover aspects of design, handicraft, music and perhaps drama and dance. Junior and secondary schools must offer music, design and handicraft. In **France**, new curriculum guidelines introduced in the mid 1980s specify five hours a week of artistic education at primary and secondary levels. In **England and Wales** the National Curriculum includes music and art within the ten compulsory foundation subjects. In most countries literature is included within mother tongue teaching. This pattern of provision was broadly confirmed in a survey in 1990 by Godfrey Brandt for the Council of Europe. Reviewing returns and information from nineteen Member states Brandt (1990) concluded that,

> ... all countries traditionally perceived visual art and music as the most important for the purposes of schooling. These have received most attention and resources. In most countries where there is training for teachers of the arts, there has only ever been training in these two art subjects. Dance has almost always been relegated to the margins of state education and tends to be included within physical education. Drama has been almost equally marginalised (although) its value as a tool for learning is increasingly recognised in most countries and as a subject in its own right only in some.

The common emphasis on visual arts and music illustrates a partial conception of the arts. The roles of the arts are often further limited by inadequate time and facilities. Schools tend to plan the teaching of all subjects in standard blocks of time even though learning in different disciplines often needs different rhythms and amounts of time. Learning a language or an instrument may best be done in regular short periods, perhaps of fifteen or twenty minutes daily: work on group projects in the sciences or in the arts may need half or one day blocks to allow a more sustained development of ideas. A cycle of constraint can be identified in schools. The arts are often poorly provided for on the timetable; as a result, too few pupils experience the potential benefits of a full and balanced arts education; as a result, too few staff or parents recognise the value of the arts in schools; as a result, the arts are poorly provided for on the timetable. This cycle of constraint needs to be broken by more appropriate allocations of time to the arts and by more flexible approaches to timetabling for the curriculum as a whole.

Specialist work also needs special facilities. This principle is readily accepted in the sciences and technology; it applies equally in theatres. Dance needs appropriate space and flooring just as visual arts teaching requires an adequate range of paints, clay, design and reprographic equipment. Some specialist facilities and materials are necessary for the work to be done at all. They are also important in creating an appropriate working environment for the arts. Like laboratories and technology workshops, specialist drama and art studios lend a mood and sense of significance to the work which can greatly enhance the motivation and achievement of pupils.

The present levels of provision for the arts in education may be further reduced by the need in many countries to cut back on public spending. Resources for education in many countries are under strain. It is to be expected that arts education should take a fair share of any necessary cuts. Usually they do more than this, suffering disproportionately from cuts in provision, and failing to benefit as they should from special project funding. The essential problem is not the overall level of resources that are available for education, but the priorities that guide their allocation, and the assumptions on which these priorities are based.

Provision for the arts is rarely comparable with other major areas of the curriculum. Some Member countries have recognised this and developed specific policies to redress the balance. In **Sweden** the national government has adopted an explicit policy for cultural development. This policy has provided the framework for over 5,000 practical projects in schools, each informed by a view that cultural policy must:

-- help to protect freedom of expression and create genuine opportunities for the use of that freedom;

-- give people opportunities to engage in creative activities of their own and promote interpersonal contact;

-- counteract the negative effects of commercialism in the cultural sector;

-- promote a decentralisation of activities and decision making functions in the cultural sector;

-- make more allowance for the experiences and needs of disadvantaged groups;

-- facilitate artistic and cultural renewal;

-- ensure that the culture of earlier times is preserved and revitalised;

-- promote an interchange of experiences and ideas within the cultural sector across linguistic and national boundaries.

The urgent need is to conceive of the curriculum as a whole and to recognise relationships as well as differences between disciplines. Too much is sometimes made of the distinctions between the arts and sciences, for example. The basic processes of work in the arts and sciences have a good deal in common. Both are potentially highly creative, and the processes of creativity are strikingly alike (Polanyi, 1969). Aesthetic considerations can be deeply important in science and mathematics as they are in the arts, just as objectivity of judgement can be essential to the processes of artistic production. For these reasons, the arts and sciences should not be seen as at opposite extremes of the school curriculum.

A better way is not to allot subjects as such on different sides of a demarcation, but to accept that the same area of human experience or activity is of interest to different kinds of study and that what distinguishes the humanities and sciences is the kind of questions they ask, the range of evidence they are prepared to accept and the kind of answers to which they attach importance. (Bullock, A. 1990)

There is an obvious and crucial difference between the language of the understanding and the language of the imagination, and yet there is also a paradoxical similarity between them. Where the scientist is concerned with the truth and falsity of propositions, the poet is concerned with the appearances and realities of the world, and so the problem with the one deals with under the rubric of error the other must consider under the heading of illusion. Both Einstein and Cervantes are concerned with the nature of relativity, but scientifically the problem of the tensor calculus is what its application will yield in errors of physical measurement, while the poetic problem of the mind of Don Quixote is just the natural history of those illusions which stem from the inability to distinguish fact from fiction. (Levi, A. W., 1970,)

In planning for the arts in the whole curriculum, it is important to distinguish between learning in and learning through the arts. The arts provide vivid methods of teaching and learning in many areas of the curriculum. Drama, dance, visual arts and music can be used to explore ideas and issues within many themes and subject areas. The study of the arts is also an essential way of coming to understand other cultures and periods of history A good deal of learning through the arts is encouraged in many primary schools and in some secondary schools. The opportunities to develop links across the curriculum are evident and can be pursued in all schools. It is equally important to provide for the teaching of the arts in their own right: for learning the skills and concepts of artistic production and appraisal for the intrinsic benefits they bring. In planning for learning in the arts, it is essential to provide a balance of opportunity between the different modes of arts experience.

What range of arts provision should be available to young people at school? We commented earlier on the difficulty of defining the arts by art forms and suggested that the arts should be seen as modes of understanding. In a classification that corresponds closely with Howard Gardner's account of multiple intelligences (Gardner, H., 1989), the arts in Schools project for England and Wales suggested that underpinning the wide range of arts practices in different cultural settings there are a number of basic modes of practice.

These include:

the aural mode	-- using sound and rhythm
the visual mode	-- using light, colour and shape
the kinaesthetic mode	-- using movement, space and time
the verbal mode	-- using words
the enactive mode	-- using imagined roles

Ralph Smith, describing the work of the Getty Centre for Education in the arts in the USA, has advocated a balance of related approaches:

"teaching about the visual arts can be rendered more effective through the incorporation of concepts and activities from a number of interrelated disciplines, namely, artistic creation, art history, art criticism, and aesthetics. The resultant discipline-based approach to art education does not, however, mandate that these four disciplines be taught separately; rather, the disciplines are to provide justifications, subject matter, and methods, as well as exemplify attitudes, that are relevant to the cultivation of percipience in matters of art. They offer different analytical contexts to aid our understanding and aesthetic enjoyment, contexts such as the making of unique objects of visual interest (artistic creation), the apprehension of art under the aspects of time, tradition, and style (art history), the reasoned judgement of artistic merit (art criticism), and the critical analysis of basic aesthetic concepts and puzzling issues (aesthetics)."

These different modes of artistic experience are available to young people as innate capacities. A central point is that most people are not equally sensitive and productive in all of these modes, concepts or activities. The first task of education, especially in primary school, is to offer opportunities for young people to explore them all through a wide variety of arts practice. In the secondary school, the curriculum can open up possibilities for individuals to specialise in those areas where they feel most able and productive.

As in other areas of the humanities, attempts to describe and analyze the arts curriculum across Member countries have been limited. This has inhibited the identification of common interests and concerns around which programmes of international co-operation can be built. There is, for example, an important need to establish some framework for looking at the way resourcing in the broadest sense (buildings, equipment, teacher in-service support and so forth) facilitate or inhibit arts provision. These and the other issues considered in this section represent an important dimension to redefining the curriculum across all Member countries.

IV. Alternative Approaches to the Teaching of Values

The extent to which the development of values is explicitly acknowledged in the school curriculum varies between, and even within, national education systems. In part this is historical. The relation of church to state. For example, changes from one country or region to another leading to contrasting traditions of state, school, family and parental authority. Across these different traditions the humanities and arts education programme has identified two common concerns. First, the renewed interest in the teaching of citizenship as part of a subject based curriculum (see for example the discussion of social studies in the USA in Section II) or as a theme developed through the whole curriculum (see the discussion of the English National Curriculum below). And second, the attempt through a number of different approaches to make values education a specific activity, even subject, within the school curriculum. The teaching of religious education, where there is a substantial international literature (Anderson 1986, Hussain and Ashref 1979, Miller 1977, Tulasiewicz 1988) represents a further area of enquiry that was not within the scope of the three workshops contributing to this review.

In looking first at the issue of citizenship numerous attempts to develop and reappraise the concept can be identified. In England and Wales in 1989 The Speakers Commission on Citizenship (HMSO, 1990) carried out a survey that showed that although 43 per cent of schools in the survey had an agreed policy, curriculum document or written statement about citizenship studies, there was no systematic teaching of citizenship. In terms of curriculum content, the schools were teaching a very wide and diverse range of topics under the heading of citizenship or community skills and the amount of time devoted to the issue varied substantially between schools. The Commission adopted T. H. Marshals definition of citizenship (1950) which identified three elements to the concept:

-- civil (the rights necessary for individual freedom: personal liberty; freedom of speech, thought and faith; right to own property; right to justice);

-- political (the right to participate in the exercise of political power, as an elector or as a member of a body carrying political authority);

-- social (a spectrum of rights, from the right to basic economic welfare and security, to the right to share fully in the social heritage. These rights are closely connected with the education system and social services.)

The National Curriculum Council (NCC) for England, building on this work, identified the aims of citizenship study as (NCC, 1990):

-- to establish the importance of positive, participative citizenship and provide and the motivation to join in, and

-- to help pupils to acquire and understand essential information on which to base development of their skills, values and attitudes towards citizenship.

Carr (1991) has been critical of the passive political perspective adopted by the NCC and Gillett (1992) has also argued against a quasi official perspective based on civil, political and welfare entitlements and for an approach which stresses greater participation in the cultural economic dimensions of everyday life.

There are a number of projects and initiatives in this area in Member countries. In the USA the Civic Achievement Award Programme was established by the United States Congress in 1987, is designed for middle school students (Grades 58) and currently involves one million children nation-wide. The emphasis of this programme is participation with students selecting a civic problem after studying a programme of American history and geography, government, economic systems and the research skills. The problem is a focus for class enquiry with students co-operatively conducting research into possible solutions to the problem, assessing the consequence of the solutions and choosing courses of action. In a more centralised tradition France in the early 1980s attempted a comprehensive reappraisal of the curriculum requirements for the *éducation civique*. This sets out a specific programme across the different phases of education with specified time requirements and a distinct place in the school curriculum. English, American and French examples therefore represent distinct forms of curriculum organisation. In England citizenship education is seen to infuse the subjects of the National Curriculum whilst in he USA the social studies programme of many schools provides a legitimate subject base for exploring the issue. In France citizenship becomes a subject in its own right with limited reference to the syllabuses and methodology of other related and prescribed subjects. Citizenship, what ever the terminology used, is high on the educational agenda and appears increasingly codified in mandatory or regulatory programmes. Statements such as the Georgia State Board Mandated Statement of Values (set out in the full report) indicate the increased importance given to policy development in the area of values.

Ruth Jonathan (1991) has described the background to this concern.

Just as awareness of the complexity of the educational process makes attention to the question of values in education unavoidable, so our awareness of social change makes it urgent. There is no need to rehearse the social problems arising from the changing nature of parenthood and the family, from social and geographical mobility, and from the decline of authority and tradition. Nor is there need to expand on the commonplace statement that just as the young have less guidance from the past than in former times, so the exponential growth of knowledge and the accelerating place of change dramatically increase the choices by which individuals and whole societies are faced, so that as value-security diminishes, it is increasingly required.

Over the last two decades values education has increasingly developed as an inquiry programme in its own right. Ivor Pritchard on behalf of the OECD/CERI project prepared a preliminary draft of a paper (reproduced in the full report) which looks at the field and explores the ancient question that researchers still seek to answer whether virtue can be taught. He points to the aim of values education as influencing what students actually do.

Values education commonly addresses not only the question of whether the student knows what honesty is, or how to reason about honesty, but also whether the student behaves honestly or not.

Feinberg (1991) has suggested a threefold classification of the different approaches surveyed by Pritchard.

The first connects value education to some larger system of beliefs and contends that the beliefs are foundational to the values. For example, to discuss the institution and obligations of marriage without a discussion of God and the Bible, would, to a religious fundamentalist, be to distort the fundamental value of the institution. Here values education consists in instruction into the source of values and in the case of the fundamentalist, that source is God.

A second perspective, sometimes termed values clarification, consists in enabling children to learn how to clarify and articulate their own values. In other words, values education under this conception is no different than any other education involving a skill. Although such educators reject the fundamentalists notion that there is a single foundation for values and accepts the view of the value clarification movement that valuing is a developed skills, it rejects the suggestion implicit in the value clarification approach that values are ultimately a matter of taste and are therefore relative.

This objection is associated with a third perspective, the view of moral education associated with Lawrence Kohlberg. It argues that valuing is a developmental activity, that it can be enhanced by instruction and that there are less and more mature forms of valuing. According to this view value education consists in instruction that enable children to move from a less to a more mature form of valuing. In this case maturity is evaluated in relation to the child's ability to reason according to universal principles which are consistent with certain philosophical standards. Instruction involves introducing ever more complicated cases and examples that stretch the child's present level of moral comprehension and require a higher level to resolve. Kohlberg's work has inspired a range of developmental projects. Heinz Schirp is North-Rhine Westphala, for example (1989) claims empirical evidence to substantiate the *Kohlbergian* approach, although as Pritchard points out there is no evidence one way or the other as the extent to which this extends to actual behaviour.

The emergence of a debate around values education, particularly in the USA, Britain and Japan has also been associated with a harking back to what many politicians see as the unproblematic virtue that characterised a more bonded social and family structure. Former US Secretary of State William Bennett for example (1986) suggested that the school, with the family was a primary moral institution responsible for developing the following virtues:

"strength of mind, individuality, independence, moral quality, thoughtfulness, fidelity, kindness, diligence, honesty, fairness, self-discipline, respect for law, and taking ones guidance by accepted and tested standards of right and wrong rather than by, for example, ones personal preference."

These virtues, drawn from what Bennett sees as the "norms of society", inculcated through experiences with exemplary role models in communities such as schools re reinforced through habits, rituals and traditions. The search for "cores" or "foundations" has been particular feature of developments in the 1980s particularly in the USA with people such as Bloom and Hirsh (op cit.) arguing against what they see as the disintegration of culture and knowledge, with its accompanying moral relativism.

Such fervent foundationalism comes at a time in the history of many developed countries when issues of multiculturalism and diversity have never been so prominent in public educational discourse. The conversations (and at times confrontations) have moved from the relative niceties of melting post pluralism to much more forceful demands for and acceptance of differences among cultural identities. No longer are "minority" groups willing to accept what they see as their marginalization by those in power at the centre. No longer will they allow their unique cultural identities to be subsumed under the rubric of "national culture" in the service of some "common national experience".

So, not only are there tensions between the demands of the individual versus. The needs of the collective, but now within that very collective, there are further schisms undermining the very premises upon which a "common national culture" can rest. Moral educators and public school educators find themselves smack in the middle of these debates as do philosophers who have engaged with the school system.

Matthew Lipman (1981), in the USA for example, has developed a number of critical thinking programmes that have characteristics in common with the ideas being advanced by Schirp in Germany. Lipman's work has been developed and reported within a parallel project being developed within The Curriculum Redefined Programme of OECD/CERI (Maclure and Davies, 19..). Perhaps one of the most interesting and challenging issues, and one that is only beginning to touch and challenge the world of schools is the influence of contemporary post-modernist thought and perspectives on the debate about values education. Extracts from a commentary prepared by Wendy Kohli, who contributed to the formulation of this review, addresses this issue.

"The political controversies surrounding values education have occurred in what has been called by many theorists, the "post-modern era"; an era in which many of the assumptions upon much of educational theory and practice resent ("conservative" or "liberal" labels notwithstanding) are being questioned. Whether we are committed to creating a "just society" or to developing "moral judgement" in children, or even to sustaining some form of "common culture", we act from explicit and implicit assumptions about what counts as "good", "true", "right", and "free". A normative framework informs our actions -- a normative framework that we hold to be true for most, if not all persons. Many doing moral education, regardless of their particular strategy or orientation, see "morality as universalizable, prescriptive and principled thought and action" (Chazan, 1985, p.35).

Current post-modern theory is disrupting our notions of education and values. It is challenging our received orientation to moral reasoning and action; to our taken-for-granted concepts of the Western intellectual tradition.

These challenges are worth attending to: challenges that raise the ethnocentrism, Eurocentrism, androcentrism of our philosophy; challenges that require us to examine our worldview(s) and our "first principles", if you will; challenges that question any notion of "core values", "universal theories", or "ultimate foundations"; challenges, for example, that declare an end to the "enlightenment" and to the humanism upon which that project rests.

In the wake of this disruption, those who have allegiances to modernity and to Western philosophy have had to come to terms with this attack on "meta-narratives":   those explanatory theories that provide us with some coherent understanding of the world.   Neither conservatism, liberalism nor Marxism escapes the critical dismissal of post-modernists.   The universal assumptions embedded in these frameworks are suspect as are their tendencies to obscure differences and discontinuities in history.   Post-modern discourses of marginality and power supplant the modernist language of consensus and contradiction.

Liberal, conservative and radical educators alike, whether or not they rely on Aristotle, Plato, Marx, Dewey or Freire for their moral and intellectual force (have been influenced) the implications of this post-modern moment, even if we do not fully embrace the theoretical positions associated with it.   The very foundations that ground our actions and thinking are being criticised.   No longer are we able to accept naively the notion of the sovereign, rational individual or the Marxist commitment to the revolutionary proletariat as the "true" maker of history.   Core values, essential identities, and ultimate foundations are subject to interrogation.

What is at stake in all of this?   What does it mean to "do values education" in a post-modern world?   Can or should we speak of universal principles of truth, justice, equality and freedom? Can or should we speak of any universal principles?   How are we to act in the world and what will guide our actions?   Our ends?   Must we, as Annemiek Richters asks, "accept some overarching framework, some permanent standard of rationality, some meta-narrative to which we can appeal in order to understand and evaluate competing claims?" or "is there really no alternative but to turn to fashionable varieties of relativism which tend to culminate in cynicism and growing powerlessness?".

(Extracts from a paper reproduced in a full report.)

V. Conclusion

Sections II and IV have set out brief reviews of the substantive reports formulated during each of the three exploratory workshops.   Experts who contributed to these saw this work as an important foundation for further enquiry and activity.   Four aims for such work have been suggested.

First, to provide a description and analysis of the way the form and the structure of the humanities curriculum and values education are developed across Member countries.   Ten themes have been developed through which such information will be organised.   These are set out in the appendix to this report.

Second, to identify within the different curriculum structures and organisation areas of common interest and concern to humanities educators examples might include the relationship of different art forms in the building of an arts curriculum or the teaching of controversial topics in history.

Third, the programme will attempt to establish the extent to which particular forms of pedagogy could be further developed in the teaching of the humanities or constituent fields of enquiry. Is it for example appropriate to think of a distinct pedagogy for the humanities?

Fourthly, there is a need to disseminate examples of practice in all aspects of the teaching of the humanities. Some earlier OECD/CERI publications which did this (OECD 1975) have now been superseded by a range of initiatives and developments that often go unpublicised outside Member countries.

Annex

Proposed framework of theories for the description and analysis of humanities and values education in OECD countries.

1.	Policy priorities	--	Can a policy framework for the improvement of the humanities and values curriculum be established?
		--	Is it possible to identify an international dimension to such a framework?
2.	Definitions	--	Can international discussion and co-operation be enhanced by through greater awareness of national terms and definitions?
		--	What common ground is there amongst the different interpretations of disciplines and issues?
3.	Rationale	--	What common themes emerge from the different forms of advocacy advanced for humanities and values education?
		--	Is the degree of converge sufficient to create a cross national rationale for curriculum development in this area?
4.	Curriculum	--	What is the relationship of the humanities and values to the education organisation of the curriculum as a whole?
5.	Process and Pedagogy	--	Are there any processes of teaching and learning that are unique to this field of enquiry?

| | | -- | Are experiences of pedagogical development in other curriculum areas relevant to work in the humanities and values? |

6. Assessment

-- Does the humanities and values curriculum throw up particular challenges for assessment?

-- Is there evidence of assessment techniques and methodologies that are particularly appropriate to work in this area?

7. Resources & conditions in schools

-- Are there criteria that would inform appropriate curriculum resourcing in the humanities?

-- What conditions in schools (environments, buildings and so forth) are necessary to implement a curriculum in the humanities?

8. Research

-- What is the evidence from the research community that can inform development in the teaching of the humanities and values?

-- Are there ways in which existing programmes can be co-ordinated, enhanced?

9. Teacher development

-- What is the record of initial teacher education in the area?

-- What are the implications for teacher development of new approaches to teaching and learning in the humanities?

10. International co-operation

-- What are the existing means of facilitating international cooperation between humanities education.

-- Can proposals for improving such co-operation be brought forward?

MEDIA EDUCATION, TRENDS AND EXPERIENCES -- SEEN FROM A HUMANISTIC POINT OF VIEW

Birgitte Tufte

In the OECD background document for this conference as well as in the summary paper about humanities and arts education made by Professor Moon there are some key concepts that I see as crucial in relation to the research and development work I have been involved in in Denmark during the past 10 years. These key concepts are the following:

-- Basic knowledge and skills;
-- Literacy;
-- Technology;
-- Communication;
-- Humanities;
-- New ways of teaching;
-- New possibilities for education in the information society.

As an example of a new trend -- being part of the curriculum, although not compulsory -- and as an example of new ideas in teaching, I shall describe the results of the evaluation of 35 media education projects in the Danish primary and secondary school. The project is part of a bigger development programme involving in all 7.500 schools, which has taken place from 1987-1991.

However, first of all I would like to comment on a video, that we -- a team of researchers -- presented to a group of 14-15 year olds last week. It is a video made by a group of young people, defining themselves as belonging to the hip-hop culture. It is a rock video criticising people's use of television. The idea of our present project is to develop teaching material based on the taste, preferences and competence of the pupils, as we consider the "parallel school" of the media as important. Four out of the eight young people we interviewed had seen the video before -- on MTV -- and all of them understood the critical content.

Talking about introducing this kind of material in the school -- i.e. another culture than the book-oriented culture of the school -- they had clear opinions: It would be a good idea to use videos in the classroom, but they ought to be chosen by the young people themselves, because you cannot expect the teacher to know much about it. It should be the best -- and critical -- videos, so that there would be some content to analyze and discuss. They suggested to use that kind of material in history, music, art, english and Danish. My point is that there exists a "parallel school" as it is called in a UNESCO report, a school of the media where children daily get pieces of knowledge, a knowledge that they bring with them to school, but which is not accepted and integrated by the school.

My impression -- after several projects of that kind -- is that the pupils have a knowledge about the new forms, content and aesthetics of the new intercultural products on the television screen, but that they do not have the literacy and skills necessary and relevant in a communication and information society that should aim at maintaining democracy and insight.

And how can we help them to obtain that? This is where the media education projects come in.

Media Projects in the Danish *Folkeskole*

The 35 projects classified by the Council for Innovation and Development, who made the project possible, as media education development projects were categorized by the evaluation team in the following categories:

-- media as a separate subject;
-- media integrated in existing subjects;
-- media workshops;
-- media in school and local community;
-- interactive media.

The motivations for the teachers who had applied for money to the projects were different, but there were three main concerns:

-- children's use of the media;
-- the media and the school;
-- the media in relation to culture and society,

and the majority of the teachers were concerned with the children's use of media -- particularly television -- and typically, and in line with the moral panic trend, that is still existing, television was considered partly to be dangerous for children.

Regarding the second concern -- the media and the school -- several teachers argued that media education is a neglected area in school, that instruction in the subject is necessary to enable children to fully understand media images and to use media actively, to strengthen its practical and creative aspects, and to break down traditional borders between subjects.

The motivations comprising the media in a cultural and social perspective were concerned with the opportunities that exist in the Cultural Centre idea and in the local t.v. and radio networks.

It is characteristic that many of the projects include as well analysis as media production (by the pupils) as part of the didactic approach.

Results

I do not have the time here to describe the projects in detail but shall refer to the English summary. However, I shall mention that part of the conclusion that is pointing to the future, as that is our emphasis.

Media education has to be based on a combination of practical media work and analysis across the curriculum.

At an organizational level, the basis for a future model for media education could be to define media education as a separate area in which teaching could take various forms, and where one form does not necessarily exclude the other. These forms could include:

-- media education as a separate discipline;
-- cross curricular collaboration (integrated into different subjects such as art, music, foreign languages, Danish, history) throughout the whole school year;
-- day or week-long courses;
-- both day or week-long courses and cross curricular (integrated) with several existing subjects.

Media education must comprise work with pupils' own production, their discovery and analysis of it as well as that of others, from both practical and theoretical perspectives. All types of media must be included (print media, radio, photography, t.v., video, film, computer graphics etc.).

From a democratic point of view the projects related to local t.v. and radio are interesting, and the conclusion is that whenever possible cooperation with local t.v. and radio should be established so that pupils get the chance to produce for a larger public, which among other things will enable them to experience the conditions for public media production and the importance of media in the democratic process.

A must for media education is a media workshop, with the permanent assistance of one or more teachers with special expertise in media and media education. The media workshop is suggested to be established in close connection with the school library.

As to the teachers' background one third of them were self-taught and some of them had had some media training, courses and media analysis. In the interviews with the teachers on the media education of the future it was a common theme that they would appreciate media courses, that there is a great need for in-service courses and that it should be integrated in the teacher education.

An important part of the conclusion suggests changes in the present sharp division between subjects. Possible alternatives are courses or projects in media education, cross curricular teaching and the integration of media education into several school subjects.

I have been encouraged by the results of video production in the 35 projects. For example, the production belonging to a project on t.v. commercials, where they have been analysing and producing t.v. commercials. The productions are simple and absolutely not professional but they show how children can work on the basis of traditional t.v. genres and then -- using their creativity and fantasy -- change them by means of humour.

Conclusion

Coming back to the key concepts I started with, my opinion is that -- in an international world of communication where information and values are transmitted through the media every day and from all parts of the world -- it is a must that the humanities necessary for survival of democracy are taught.

One way of trying to do that is by giving the pupils insight in the aesthetics, language, production and reception of the traditional and new media. New teaching methods have to be used and further developed, methods that accept and integrate the competence and skills of the pupils in this field (media and computer skills).

As I started to say the pupils do have skills in this new field, but they do not have literacy, media literacy, so -- seen in relation to the school -- it is, among other things, a question of redefining literacy and basic skills if we -- as teachers, researchers and decision makers -- want to qualify the children for the 21st century.

Literature:

The Curriculum Redefined. Schooling for the 21st Century. Background Document. OECD. 1993.

Humanities and Arts Education. Summary paper reporting a review of issues prepared as part of the OECD/CERI project. 1993.

(Bazalgette, C. et al. ed.): New Directions - media education worldwide. British Film Institute, clemi, UNESCO. 1992.

(Morsey, Zaghlone, ed.): Media Education. Unesco. Paris. 1984.

(Tufte, B., Holm Sørensen, B., Scoubye, J., Løkkegaard, F., Cornelius, H., Arnov, J.): Medieundervisning. Copenhagen. Danmarks Lærerhøjskole. 1991.

(Tufte,B. et al.): Summary of Evaluation Report for the Innovation Council of the Folkeskole: Media Education. The Royal Danish School of Educational Studies. Copenhagen. 1992.

4. Changes in Teaching and Learning

As mentioned before, the current situation poses quite new challenges for the schools: to educate almost the entire age-group to high levels. In schools in the past, those who did not succeed in their studies left school to find full-time and continuing employment in the local community. Those who continued on and succeeded in school were able to go on to higher education and qualify for professional jobs. The divisions between those who left and those who stayed were as much social as intellectual, with those from economically deprived backgrounds generally performing worse and leaving earlier than others. The school experiences frequently magnified the differences originally linked with social background, with the more advantaged students generally performing better in schools and extending their original advantage. In today's schools and those of tomorrow it is no longer acceptable for so many students to be deprived of opportunity by the accident of social background. The schools now have to find ways to succeed not only for those students who have been effective in the past but for those for whom school has been an experience of failure and dissatisfaction.

The problem is graphically illustrated in the very substantial longitudinal study of three Tasmanian school cohorts, involving over 20,000 students (Abbott-Chapman et al., 1991). The study related school performance, further education and employment with social factors, particularly home background. For the great majority, some 84 per cent of the students, their performance, both in school and in further education, was most strongly related to their social background. The early performance for this group correlated closely with social background, as did later performance. The gap between upper and lower achievers, however, increased substantially during the period. This is a dispiriting story seeming to confirm the claims of Marxist writers that schools confirm and strengthen social handicaps. For a substantial minority, however, the story is different. A significant group of socially disadvantaged students, some 16 per cent of the cohort performed better than their predicted level of success. In their case, a major factor proved to be the links with particular schools and particular teachers. There is, then, no automatic failure attached to social disadvantage. Particular approaches in teaching can be of significant help. Particular aspects of school organisation can also be of help. It seems certain, too, that recent studies on intelligence and thinking open up new ways in which better learning may occur.

Intelligence and thinking

One of the profitable lines of progress comes from research in thinking and learning, as indicated in the OECD publication *Learning to Think: Thinking to Learn* (OECD, 1991). This reports on some of the research in linked areas of psychology, technology and artificial intelligence. From this research a number of initiatives have emerged, particularly in the "skills approach" which seeks to disentangle thinking from the traditional disciplines and teach thinking skills directly. One such approach was developed in Israel and has been implemented in France, Professor Feuerstein's Instrumental Enrichment (IE) programme. Debray (1991) describes this approach where psychologists train teachers to develop a wholly new pedagogic approach, based on new concepts of children's thinking and with the direct aim of developing the learner's intelligence. A different approach has been developed by Edward de Bono, the CoRT (1973) package, which develops in students a set of thinking skills or tools to apply intelligence more effectively. The key competencies approach developed in Australia through Finn and Mayer, as an attempt to develop generic vocational skills, belongs to the same approach, even though it has a very different rationale.

A major criticism of this approach lies in the failure so far to demonstrate "transfer", i.e. to show that knowledge and skills developed in one context can be used to solve problems presented in a different form and context. Further, the same name may not always designate the same activity:

critical thinking in history bears little relationship to critical thinking in physics. In other words, the very attempt to disentangle skills from content may make them of little practical use. Nevertheless, further study seems warranted in terms of the benefits to be gained from a breakthrough in this area.

A different direction lies in new ideas about intelligence, for example the work of Howard Gardner at Harvard. Gardner contests the assumption of a unitary intelligence and puts forward the concept of "multiple-intelligence", a "capacity to solve problems or to make something that is valued in at least one culture" (Gardner, 1983). Under this approach intelligence can be "linguistic, logical-mathematical, musical, spatial, bodily-physical, interpersonal, and relating to internal self-knowledge". One of the values of this approach is that it places a value on many dimensions of human performance beyond our traditional academic achievement. Our past emphasis has been on the conventional logical and linguistic skills, long called IQ. In a society where we require a greater range of performances we cannot afford to limit ourselves. What Gardner calls the 'personal intelligences', the capacity to know oneself and the capacity to relate to others are recognised as vital in daily life. Their acknowledgement as abilities to recognise, develop and encourage is overdue. This broadening of emphasis may be a valuable approach at a time when we are educating a wider range of students for a future which will demand more varied and flexible approaches.

A reconsideration of school organisation

The pattern of organisation in schools has changed very little over the years. The size of classes, the range of available equipment, the decor of classrooms have changed but the basic form in which teaching occurs has changed very little, particularly at the secondary level. Albert Shanker, the US educator, comments on the unsuitability of the pattern in secondary schools, when considered from the viewpoint of organisation of work.

> "Charles Handy, a British authority on organisations, suggests that secondary schools are certainly not encouraging students to be active learners...he asks us to imagine an office in which a new employee is seated at a desk and told who his or her supervisor is and what job is to be done. The new employee is surrounded by 20 or 30 others at similar desks... Every 45 minutes or so, the new employee is told to move to another desk in another room where there will be a different supervisor (with a different personality and a different set of expectations), a different task to do, and a different group of 20 to 30 employees working at their desks.
>
> 'How many of us', asks Handy, 'if asked to organise an office, would so arrange things that people worked for eight or nine bosses in a week, in perhaps five different work groups...?' How much work would get done under these conditions?
>
> Handy points out that this system doesn't make sense if we consider the student as a worker, but it makes perfect sense if we consider the student as raw material that adults are turning into finished product. 'Raw material', he says, 'is passed from work station to work station, there to be stamped or worked on by a different specialist, graded at the end and sorted into appropriate categories for distribution" (Shanker, 1990).

Vocational education

More fundamental differences to the above are suggested by those deeply involved in vocational education. Their experience in dealing with people who have not been successful in general education can be of great value more widely in the changes occurring in schools, not only in vocational education. Raizen, speaking at an OECD Seminar in 1991 made the following comments:

"The research involving analyses of individual performance has resulted in greater attention to the several types of knowledge (and their structure and inter-relationships) that competent individuals display; the research on situated learning and socially constructed knowledge highlights the need for providing a real-world context (both physical and social) for education and training intended for the world of work. An optimal educational response welding these requirements would appear to be learning environments that make task knowledge and problem-solving procedures explicit and that provide for feedback and tutoring by more experienced co-workers" (Raizen, 1991).

This approach would suggest organisational changes of quite a different sort, involving links between schools and external organisations.

In Paper 13, Phillip Hughes explains the implications for curriculum reform of OECD studies and projects in a number of fields, in particular:

-- lifelong learning;
-- vocational education and training;
-- environmental education;
-- children with special educational needs and students at risk.

Paper 13

IMPLICATIONS FOR CURRICULUM REFORM FROM OECD ASSOCIATED PROJECTS

Phillip Hughes

LIFELONG LEARNING; VOCATIONAL EDUCATION; ENVIRONMENTAL EDUCATION; CHILDREN WITH SPECIAL EDUCATIONAL NEEDS AND STUDENTS AT RISK.

The Central Project

The project entitled The Curriculum Redefined is to be the focus of the OECD Conference of April 5-8 1993, in Paris. The project derives from an OECD/CERI study initiated with the support of Member countries in 1987 and resulting in a major publication indicating current thinking and policies, *Curriculum Reform: An Overview of Trends* (Skilbeck, 1990). This study initiated five OECD programmes: Learning to Think -- Thinking to Learn; Core Curriculum; Pupil Assessment and Curriculum Evaluation; science, mathematics and technology; and, humanities and values. The commitment of OECD to curriculum reform as a major initiative was further underlined by the report of the 1990 Conference of Ministers, significantly entitled, *High Quality Education and Training for All* (OECD, 1992a). That commitment was affirmed by a realistic assessment of the breadth of the necessary re-conceptualisation:

> "It is one matter to analyze trends and problems and to pose ideals to which education and training policies might aspire, conveniently buttressed by the supporting arguments in their favour, whether these be educational, social, or economic. It is quite another to match these ideals against existing realities, with all the dilemmas, conflicts and problems that then naturally arise" (OECD, 1992*a*).

It is in pursuing these ideals against the existing realities that OECD and the Member countries have established a number of programmes which explore the implications in particular areas or sectors of education. These programmes include: Lifelong Learning, Vocational Education, Environmental Education and, Children with Special Educational Needs and Students at Risk.

The clear link between all these initiatives is the ambitious theme: high quality education and training for all. This theme comes as a calculated response to social and technological changes. Rather than reacting to individual aspects of these changes, OECD has chosen a more proactive approach, to enable education to play a positive role in societal development for the future, including the key function of education in broadening the capacity of individuals to make choices.

High quality education and training for all can easily become a slogan. High quality education and training has always been a reality, but for some students, not for all. In no country is it a reality for all, although many OECD countries have set specific targets for achievement at particular times. It is not only the breadth of the population that poses a challenge, i.e. the commitment for all students, but also the breadth of the task. For the period of compulsory education, that task involves a commitment towards three major emphases: personal development, social development and vocational development. In this period, these are not separate strands but complementary ways of describing the aims during the compulsory years of schooling. The various elements of the curriculum make their contributions to all aspects, sometimes with differing balances for individuals. Thus, the study and practice of language are clearly important for all three. It is important to the person, as language expresses and enhances thinking and is one of our major links to others. It is important to the citizen, in enabling understanding of civic issues and providing a capacity to contribute. It is important vocationally, where communication plays an increasing role. For the journalist, for the engineer, for the banker, for example, it will play specific as well as general vocational roles. Increasingly, the compulsory period is to provide the general base for developments, enabling more specific knowledge, skills and understanding to be achieved as needed. The case for this broad development is covered thoroughly in the recent Swedish Report, *A School for Life* (1992).

The commitment to a task of such dimensions, in breadth of participation and in quality of achievements, requires a reconceptualisation of education. It will not be a matter of simply doing more of the same. Trying harder at what we currently do, will not be enough, in the ways we organise and structure education, in its methods and approaches. Particularly, we need to recognise the special challenge of the disadvantaged students. For these students, our current processes have not been a success. They will suffer particularly if those processes are simply extended. It is for these reasons that we consider in more detail the implications of the programmes in lifelong learning, vocational education, environmental education and children with special educational needs. There are, then, strong interrelations between these initiatives.

Lifelong Learning

a) A conceptual change

The most crucial aspect of lifelong learning is that it is not a new structure for education but rather a new viewpoint as to what is involved. In one sense it is an ancient idea. In hunting and agricultural societies, learning continued through life, as a normal part of experience. What was being learned was what was already known, the accumulation of the experiences of others. The elders of the society were the wise people, for the more experience, the more wisdom was possible. This pattern was broken by the industrial revolution where the workers, including children, learnt new skills, skills unknown to their elders. In the other areas of personal development, of social development, more traditional patterns still survived. Our information society has brought a total change. It requires the capacity not simply to learn new skills, but to keep on doing so and to learn new concepts, new ways of organising society, new views on what is valued and worthwhile. It is in this context of continuing change in all aspects of life that lifelong learning takes on a new and special meaning. What is involved is not merely continuing to learn what is known, but to be capable of continuing to learn; new knowledge, new skills, new attitudes and values. Lifelong learning then involves not just new learning but new sources of knowledge and, correspondingly, new structures of authority.

The early concept of lifelong learning was as a form of recurrent education, a means of enhancing the opportunities for adults. The restructuring of employment has given another dimension, one which affects many aspects of society. With the rapid disappearance of unskilled jobs, the requirement is for a work-force which is more flexible, more skilled and capable of continued learning. This increased complexity through change applies not only to our work but to our individual lives and our opportunities and responsibilities as citizens. In these three aspects of our lives, the person who is able to continue learning is substantially advantaged over the person who does not. The net result of a society where high quality education and training for all is not a reality, will be a deeply divided society. The divisions will come between those who can continue to gain work opportunities and those who do not; between those who can adequately manage their personal lives and those who can not;

between those who can cope with more complex tasks of citizenship and community living, and those who can not. If these dividing lines were to become deep and lasting, as is entirely possible, our society would be very badly affected. It would bring into being what some writers call "a permanent under-class", continually shut out of genuine participation in the wider society and dependent on social welfare on a lasting basis. Large-scale, increasingly chronic adult unemployment will have significant implications for lifelong learning. So too, education for leisure will be an important issue, whether or not the unemployment issue is resolved.

b) *Engagement in learning*

The idea of lifelong learning is something undertaken as need and opportunities arise. Since it has not, as yet, been systematical or built into the formal education structure of countries, it is in contrast with the definitive stages currently involved in most schooling and further education. Nevertheless, it has strong implications for compulsory education which, under this approach, is viewed as the foundation for continued learning. For this element to act effectively in such a role it needs to provide not only the means but the motivation (OECD, CERI\CR(93)3, 1993).

The means suggested in the wider project is the core curriculum: those essential learnings thought to be necessary for all students, for living in society both now and in the future. They will consist of the knowledge and the conceptual and methodological tools needed for students to continue their own learning. They will result from substantial societal debate and significant cultural analysis and will always represent temporary and changing choices. The core curriculum is not a final statement but one that continually develops.

These basic learnings are not enough. What is needed also is an engagement with learning, a desire to continue. For many students growing up has been signalled by leaving school. The school association is seen as a part of dependence and leaving school means leaving learning. Unfortunately, many school leavers see their school years as demeaning experiences, a continued experience of frustration and failure, where what was valued they could not do, and what they could do was not valued. In this sense, reforming the curriculum towards lifelong learning means not only reconsidering the aims and content, but also reconceiving the process. In what ways can our core curriculum deliver not only the capacity to continue but the active will to do so? That active will is a lively feature of early education. In that period children actively enjoy learning, with very few exceptions. Also with few exceptions they achieve dramatic results. The significant achievement in language learning in the early years represents one of our major human achievements. Can we continue and build on these achievements or do we accept the self-judgement of so many students who describe their education as a failure?

The early learning which is characterised by such achievement and such enthusiasm is a period where children are immediately conscious of the value of what they have learned and of the ability to succeed in new things -- reading, writing, constructing, story-telling, playing, making new friends. For adults in successful adult learning, something of the same is true. They are acquiring new knowledge and skills which they need -- of counselling, first-aid, furniture-making, a new language, new work skills. In much of schooling after the early years this sense of engagement, of increased powers is gone. The traditional question and answer: "Why do we have to do this?" "Because it's in the exam!" may once have brought silence but was never a satisfactory answer. For those students who have long-term goals it may suffice as a step in the desired direction, a way over a necessary hurdle, but even there it is accepted often as something that has to be done, not as a satisfying step in itself. The importance of establishing a meaningful reason for learning was pointed out by Dewey, many years ago, in his book

Democracy and Education. He conceived of education as: "that reconstruction or reorganisation of experience which adds to the meaning of experience, and which increases the ability to direct the course of subsequent experience". He continued: "The scheme of a curriculum must take account of the adaptation of studies to the needs of existing community life; it must select with the intention of improving the life we live in common so that the future shall be better than the past" (Dewey, 1916).

In the task of succeeding for all students, schools cannot afford the loss of enthusiasm, of involvement, that signals that many students are turning away from learning. Can a greater involvement in the learning process help in this situation? Is it desirable to involve students more in deciding on the aims and objectives and how these might be achieved? One of the paradoxes of education is that the greatest freedom of choice goes to the youngest pupils. In early childhood classes there is a variety of modes of working: reading, listening, building with blocks, printing, cooking, playing on equipment, working with a computer. The progressive approach has increased the flexibility of this pattern so that children can choose their activity and move about. Even in a more closely organised pattern, there is a great variety of activities. At the end of the secondary school, the major choice is on which path to follow. A student heading for law or medicine or engineering has few choices left, because the prerequisite studies are so demanding. Yet, one of the most basic aims of schooling is to increase the capacity to make responsible choices. One implication of lifelong learning, then, is a reconsideration of the involvement of students in the process of learning. A further implication, in the context discussed here, is that we should reconsider the nature of secondary education. After the expansive years of primary education, the formalisation experienced in the early secondary years is one reason for the progressive disillusionment of students with that experience. The curriculum framework for the compulsory secondary years is one that is suited to the most highly motivated but poses severe problems for others for whom schooling may seem increasingly irrelevant. Again, Dewey's words are relevant.

"In the case of the so-called disciplinary or pre-eminently logical studies there is a danger of the isolation of intellectual activities from the ordinary affairs of life. Teacher and student alike tend to set up a chasm between logical thought, as something abstract and remote, and the specific and concrete demands of everyday events. The abstract tends to become so aloof, so far away from application, so as to be cut loose from practical and moral bearing" (Dewey, 1933).

It is not the pursuit of intellectual activities which is criticised here. It is the failure to link them with the ordinary affairs of life, which is seen as leading to a lack of engagement with learning.

c) *Content and process in the curriculum*

There is considerable controversy on the issue of content in the curriculum. Many countries have always been prescriptive as to the content to be taught. Now, countries such as England and Wales, USA, Australia and New Zealand are moving closer to this pattern by defining what areas of study should be followed and providing detail as to the content in these areas. The argument is that there is useful knowledge in key areas such as science, mathematics, geography, history, politics, literature, health, and that it is the responsibility of schools to ensure that this is learned.

This argument is not new and has moved in different directions at different times. In the traditional pattern of the curriculum, knowledge was the dominant aspect and success involved the capacity to reproduce the knowledge accurately. Two aspects changed this approach. One was the flood of new knowledge which made it unreal to cover the field and made it necessary to select "the most

147

valuable" knowledge. The other aspect was the emphasis on higher level purposes, the importance of applying knowledge, of presenting it in different forms for different audiences, of evaluating its validity, or its relevance to new situations. This was the stress on process which became the new orthodoxy. Rote learning was out, problem-solving was in. The argument ran that since the process could be developed with any knowledge that it was not crucial what knowledge was used.

This emphasis on process is itself a subject of criticism. Where students once learned to recite the bays, rivers and main features of all the continents, the critics claimed that students could not now place other countries on the map and did not know their capitals. The current emphasis in England and Wales, and the more recent initiative in the USA, is to prescribe those things that should be known and to assess their achievement. This is one approach to the idea of a core curriculum, of essential learnings. This idea, however, is more complex. It accepts the notion that some knowledge is of value to all students, but is equally concerned that students should be able to apply knowledge; to solve problems, to communicate clearly. The core curriculum is a content-and-process curriculum, one that is conscious of the delicate balance between the two. That balance is crucial if learning is to be a successful process for all students. Students who have difficulties with learning benefit from the chance to be able to assess their progress regularly, to have a sense of continuity and purpose, to see the applicability of what they are learning to aspects of life that do or will concern them. Paradoxically, the effective core curriculum may well involve less knowledge than traditionally, but a greater emphasis on assessing that knowledge, on applying it in familiar circumstances, on applying it in novel situations, on finding ways of communicating it to different audiences.

d) Wider links and outlooks for the school

A further implication of lifelong learning is the need to reconsider the role of the school. If schooling is to be part of a wider process, and not an enclosed experience for young people, the more it is seen as part of the normal community, the better. Part of the dissatisfaction of young people with schools comes from their feeling it is isolated from normal life. Many initiatives now are beginning to change their perception.

One of the promising initiatives has been the link between schools and businesses, documented in a recent OECD publication, *Schools and Businesses: A new partnership* (OECD, 1992b). The purpose of such partnerships is threefold. One is to permit students a close and continuing link with work, providing a real setting for much of the learning that has a vocational emphasis and encouraging schools to have a wider range of activities. A second is to help secure particular changes in schooling seen as relevant to business, for example the development of generic vocational competencies, such as communication, useful in work and in other areas of life. The other is to provide business with an insight into schools and an appreciation for the full sweep of the curriculum. So far, the initiatives are not generalised or fully integrated in the curriculum except in a few countries, such as Germany. Careful and systematic development offers possibilities of a valuable association. That association must recognise the two-way nature of the process. Business has frequently been critical of schools in their efforts to cope with change. This criticism has often been uninformed and closer links would provide a better basis for dialogue. Business, too, has much to gain through this process for its own benefit and would be unwise to approach it from a position of assumed superiority. Partnership is the appropriate term.

Schools have been isolated from their own communities as well as from business institutions. One of the features of initiatives in many OECD countries, such as France, the Netherlands and Sweden, to take examples, is to increase the strength and effectiveness of the links between the schools and their communities. This tendency is strengthened by the concept of lifelong learning which envisages the whole community as a learning community, with the schools playing a central role, both physically and organisationally. An initiative in Alberta, Canada has helped some schools to become community schools, involving both students and community members as teachers as well as learners. The community colleges in some countries, such as the US and Canada, have also developed useful initiatives.

Lifelong learning is seen as a necessary consequence of the society in which we live. It opens up quite new concepts on schooling: the role of the school, the nature of the curriculum, the learning process, the nature of the associations of the school with the community. This is an area where there are many initiatives but so far a lack of a clear set of purposes and priorities to orient future activities. It raises many questions and issues for further consideration. In what ways can we introduce a greater focus in the curriculum on the applications of learning? What sorts of partnership between business and education might be appropriate? What are the most fruitful forms of co-operation between the schools and their communities?

Vocational Education and Integrated Learning

a) A changing role

The OECD Education Committee stressed the impact of change on vocational education through the establishment of their programme, VOTEC, The Changing Role of Vocational and Technical Education and Training. This is an important area in its own right in view of the impact of the changes in employment structure on so many areas of individual and social life. Here, we will be concentrating particularly on the implications of the changes, both for the period of compulsory education and also for the post-compulsory secondary years.

A major factor in the changes in vocational education comes from the responses to technological and social changes in the workplace. Earlier OECD/CERI studies described these changes in the following ways.

-- The new technologies tend to eliminate repetitive and routine jobs. One result seems to be a general up-skilling of jobs. Another result, about which some controversy continues, is a reduction in employment opportunities for young people.

-- There is a clear tendency towards more team-work. The man-machine relationship is being replaced by an interaction between teams and technical systems. As a result, increased emphasis is put on social skills and communication to complement technical expertise.

-- Increasingly, employees are expected to perform a greater variety of tasks ranging from planning to evaluation. There is an increased emphasis in the more progressive enterprises on polyvalent skills, on the multi-function employee. On the other hand, changes in work organisation are needed to provide more scope for the exercise of these professional skills.

-- The intervals between training and work are becoming shorter. As a consequence the readiness for continuous learning and its cognitive and attitudinal correlates are considered more and more important. (See, for example: OECD, 1986).

With these trends, there is also an increasing pressure for participation in decision-making, stressing the importance of more dynamic personal qualities as well as a capacity to learn from experience in a way which transforms experience.

These changes in work, actual and potential, have a dual impact on education. Most obvious is the effect on vocational education and training. A limited training with a fixed set of skills is no longer enough; the person will require not only higher skills but the capacity to adjust to and master new technical and social situations. This calls for a broadening and strengthening of the nature of vocational education and has a particular impact on people currently at work and those preparing immediately for it. This aspect is being addressed through a substantial restructuring of vocational and technical education including its relationship with general education. Our concern focuses on the impact of these changes on general education, including primary and secondary schooling. In those areas, while there are important structural changes to improve the links with vocational education, the more important change may well be one of process. The recent developments in vocational education, made to cope with more forward-looking business, may well be ahead of the developments in many fields of enterprise. The interactive process must apply on both sides of the education-industry link.

b) *The learning process*

One major factor of secondary education, linked largely with employment changes, is the growth in participation rates at the upper secondary level. This is not only the result of increased individual aspiration but of deliberate government policy, justified largely by governments on the need for a more productive work-force. As discussed in the Background Paper, equally powerful arguments can be mounted for personal and social requirements, with all three emphases being complementary. The fact remains, as indicated in the Background Paper, that participation is rising rapidly. This brings its own problems.

In many countries, the major thrust of upper secondary education has been academic in nature, focusing on higher education. With participation rates of the order of 25-35 per cent such patterns were acceptable, even though restricted in emphasis. With a broadening of participation to the levels of 75-85 per cent, an actuality in some countries and a target for many others, that provision is less satisfactory. Reports are already indicating large drop-out rates and considerable numbers of students who leave without any qualification. The greatly increased student population also puts at risk those who have formerly found secondary education to be of value. What is desperately needed is a pattern of education for the whole secondary population that is seen by them as of value, and is of worth to society also. This requires a comprehensive approach involving structural change, a reformed curriculum and a new pedagogy. Vocational education feels it can contribute in all these areas. We shall concentrate here on pedagogy.

A major part of the approach with the "new population" of secondary education must be to provide them with the motivation to learn and the confidence that they can learn. These are students who have been increasingly alienated by their school experience, partly through its perceived irrelevance, partly through an experience of continued failure. Thus, the impact of this thinking relates not only to helping upper secondary students who have a history of failure but also of addressing the issues which cause that situation. An approach strongly commended by vocational educators, is the integrated learning process.

c) Integrated learning

At the joint seminar by OECD and the US Department of Education, **Linkages in Vocational-Technical Education and Training,** Raizen (1991) developed the concept of "situated learning" as a means of integrating learning more closely with practical activity. She pointed to the failure in the US for either general or vocational education to deal with the issue of disadvantaged students, forecasting a distressing social divide unless their learning needs could be met effectively.

Raizen summarised the findings of cognitive research over the past 25 years, to indicate that approaches were available that schools and colleges are not currently using. Her summary:

-- "It is not sufficient to teach knowledge and procedures; instruction must also focus on conditions of application of the knowledge and skills being learned.

-- Instruction must intermingle context specificity and generality, including the development of self-regulatory skills and performance control strategies.

-- Instruction should take into account the learner's original ideas, stage discrepant or confirming experiences to stimulate questions, and encourage the generation of a range of responses with the opportunity to apply them in various situations.

-- The most effective learning takes place through 'situated activity' using the physical environment and the tools it provides, the co-operative construction of knowledge among groups of workers doing a common task, and the culture of the specific work community". (Raizen, 1991).

The concept of "situated learning" or "integrated learning" offers a new and hopeful approach to a problem that is deeply rooted in schools and will require a major effort to solve. It is not however a simple concept to implement as it raises questions about almost every aspect of schooling. The principles outlined are by no means self-evident and are very different from current approaches to teaching and learning. Is it possible to make such a significant change to current approaches? At what stages should such an approach be developed and for which students? To what extent can this be done in schools and to what extent does it require work settings? The answers to these questions are not obvious. On the other hand, the task of achieving quality for all is so demanding that we need to be prepared to consider quite new and radical approaches.

d) Pathways for the future

Efforts for the future need to be directed towards the priority issue, already identified in the section on Lifelong Learning. The aim is to provide all students with the basis of knowledge, skills and understanding required for continued learning: it is also to provide the motivation to continue. One of the strongest arguments for the further consideration and development of the integrated learning approach is that it does address the key issue. That issue relates to the need for students to see that what they are learning in the classroom is of relevance to their current or future interests, personal, social or vocational. For some students a sense that it will prove to be so in the long run is enough. They will accept distant goals. For many students, the connection must be more obvious and their feeling of success, of achievement, must be equally clear. A continued diet of failure or irrelevance is fatal to self-confidence and interest and thus to continued learning. Further, a greater variety of situations and

151

learning conditions will help, rather than assuming that lessons dominated by speech and writing are effective for everyone.

It is important to recognise that the case for situated learning or integrated learning relates not only to direct vocational education and training but to general education for many students. Resnick (1987) comments on the artificiality of the school setting in contrast to work:

"A school stresses individual as contrasted to group performance; school expects performance on the basis of unaided thought whereas work provides cognitive tools; school emphasises symbolic thinking rather than using objects and situations to aid problem-solving; school aims at general knowledge and skills rather than knowledge and skills linked to a particular situation, as is the case outside school".

This approach is being put forward as a possible help to the many students for whom school is currently not a satisfactory solution.

For integrated learning to become a more important part of education will require a reconsideration of the essential aspects of the process and its potential. Part of this will involve substantial re-thinking on the part of both schools and business. Schools have long recognised this challenge. As long ago as 1968, Hargreaves (1968) pointed out the failure of comprehensive schooling to reach effectively a significant slice of its population. With the further extension of schooling and the increase in participation rates, this problem is even more urgent. Business and industry will have to reconsider their roles with equal thoroughness. They have been frequent critics of the schools, not always in constructive ways. Now they are being called on for an effort in co-operation to meet a major social need. The cohesion and purpose of our society will depend heavily on the fruitfulness of such co-operation. The VOTEC programme is addressing these issues in the context of the needs of vocational and technical education and training (OECD, 1992d). The same attention, radical in its nature, needs to be addressed to general education, where the concept of integrated learning has much to offer.

The question of motivation for learning will be quite vital. For all students, the perceived relevance of education for vocations has always been a powerful factor. For many students in the past, leaving school early in the secondary years, they were able to go directly into employment. These were mostly unskilled jobs, but often provided opportunity for further development and on-the-job training. Those opportunities are gone. Those students now continue further in education since there are no pathways for 14/15 year-olds to move directly to paid work. The motivation is now unclear. The possibilities for work in the future seem uncertain and, at the best, are distant. How can schools avoid the growth of a frustrated cohort of young people who see no value in education for themselves and may well distract or disrupt the opportunities of others. Can we provide practical, work-type situations which can challenge young people and provide sensible and worthwhile applications of their learning? This would give the concept of integrated learning an additional dimension.

Environmental Education in the Curriculum

a) Environmental education and the core curriculum

The OECD/CERI programme, Environment and School Initiatives (ENSI) is substantial, involving 19 Member countries. Again, as with vocational education, it relates to a major social issue, one with dramatic global implications as well as having a significant impact at national and local levels. Environmental awareness is also a very complex issue, raising important scientific questions, with economic impact through the concept of sustainable economic development and of political significance, as it raises questions of international co-operation as well as of local action. The links between environmental change and the economy have been documented over a substantial period (Barde and Gerelli, 1977)

Environmental education raises important issues for the curriculum, especially in a climate of curriculum reform. Is it to be a part of the core curriculum, of the essential learnings for all students? Or is it something which is an optional extra, to be a matter of choice at the local or school level? At the moment the work of ENSI proceeds through particular schools, with the curriculum created through the choices of teachers and students rather than having objectives clearly specified beforehand. It does, however, raise much more general questions.

The paper prepared for this conference on the CERI/OECD Project on Innovations in Science, Mathematics and Technology Education (Atkin, 1993) points out that these areas have been identified as a priority in almost every country, and that the new curricula are increasingly incorporating practical applications and implications, with a new receptivity for cross-circular links. Atkin continues:

"Another contextual influence of increasing importance in setting the direction of change in SMT education arises from social concerns about environmental quality. In a few countries, a new subject, environmental studies, has been created. In many places, the better-established subjects have been modified to incorporate environmental issues. Almost always, this development entails probing connections between scientific and technical fields, on the one hand, and political/social/economic considerations, on the other".

Thus the key question with respect to the core curriculum is not whether a subject called environmental studies is included. The question is whether environmental education involves either a core area of knowledge and experience, or a core learning process, to put it in the terms of the Background Paper. The nature of possible contributions is illustrated in the ENSI project itself.

b) Emphases of the ENSI Project

The ENSI Project does not set overall knowledge objectives for the co-operating schools. Its approach, however, has important implications in that the schools selected are required to set their own knowledge objectives, relevant to their particular situation. In addition there is a requirement which applies to all schools: pupils or students are required to take an important role in the project, defining it, being responsible for its management and progress, and to take as the objective of their work to change something in the local environment. Implicit in the activities of all the Member countries is the understanding that young people can contribute to their societies through activities that are respected and that they can influence the world in which they live. There are, then, significant and tangible objectives at the heart of the ENSI project. One is the joint development of knowledge necessary to understanding and action. The other is to obtain social participation, in particular the sense that students can influence their surrounding society. These are both important objectives for students in the context we are considering at this conference.

ENSI established four targets which would be possible bases for the school projects:

-- to envisage the environment as a sphere of personal experience;

--   to examine the environment as a subject of interdisciplinary learning and research;

--   to shape the environment as a sphere of socially important action;

--   to accept the environment as a challenge to initiative, independence and responsible action.

Here again there are strong implications for the nature of such projects, to be socially relevant, interdisciplinary, and requiring strong personal qualities and initiatives.

The projects provided ENSI with the opportunity to explore a number of important themes: One of these was to determine ways of overcoming some of the main barriers to the teaching and learning of environmental issues. They also provide information on a variety of forms of interaction between teachers, students and the community and on the changing roles of teachers and students in environmental education. A further issue is the integration of various disciplines and the question of standards of achievement. At the heart of most projects is the aim to foster and assess "dynamic" qualities in students: responsibility, initiative, co-operativeness, creativity. These themes develop further the central objectives of ENSI. One is to develop the personal qualities of students, in particular those qualities relating to social influence, to affecting their surroundings. The other is to promote environmental awareness, including the capacity to construct knowledge through experience not only in schools but also in local communities. As has been pointed out in the programme itself, there is some tension between these two objectives, with the latter more passive and emphasizing qualities such as understanding. The former emphasis is on initiatives on responsibility, on taking action. In the projects themselves, sometimes one emphasis predominated, sometimes the other and in some, both aspects featured.

c) The ENSI school projects

A large number of case studies has been developed from the projects. By the nature of the programme, the projects were diverse. They depended on a local setting, with some environmental significance. They were shaped by the teachers and students in each school. Thus, both the issue itself and the way of dealing with it were peculiar to the setting.

At Serre in Italy two primary classes became involved in the issues of local industrialisation and the impact that might follow these processes on the oasis, a local endangered wetland area. Their involvement led to a significant amendment in the process.

At Evo in Finland, the vocational forestry school planned and set up a nature park, obtaining the co-operation both of the city administration and local industry. Their activities, in contrast with Serre, were carried out as a part of regular lessons.

At Bredstedt, in northern Germany, a study group of teachers and secondary pupils converted a disused school into a nature information centre providing exhibitions and courses and undertaking public relations. Its success was such that it was taken over by the city administration as a tourist attraction, thus retaining the community service and creating new jobs.

Not all projects had such immediate results. At Herning in Denmark pupils aged 12 studied a lake which had been heavily polluted by the waste water of a sewage purification plant. Studies of the history and ecology of the lake were the basis for a report, including proposals to the local authorities for the future utilisation of the lake.

In the variety of processes and situations involved, the success depends only partly on the outcome. Clearly it is important that significant outcomes sometimes, even frequently, occur. After all, the rationale of the projects is based on the belief that individuals and groups can work to influence events in their society. Yet provided successes do eventuate with reasonable frequency the projects can succeed in other ways all the time. What the project has developed is a constructive way of learning and teaching, here to some extent all are teachers and all are learners. It is in these elements of environmental education that lessons are to be learned for all education.

d) *Implications for the curriculum*

The future role of environmental education in the formal sense is still unclear. As already mentioned, some countries have included a specific subject of environmental studies, others have amended existing courses such as science or social studies to include aspects of environmental education. In some countries the area is included specifically as parts of the core curriculum. Regardless of the final outcome of this process, and that may continue to take different forms in different countries, the ideas behind the development will have increasing significance.

The importance of these ideas is that they address issues which are central to curriculum reform. As has been emphasized in the Background Paper, decisions made outside the school are vital in their involvement of the wider society and in obtaining wide consensus on purposes. They will still not be practically significant if they do not result in changes in the classroom. A major difficulty here is that many students become progressively detached from their school learning, seeing it as unrelated to their interests or as beyond their capacities, or both of these. A major need if this substantial group of students is to truly engage in learning is to involve them in pursuits in which they have a genuine interest, but which are also capable of extending and deepening their knowledge and skills and, particularly, to be able to apply them.

The approaches of environmental education have much to commend them as a regular aspect of the curriculum. At the moment this area is rather marginalised, being seen more as a means of social activism than as a genuinely educational approach. This strengthening of the initiatives tends to be responded to in kind. Many environmental educators put forward an over-generalised view of other areas of education. This view describes the extremes of traditional education: authoritarian teachers; knowledge presented in isolated packages, beyond dispute and debate and therefore partly irrelevant; students operate as individuals, with communication and co-operation seen as dysfunctional. Both stereotypes are unjust to the reality and hinder the active debate that needs to take place. Only through such a debate can the understanding develop which sees environmental education as part of the mainstream, with that mainstream much richer for the inclusion.

A further contribution of environmental education to the curriculum could be through the exhibition of interdisciplinarity in practice. While in the primary schools subject divisions are often not sharp, in secondary schools both the organisation of the curriculum and the training of the teachers makes for strong boundaries. Even the development of effective working links across those boundaries is difficult, partly through the logistic difficulties of joint planning but also due to the established tradition of separateness.

Environmental education at its best is an excellent example of interdisciplinarity, of the growing need to cross disciplinary boundaries in problem-solving and research. Much of what passes for interdisciplinary work is merely a lack of disciplinary contribution, a *melange* lacking cohesion or rigorous thought. If environmental education is to be successful it requires true interdisciplinarity: the combined contribution of disciplines focused together on a problem of common interest.

In addition to the intrinsic merits of environmental education as part of the contemporary curriculum, it illustrates and illuminates many of the issues which arise in other initiatives which cross traditional curriculum divisions. These issues are similar to those which arise in health education or in moral or civic education. While the important value questions which arise in such areas are given an implicit role in many of the traditional subjects, the major attention focuses elsewhere and particularly on those aspects which are likely to be assessed. The merit of considering in detail an area such as environmental education is that it raises controversial issues as the central theme. While we continue to bypass issues of major social and personal concern, or to deal with them in technical or abstract or impersonal ways, we miss a major opportunity to demonstrate the relevance of education. We also under-emphasize one of the major aims of education.

Children with Special Educational Needs and Students at Risk

a) Context of the issue

Children with Special Educational Needs (SEN) and Students at Risk are important tests of our sincerity in proclaiming the aim of a high quality education and training for all. In the past many children with special educational needs were in separate institutions and thus had no access to the regular curriculum while Students at Risk (STAR) tended to segregate themselves from opportunity by failure to keep up with the pace of the curriculum, by early drop-out, by inattention or disruption. If the goals of education are to be the same for all children, which is our assumption here, and if education incorporates basic essential learnings and aspects of socialisation, then it is difficult to justify a segregated provision for these students. Limited access means limited opportunity. Yet the task poses severe difficulties, when accepted. The issue is highlighted by the case of the most severely handicapped children, who in some countries are still considered as outside the system.

It is important to be clear on the focus for our consideration, which is that for the OECD/CERI studies. Children with special educational needs belong to two groups: those who form the categories of handicapping or disabling conditions and those who for one reason or another have fallen behind their peers in their educational achievement. As no consistent classification is used in OECD countries, the percentage of children recognised in this group varies between two and six per cent. Remedial and slow learners are those who are functioning significantly behind their peers (e.g. two years or more), with no known aetiology. These two groups taken together make up 16-20 per cent of the school-aged population, i.e. in a non-selective class of 30, averaging between four and six (OECD, 1992c).

The OECD/CERI study defines students at risk as "those children and youth from disadvantaged backgrounds, especially those living in poverty or who are members of minority groups, who are failing to make the educational, social and vocational progress that might be expected of them" (OECD, 1990). Estimates of the size of this group range about 30 per cent: there is substantial overlap between children classified as having special educational needs and those considered at risk. The entire group with whom we are dealing here thus represents a major individual and social concern. In terms of individual equity, of social cohesion and economic productivity the situation must be addressed.

156

b) Reasons for reform

In the past, the failure of these students was explained in terms largely of individual deficits. Taking the distribution of intelligence on the Gaussian curve as "normal", and regarding IQ as fixed, a substantial proportion of people was bound to be "retarded". This reasoning was the base for separate provision, which was also available for those with physical disabilities. Currently, while the facts of performance must be kept in mind, there is a strong pressure to provide access for these students to the same opportunities.

The change of attitude leading to reform comes for a variety of reasons. One is the inequity of denying access to an individual, in a society where such access is accepted as a democratic right. On a social basis, there is a waste of human potential if we permit such a large group to remain unable to participate effectively in society. Too many such individuals have succeeded in spite of the system, for the opportunities to be limited for ever. There is also a pressing economic reason, and the more cynical might regard it as crucial. With the increase in the proportion of the elderly in the population, and the decrease in the birth rate, industrial societies see a demographic trend towards fewer productive workers and more people on welfare. The full productive potential of those societies will be required to support their economies, and no society could afford 20-30 per cent of its working-age citizens to be unproductive. Even currently, there are sections of the population aged 16-25 in many countries in which unemployment reaches or exceeds these levels.

c) Potential for reform

Education is not the only route to reform. Better physical assistance and supportive social programmes can help. In an information society, education will remain crucial and the curriculum will be an important factor. Many of the factors discussed earlier help the situation. The idea of a learning society implies more avenues for learning than our current patterns of schooling and new information technology provides a range of alternative means. The concern here, however, is the curriculum, particularly in view of the argument developed that the core curriculum must be the enabling process for lifelong learning. This is the basis for the assumption in the opening paragraph, that the goals of compulsory education should be the same for all children. This is the very basis for them to be able to make diverse choices. The key requirement for both groups is access to the curriculum.

Access has many aspects. One is physical: arrangements for the movement-impaired, the hearing impaired and the visually impaired can effectively overcome these problems, through building design and the provision of facilities, such as Braille, signing systems and personal computers. Secondly, the curriculum materials can be redesigned to make them more widely available. Third is the support given to teachers to assist their understanding of the issues and their capacity to manage it, for example in better assessment of student progress. Thus, while the curriculum remains basically the same for all, access to it and means of delivery may be significantly differentiated, as may be the pace of progress (Evans et al., 1989). A careful analysis of the needs is given in the recent Irish Green Paper, *Education for a Changing World* (Irish Ministry of Education, 1992).

d) Curriculum differentiation

The essential reason for curriculum differentiation in the sense we are using it, differentiation of the means and processes of delivery, is the extreme heterogeneity of the group under consideration. There is a danger in grouping under labels, of under-estimating the differences. A little reflection on the diverse conditions of the visually impaired, the hearing impaired and the motor impaired will

157

indicate much greater diversity than in the non-disabled population. Differentiation will have many aspects, according to its purpose.

One aspect is time differentiation, "stretching the curriculum". Early childhood programmes in many countries have demonstrated their effectiveness in reducing perceptual or linguistic delays or problems of socialisation. The first five years of life is significant in this regard. Exploration is underway and needs to be further developed on the extensions for older students. As more precise expectations of competent performance are developed, these can become targets disassociated with ages or grades. There is no logical reason to assume all students should progress at the same rate in the various fields. Again this has substantial implications for the organisation of schooling. In addition, the opportunities within further education are increasing as courses are organised on more flexible bases, with criterion-referenced rather than norm-referenced assessment. Accelerated learning can also be an important aspect. In some countries, such as USA, students at risk have been found capable of a faster pace when not classified as having special educational needs (Evans, 1985).

In the past, differentiation has been largely structural, providing separate avenues for progression, as with selective schools providing essentially different curricula. This concept envisages the differentiation being made through comprehensive institutions, finding ways of differentiating the same curriculum for different ability levels. This has been the subject of much research and of even more controversy. Essentially, the basis for proceeding is the finding that in mixed ability groups the better students do as well as in more homogeneous groupings, but the less able do considerably better.

The major onus for the success of the differentiated curriculum falls on the teacher. Much higher demands are placed on the teacher by this approach, at both primary and secondary levels. What is required is a detailed grasp of the curriculum itself and of the needs and aspirations of students, plus an appreciation of the varied learning tasks and routes. This is a substantial teaching challenge but one that pays off in greatly increased opportunity and student progress.

The points made in the earlier sections of this paper on vocational education and on environmental education are particularly relevant here. In the past, the pattern for at risk students has been one of early leaving. With that option reduced by lack of employment, it becomes more important to demonstrate that staying on is worthwhile. This is so in a vocational sense and the perceived realism of situated learning, as described earlier, has particular promise here. So, too, does the emphasis put forward in environmental education, that schooling can make a practical difference to the student's own life and to life outside school. The Background Paper quoted Postman's comment:

> "In the face of all this, perhaps the most important contribution schools can make is to provide young people with the sense of purpose, of meaning, and of the interconnectedness of what they learn" (Postman, 1983).

This is no less true for the students considered in this section. Arrangements in the past have drastically reduced their educational opportunities. We have a unique opportunity to help those horizons expand.

In the book *Education for Capability* (Burgess, 1985), Weaver argues for an extension of the explicit aims of education. He spoke of cultivation as an awareness of and involvement in culture; of comprehension as the development of understanding; of competence as the capacity to form purposes and act on them; of capability, as being able to manage one's life, to cope with situations and learn from them; of creativity, as the power to originate, to envision, to develop or construct; finally, he mentions communion, as the sense of belonging, of responsibility and commitment to a general welfare. His argument is that the emphasis of schooling has been too much at the culture and comprehension end, too little at the competence, capability, creativity and communion end of the spectrum.

Weaver's comments describe a reality that many observers have noted. Much of the knowledge developed in school, and many of the skills, find no application in everyday life. There seems to be a failure to apply in one context what is learned in another. In the approach of environmental education it is the application in a real context that is the essential element, and in problems that are real and are seen as socially useful. The concept has much in common with the idea of situated learning or integrated learning discussed in the last section. It also links with the remarks of Whitehead in his essay, *The Aims of Education*. Speaking of the dangers of "inert ideas", he says:

> "...ideas which are not utilised are positively harmful. By utilizing an idea, I mean relating it to that stream, compounded of sense perceptions, feelings, hopes, desires, and of mental activities adjusting thought to thought, which forms our life" (Whitehead, 1962).

Conclusion

Each of the four associated projects raises issues which are central to the major concern of the conference, The Curriculum Redefined. This, of course, is no coincidence as they seek to address the same contextual factors and are committed to the same universalist aim, which are central to the conference. The situation, however, stresses further the breadth of the approach which is necessary if the concerns of general education for the period of compulsory schooling are to be addressed. It is encouraging that approaches in such diverse areas should indicate so many common concerns.

The concept of lifelong learning places compulsory education in a new setting. Rather than being the unique period of schooling leading on to vocations or further education, it is a phase in a life-long process. That phase, however, has two key requirements: one is to provide a basis for further learning; the other is to ensure a continuing motivation for it. This may imply a greater organisational variety and more flexibility in approach than is the case with current schooling. It certainly implies the need for greater and more constructive student involvement in the planning and conduct of their education.

Vocational education and training will make an impact on general education in many ways. The organisational and structural links need further strengthening. Our particular interest here was on the relevance more widely of the current concerns of vocational education for integrated learning. The factors which raised the interest of vocational education in that concept apply with equal force in compulsory education. In that phase we have a substantial group of students who see little value in their education and who now, because of external factors, continue on to post-compulsory education with that negative attitude and, often, substantial gaps in knowledge and skills. The basic assumptions of integrated learning, which links them with practice, thinking with doing, and seeks an active involvement by students in the planning of those links, offer an important potential for study and development.

Environmental education poses both challenges and opportunities for those concerned with curriculum reform. As a major social concern it makes a valid claim for inclusion in the curriculum, perhaps in the core curriculum, either as a special subject or as a linking process involving a number of subjects. In that latter role it offers a valuable exercise in interdisciplinarity. Equally importantly, the process of environmental education, with its emphasis on using a significant knowledge base as a

159

platform for co-operative social action, offers a valuable method for obtaining greater student involvement and engagement in learning.

The concerns for children with special educational needs and students at risk pose a sharp challenge to the sincerity of commitment to an aim such as high quality education and training for all. If that aim is accepted fully, as part of a commitment to equity, a requirement for a democratic society, then we need to consider the organisational form and the changes in curriculum and pedagogy, which will provide substance to that purpose. The most obvious issue is one of inclusion, providing the same opportunities as others. This issue brings with it physical and organisational requirements, to make those opportunities realisable. In addition, the concept of curriculum differentiation offers possibilities of more flexible and more effective learning for all students. It is also vital to acknowledge, in this and each of the other initiatives, the central need for greater involvement of students and teachers, in the reconceptualisation and also in the realisation.

Bibliography

ATKIN, Myron (1993), Paper prepared for Conference on CERI/OECD *Project on Innovations in Science, Mathematics and Technology Education,* CERI/OECD, Paris.

BARDE, J-P. and GERELLI, E. (1977), *Economie et Politique de l'Environnement,* Presses Universitaires de France.

BURGESS, T. (Ed.), (1985), *Education for Capability,* NFER-Nelson, Windsor.

CERI (1993), *An Introduction to Learning -- Redefining the School Curriculum in a Lifelong Perspective.* Room Paper for the 1993 Conferences on The Curriculum Redefined.

DEWEY, John (1916), *Democracy and Education.* Macmillan Publishing Co., New York.

DEWEY, John (1933), *How Do We Think?* D.C. Heath & Co., Lexington, Mass.

EVANS, P. (1985), *From Coping to Confidence: Unit on Assessment,* NFER: Nelson, Windsor.

EVANS, P., IRESON, J., REDMOND, P., and WEDELL, K. (1989), *Pathways to Progress. Developing an approach to teaching the National Curriculum to children experiencing difficulties with learning in the primary school.* Institute of Education: University of London, London.

HARGREAVES, David (1968), *Challenge to the Comprehensive School,* Routledge, Kegan, Paul. London.

IRISH MINISTRY OF EDUCATION (1992), *Education for a Changing World,* Stationery Office, Dublin.

OECD (1986), *New Technology and Human Resource Development in the Automobile Industry,* OECD/CERI, Paris.

OECD (1990), Children and Youth at Risk. *A preliminary synthesis of country reports (revised).*

160

CERI/CY/90-15. OECD, Paris.

OECD (1992a), *High Quality Education and Training for All.* Report of the 1990 Conference of Ministers, OECD, Paris.

OECD (1992b), *Schools and Businesses: A new partnership,* OECD, Paris.

OECD (1992c), Active life for disabled youth: integration in the schools. Chapter 3 in *Classification statistics and terminology.* CERI/DY(92)4. OECD, Paris.

OECD (1992d), *New Approaches to Integrated Learning:* Issues Paper DEELSA/ED/WD(92)46, OECD, Paris.

POSTMAN, N. (1983), *Engaging Students in the Great Conversation.* Phi Delta Kuppan, New York.

RAIZEN, Senta (1991), *Learning and Work: The Research Base,* OECD, Paris.

RESNICK, Lauren (1987), Learning in School and Out. *Educational Researcher,* Vol. 16, No. 9.

SKILBECK, M. (1990), *Curriculum Reform: An Overview of Trends,* OECD, Paris.

SWEDISH MINISTRY OF EDUCATION AND SCIENCE (1992), *A School for Life,* Report of the Commission on the Curriculum, Stockholm.

WHITEHEAD, A.N. (1962). *The Aims of Education and Other Essays,* Ernest Benn Ltd., London.

5. Pupil Assessment, Evaluation and System Accountability

Many years ago a medical educator wrote these comments on examinations: "At the best, means to an end; at the worst the end itself, they may be the best part of an education or the worst -- they may be its very essence or its ruin". (Osler, 1913). The way in which we assess student achievement is a vital aspect of the way we define the curriculum. The most explicit statements of what we believe to be important in the curriculum appear in the process of student assessment. This is not simply because it becomes the focus of student attention but because it is for teachers and others the definition of what schools see to be valuable.

Two distinct approaches exist, perhaps in competition, perhaps complementarily.

i) Political accountability and community support and understanding of what schools are doing both require that achievement standards are assessed and reported in meaningful terms. In this approach, assessment is used for monitoring and accountability in state or national systems, for example in terms of nationwide testing of student achievements in core areas of the curriculum. To do such testing in ways that are reliable and valid and still remain understandable to the public and to politicians is not an easy task.

ii) Integrating assessment with learning. In this approach, students' everyday work is used for continuous assessment rather than depending on formal examinations or standardized tests. These approaches include records of student achievements, portfolios, practical tests, school-based feedback to help define objectives and to encourage learners to take responsibility for their learning.

These two approaches are considered in detail in the Conference Paper edited by Nisbet, *Assessment and Curriculum Reform* (Nisbet, 1993), who comments that the first approach has resulted from pressure by politicians, parents and administrators, while the second is favoured by the professionals in education. He continues to discuss the possibility of doing both, given that both have merit but concludes that the 'high stakes' accountability procedures will soon come to dominate the 'low stakes' learning-related student assessment. He continues: "A more constructive resolution of the conflict between the two uses of assessment, the 'accountability' use and the 'institutional' use, is to seek to combine both within a single system of assessment. This implies designing national testing to encourage new or improved styles of learning and adapting new forms of instructional assessment to provide for national monitoring. Hence, we are distinguishing two levels in the use of assessment in education: assessment of the system and assessment of the process." This is a very constructive suggestion in a situation where the pressures from both points of view are very strong. Nisbet himself asks whether these two approaches are compatible or irreconcilable?

The Nisbet paper includes seven case studies of national testing and new approaches to assessment, identifying issues of concern. The countries included are France, Germany, the Netherlands, Spain, Sweden, the United Kingdom and the United States of America. This is an intriguing study, revealing constraints of approach which are deeply embedded in national cultures. The key issues are illustrated in a variety of ways, but the major question remains to be resolved.

Schools and teachers must recognise in practical ways the importance of more meaningful and comprehensive assessment and reporting of student achievement. The strong emphasis on methods of recognising outcomes is related to the powerful feeling reported by Boomer, "...that parents, by and large, wish to know with the minimum of jargon and window-dressing where their children stand, not necessarily in a class pecking order but in relation to others across the state" (Boomer, 1992). Our claims from within education that we are doing better than ever may well be true but they remain unconvincing while we do not produce any evidence.

There is a pressing need for teachers and schools to find ways of reporting meaningfully on student achievement, yet to avoid the restricting, least-common-denominator approach of many testing programmes. The light sampling method of national testing described in the French Case Study, and proposed also as part of the New Zealand changes would seem to offer the possibility of defining standards in an objective way without adopting the time and resource-costly approach of universal national testing at set stages. A further possibility of linking is to use the learning profile approach. These are detailed descriptions of what students will be able to achieve as they move through the curriculum. They are the 'output' side of the curriculum, embodying what students will be able to say, do or understand as a result of pursuing particular curriculum goals. They have the added strength of not being restricted to a particular format but include oral work, group performance, problem-solving skills, or research, for example.

This question of assessment and curriculum reform will be one of the major issues to resolve in the whole process of curriculum redefinition. Like most alternatives in education, vocational or general, content or process, the accountability -- instructional tension must remain just that. Both aspects play a vital role and the issue is to find constructive ways of achieving both sets of purposes, for both are valid and appropriate. Schools cannot turn their backs on their communities when they ask, understandably, for meaningful assessments of progress. They must, however, point out clearly the benefits and the dangers of various alternatives. In the task of achieving quality education and training for all the stakes are high. Pupils and students will be the losers if this tension is not constructively resolved.

RELATING PUPIL ASSESSMENT AND EVALUATION TO TEACHING AND LEARNING

John Nisbet

The central issue raised in this paper is whether assessment can be used as a means of reforming the curriculum. The converse is certainly true: that if assessment remains unchanged, it can be an obstacle to reform. To try to reform the curriculum without taking account of assessment will be ineffective, for the teachers and students work to the reality imposed by assessment rather than to the rhetoric of a statement of intent. But this point can be made positively: because assessment is a powerful determinant of what is taught and learned, we must plan assessment as an integral element in curriculum reform, to help implement the reforms which we see as desirable. But can we do this?

The background document for this discussion is the report, Curriculum Reform: Assessment in Question, which was commissioned by OECD in 1991. This report reviews seven countries where there have been distinctive developments in educational assessment: France, Germany, The Netherlands, Spain, Sweden, Britain and United States of America. Each of these countries has adopted a different pattern of assessment, reflecting an "assessment culture: (to quote from the report), a culture based on different values and remarkably resistant to change. But the same issues arise in each of the countries; and the report focuses on two strategies which have been used for educational reform through changes in assessment: national testing, and new forms of assessment.

i) National testing is a new political imperative in what was formerly seen as primarily a professional and pedagogical concern: the use of assessment for monitoring and accountability in national systems, especially in terms of nation-wide testing of students' achievement in basic skills or core subjects.

ii) The other strategy, new approaches to assessment, represents a paradigm shift towards integrating assessment with learning: continuous assessment using students' regular work rather than formal examinations or standardised tests, records of achievement, school-based assessment, self-assessment by students, using the results formatively as feedback and diagnostically for guidance to reinforce learning, to help define objectives and to encourage learners to take greater responsibility for their own learning.

At first sight, these two strategies appear to be in conflict, the second being favoured by the professionals in education, against pressure for the first from politicians, parents and administrators. The first is an assessment-led curriculum, based on a centre-periphery model of change; the second is curriculum-led assessment, based on a user-centred model. As a result there is an ideological divide between those who hope to raise standards by more extensive testing and those who hope to improve the quality of learning by using different methods of assessment. Can one form of assessment satisfy both these requirements? Maybe we should acknowledge that assessment performs multiple functions and therefore should adopt a variety of forms. But are the two requirements fundamentally irreconcilable? Or will the one which is seen as involving "higher stakes" dominate the other?

Our report reviews the two strategies impartially, and concludes hopefully with the aspiration that we can reconcile the two requirements, recommending a form of national testing which will support the curriculum reforms which we see as desirable, and patterns of school-based assessment which can answer to the demands for accountability and guarantee quality of learning. But in order to sharpen the debate in this session, let me declare my own preference as a challenge. My fear is that, in the attempt to reconcile these two very different requirements, the demand for accountability, for certification and selection, for hard evidence, will take precedence over the equally legitimate requirement that assessment should promote learning; that the two cannot readily be reconciled, and that, particularly in the design of national testing, accountability will take precedence over learning, because it involves "higher stakes". Much of the work of OECD in recent years has been concerned with performance indicators and methods of assessment which provide for control of the system. In contrast, in the professional field, among teachers and researchers, the outstanding development of recent years has been towards a deeper understanding of learning, towards an integration of assessment and learning, aimed at promoting growth rather than learning: in short, assessment should be viewed "as part of learning, rather than a judgement passed on performance once learning is over" (Hargreaves, 1989). The emphasis on performance indicators, accountability and national testing puts this approach to assessment at risk. It puts the interests of the learners as subordinate to the requirements of management and control.

The "new" approach (so-called, thought what is new in one country may be established practice in another) covers a wide variety of methods: continuous assessment, greater use of extended writing and substantial projects, portfolios or records of achievement, criterion-referenced measures (instead of norm-referenced), "authentic" testing (using materials or contexts similar to those in which the knowledge and skills will be applied, instead of artificial paper-and-pencil tests), an emphasis in tests and examinations on problem-solving and knowledge application rather than on recall, and greater reliance on teachers' estimates and learners' self-assessment. Using methods such as these, it is claimed, assessment will be more valid and less stressful, and, most important, will support learning more effectively.

The principles underlying this approach to assessment derive from a constructivist theory of learning. Briefly, constructivist theory rests on the premise that learners build up their own understanding of knowledge, structuring it in their own personal way, in the search for meaning and understanding. Learning involves a personal construction of knowledge.

"Learning is not something that happens to students: it is something that is done by students" (Zimmerman & Schunk, 1989).

We do not learn by being told; or rather we may seem to learn, but it is a surface learning -- verbal learning -- which is quickly forgotten and cannot easily be retrieved or applied to novel situations outside the context in which it was taught. We learn through action an interaction: interaction with the material to be learned, with the teacher, with peers and with oneself. The role of assessment is to support this interactive process.

This approach cannot readily be reconciled with national testing. There are many issues to be resolved in national testing: what aspects should be tested, at what ages or stages, by what methods, who should decide, and, most important, by what criteria do we decide on these issues? The prime criterion, I suggest, is the effect on learning. Does it have a beneficial effect on learning?

The summative and certification function tend to be associated with pressures for accountability and classification, external demands, standardised scores and high stakes testing. In contrast, the formative and diagnostic functions reflect the demand of learning and individual differences, professional interests, using profiles rather than scores and low stakes testing.

This separation expresses a tension between assessment as an instrument of management or control, and assessment as a means to support learning; between accountability to society, and the promotion of learning. The analysis can be made more thoroughly if we try to draw a cognitive map. Drawing a cognitive map involves writing down all the concepts which have been mentioned, and then trying to group these concepts into clusters, identifying linkages and overlaps, and finally searching for the underlying dimensions which analyze and explain the arrangement of the concepts. This is my cognitive map:

Cognitive Map of Concepts Associated with Assessment

POWER	ACCOUNTABILITY	RESPONSIVENESS
	Society's demands	

SUMMATIVE · DIAGNOSTIC

NATIONAL TESTING

CERTIFICATION · TEACHER AS TRAINED PRACTITIONER

HIGH STAKES · PERFORMANCE INDICATORS · VOCATIONAL PREPARATION

APPRAISAL

MULTIPLE CHOICE TESTS · PROFILES

CONTROL ══ **ASSESSMENT** ══ GROWTH

Product · *Process*

MONITORING · PORTFOLIOS

STANDARDISATION · FLEXIBLE LEARNING PROGRAMMES

MINIMUM COMPETENCY · OBJECTIVES · COMMITMENT

AUDIT

LOW STAKES · CONTINUOUS ASSESSMENT · SELF-EVALUATION

TEACHER AS REFLECTIVE PROFESSIONAL · FORMATIVE

RESPONSIBILITY	PROFESSIONALISM	TRUST
	Learners' requirements	

The East-West dimension of the map is control and growth. At the West extreme, assessment is seen as an instrument of management and control; at the East extreme, assessment is seen as a means to learning, a process of growth. The North-South dimension is more questionable: I call it accountability and professionalism, the demands of society and the requirements of the learner. (The mathematicians may point out that the dimensions are not necessarily orthogonal; but the four quadrants produced by these dimensions are of equal importance.) We can label the four quadrants by the dominant characteristics of the concepts in each group: power, responsiveness, responsibility, trust.

Thus, Country A has a system of national testing and relies on expert consultants to interpret results and advise on improving efficiency: its location is in the top left quadrant. Country B has substantial autonomy for its teachers, and uses the schools as a basis for curriculum and staff development: its location is in the bottom left quadrant. But some personnel in Country B have reservations and favour a greater degree of accountability to parents and public: their position is in the top right quadrant. Country C uses assessment for management and control purposes, but with a light touch, trying to ensure a 'low stakes' approach, avoiding the arbitrary use of test scores for critical decisions and taking account of social factors: its location is in the bottom left quadrant.

Is it possible to embrace all the various meanings and uses of assessment in one ideal position, in the centre? I don't see the map as having this function: the appropriate position for any one country depends on its 'assessment culture', as our Report calls it -- the traditional attitudes towards assessment, the distinctive historical pattern of procedures, and the attitudes and values linked with these practices, established over time which provides a necessary continuity and stability but is strongly resistant to change. If we hope to use assessment to reform the curriculum, the map makes us more aware of the gravitational pull of 'power'. The future for assessment, and for curriculum, depends on where the power lies.

My argument (*not* the argument of the Report but one to open up the debate) is that we should be more concerned with the interests of the group with least power, the learners. In designing the future pattern of assessment, the prime consideration should be the effect on learning, and decisions about assessment should be made as close as possible to the learners.

In discussing assessment systems, we tend to focus on issues of organisation and technique, neglecting the affective and social factors involved in learning. This is a common fault throughout education: we treat learning as intellectual and rational, and neglect the feelings and attitudes and dispositions which influence the use we make of our knowledge and skills, and even determine whether we learn or not. Acquiring knowledge and skills is not enough: we also have to want to use the competence acquired, and to want to continue learning. A major factor which influences our attitude to learning is the learner's self-image. Building appropriate attitudes to learning, and to one's self as a learner, is a crucial part of teaching and learning.

Thus, in addition to the direct effect of assessment in publicly defining which pupils are regarded as successful or inadequate and which aspects of knowledge and skills are regarded as central or peripheral, assessment has a powerful indirect effect on attitudes and values within the learning process. It influences the disposition to learn, to further one's learning, to use strategies of thinking, to accept rational argument, and to tackle problem solving and critical reasoning. Positive attitudes are encouraged in a climate of learning which is tolerant of questioning and exploration, and are discouraged by an emphasis on memorisation and an authoritative regime. De Corte (1990) argues for a balance of requirements in creating "powerful learning environments... characterised by a good balance between discovery learning and exploration on the one hand, and systematic instruction and guidance on the other." Assessment is a powerful factor in creating this climate of learning.

Assessment, like management, has to be concerned with both control and growth. The Educational Testing Service in USA forecasts that "Educational testing will change more in the next ten years than it has done in the past fifty years." (ETS, 1990). It is important that its development should not be a separate issue but be planned as an integral element in the context of curriculum reform, and planned with the aim of providing learning, not just of control.

References

De Corte, E (1990) Towards powerful learning requirements for the acquisition of problem-solving skills, *European Journal of Psychology*, 5, 5-19.

Educational Testing Service (1990) *Helping America Raise Educational Standards for the 21st Century: 1990 Annual Report*. Princeton: ETS.

Hargreaves, A (1989) *Curriculum and Assessment Reform*. Milton Keynes: Open University Press.

Zimmerman, B J & Schunk, D H (eds) (1989) *Self-Regulated Learning and Academic Achievement: Theory, Research and Practice*. New York: Springer-Verlag.

MASS EVALUATION EXERCISES IN FRANCE SINCE 1989

Claude Thélot

I should like to outline our recent experience with evaluation and assessment. France has opted for mass education, and to make it as appropriate and effective as possible we are introducing new education policies at all levels in the system. They naturally cover a range of aspects: changes in curriculum and in the way knowledge is assessed, and changes in examinations which include new kinds of tools for teachers, in line with the new objectives. Since 1989 we have run exhaustive evaluations of all pupils, as part of this process, and that will be my main subject here. Opting for mass education also meant opting to make the French education system more visible, both to itself and to French society as a whole. Hence, while giving our teachers new tools, we were also aiming at more public assessment of the system: for both internal and external purposes, there is a need for public evaluation of teaching units, by which I mean the whole education system, or its regional components, or the individual schools in the system.

One area, in my view the chief area, where evaluation and transparency are relevant concerns the results that our education system achieves. Results without targets are of course meaningless, and without spending too much time on setting targets they do need to be stated, recognised and understood. In France the targets have been set in democratic fashion, in a broad Education Act. A school's results have to be assessed in terms of those targets.

There is thus a twofold requirement: to assist teachers, inter alia in interacting with pupils, and to evaluate and provide transparent results. I do not believe that at the start of the process, the position we are in today, the two requirements are necessarily incompatible.

We have been running exhaustive mass evaluation exercises since 1989 at three levels of the education system in France: for children about eight, for children about 11, and at the start of the *lycée* classes, for children between 15 and 18. In each case the evaluations, run at the start of the academic year so that they are not in any sense final examinations, were introduced by the Directorate for Evaluation and Prospective Analysis as elementary schools and later the *lycées* were being reformed. Assessment in the first *lycée* classes, for instance, was introduced at the start of the last academic year, as educational reforms were brought in. It is worth stressing the link between classroom tools and a new education policy to meet targets set by the country.

The actual assessment takes place at the start of the school year. It is not intended to test what pupils have learnt, but to identify the strengths and weaknesses for the year ahead. The assessment of each pupil's strengths and weaknesses will help teachers to cope with classroom diversity, handle their classes during the year, raise the standard of their teaching practise and take full account of the differences between pupils. The assessment may deal with knowledge, or with skills. At the *lycée* stage in particular, the focus is on very general capabilities and skills (observation, foresight, identification, etc.), not on specific knowledge.

The assessment is in no sense an examination. France is of course familiar with examinations, with nationwide tests such as the *baccalauréat*. But the pooling of marks gives a distorted view of teaching practice and what pupils are supposed to know. The mass evaluation at the start of the year is based on detailed targets for the coming year, set in terms of the general objectives of the school at each level. This means that the characteristics of each pupil can be identified in greater depth, and in a manner more relevant to teaching practice. The assessment protocols are prepared by working groups made up of teachers, inspectors and officials; a reflection, to some extent, of the education system.

The protocol is issued to all classes, and teachers are invited to supplement it with their own methods of assessing their pupils at the start of the year. (Long before this scheme was introduced, of course, the profession was conducting start-of-year evaluations, so it is quite legitimate for teachers to make use of methods that they regard as reliable together with the national protocol from the Ministry.) Last, an essential point, each class and each school is provided with software designed solely to use the assessment findings to help the teacher determine his teaching approach.

The clearest example is found in the initial *lycée* class. The assessment here was not initially devised to identify the standard of the pupils, but quite explicitly to help teachers introduce the main novel feature of the *lycée* reforms, the modular system. The modules are a major innovation in education practice in France: they are periods in the teaching programme not devoted to a specific subject but designed, via the teacher's subject, to familiarise pupils with transversal rather than subject tools, methodology in particular. The teacher works here with subgroups of the class, or with subgroups straddling two classes.

The modules are intended to alter both the teacher's own practice and the exclusive classroom style of teaching. The aim is that homogeneous pupil modules should be set up on a given aspect, or with a given objective, for a fortnight, three weeks or a month; then the module is changed, that is to say the group of pupils changes, and the teacher changes his teaching as well. To enable teachers to establish the most appropriate subgroup of pupils and the most appropriate type of teaching, they can make use of the start-of-year assessment. That makes it clear that the assessment is first and foremost a tool. Naturally, this was not what happened in all cases in October 1992. But in a good number of classes the assessment did help in establishing the modules.

The mass assessments at the start of the year are also the occasion for dialogue with parents in the case of smaller children and with the pupils themselves in the *lycée* classes. The dialogue is not about the examination that has just been taken. *Lycée* pupils have recently been guided into general or vocational courses, and are entering a different and in some respects disturbing world; dialogue can then be an opportunity for each pupil to take stock of what he is, what he knows, what skills and methods he possesses, and the project that he is forging for himself. France's Education Act places pupils at the centre of the education system, and this entails a number of things: in particular, it means the gradual development of a project that the pupil personally builds up. The education system has to supply him with the relevant tools, and one is the start-of-year evaluation and the resultant stock-taking.

A number of teachers were surprised by the assessment protocol. Any mass evaluation has to be based on a very sound protocol (like a good novel, it has to stand up on its own). The teaching body has to accept the protocol as a credible tool designed to assist them; for the protocol to stand up, it must be of very high quality. Many teachers were involved, in french, maths, history and geography, english, german, industrial science and technology, tertiary science and technology, in short all the disciplines where assessment took place. In many cases the protocol was an opportunity for teachers to consider their teaching methods, and the requirements that the education system as a whole was making clear via the protocol. The mass assessments are tools for dialogue, but of course regulatory tools as well; they assist teachers with their practice, and should also help them to a fuller understanding of the requirements that the education system places on pupils and on the teachers themselves. To take one example, in southern France where the ability to speak english or german is

171

masked by the accent peculiar to French people living in that region, the modern language protocol contained an element of oral comprehension, on diskettes. This "woke up" a few of our teachers, by demonstrating the degree and nature of the requirements set by the general objective of modern language oral comprehension.

The second use of mass assessment, in addition to serving as tools in schools and classrooms, is the overall picture they provide of the condition and achievements of France's education system.

The system can valuably employ this tool (along with other assessments on sample groups of pupils) to supplement awareness of the achievements of the education system. They can help define the value added by education units, in particular the system as a whole or certain component parts of it. Value added indicators for each of France's regions were published six months ago, based on mass assessments of this kind. The purpose is not simply to record that a given region has satisfactory education results, but to compare its achievements with the results expected in terms of social structure or, more broadly, a number of characteristics of its inhabitants and pupils. To tackle the value added of a region or individual school in this way avoids snap judgements based on the results alone, by relating them to the progress achieved by the system and to its environment.

It would appear that mass evaluations can meet two objectives; no doubt more varied objectives will gradually appear. They can be teaching tools, and can form part of the overall assessment of the education system or particular parts (regions, etc.) of it. It is not clear, on the other hand, that they should be used for *public* assessment of the schools themselves, especially if confined to the results alone without accompanying value added indicators. (It should be borne in mind that mass evaluations in France are held at the start of the year; that means that they cannot be used to judge the results of the school that the child is attending when he is assessed.) But the exhaustive evaluations, published or not, must have functions other than purely educational ones. When it was stated publicly that a given region's value added was low, the authorities there and the teachers themselves were able to consider the possible reasons and act accordingly. Similarly, whether or not the results are published (and it may be better not to do so), for a school to receive its results corrected for the pupils' characteristics, together with the average results for the region or the whole country enables all those involved to see things in perspective. Although primarily educational tools, mass evaluations should also provide results which show how things really are, and hence lead on to action.

THE CONTRIBUTION OF INTERNATIONAL COMPARATIVE ASSESSMENT TO CURRICULUM REFORM

Tjeerd Plomp and William Loxley

Introduction

The OECD study entitled: Curriculum Reform: Assessment in Question (Nisbet, 1993) addresses many important relationships between curriculum and assessment using case studies from around the world. John Nisbet, Professor at the University of Aberdeen, Scotland and senior contributor to the OECD report, argues that the use of tests to monitor school standards has become a political imperative in most OECD countries. He rightly points out that redefining curricula without taking assessment into account will lead to failure (o.c. p 26). Nisbet asks to what extent can planned assessment become an integral part in monitoring curricula to achieve stated objectives or reform itself. He answers this question by categorically stating that once curricula are known and developed, assessment can and should be developed to monitor levels and change. But in addition, Nisbet believes equally in the reverse: namely, assessment-led curriculum reform. That is, assessment planned from the beginning as an integral element in monitoring curricula can contribute to curriculum objectives including the identification of a compatible learning style that accomplishes such objectives.

The above OECD study allows one to view the various assessment traditions of countries around the world to see how successful they influence change. In sum, the Nisbet study looks at the relationship between curriculum and assessment across nations and offers some general framework most educators can fully support. On the other hand, the Nisbet study does not address two major aspects of the curriculum and assessment relation. First, the study interprets assessment too narrowly by looking at only student achievement (via examinations or national survey scores), thereby emphasising student learning at the expense of classroom objectives and system wide goals. We argue that the concept of curriculum has several dimensions in addition to student achievement data because assessment procedures come from a variety of sources other than the student. Second, it was beyond the scope of the Nisbet study to ask whether international comparative assessment can contribute to curriculum monitoring and reform. That is, what value does educational assessment in the broader context of international world class standards offer above and beyond mere national assessments?

In this paper, we address the relationship between curriculum and assessment using a multi-faceted meaning of curriculum. We take the view that adding international comparative assessment will not only enrich national assessment practices, but also add a unique element to interpretation as well as shed light on alternative practices elsewhere which may lead to curriculum reform in other areas of the world.

Before presenting examples of how international comparative assessment can contribute to monitoring national curricula, we first present definitions of curriculum and assessment in their various contexts. Since examples are drawn from IEA research, the International Association for the Evaluation of Educational Achievement (IEA) mission and scope will be highlighted along with the IEA project research design and process.

The Curriculum viewed from Three Levels

What students learn is dependent on what teachers choose to teach them. In turn, what teachers choose to teach is dependent on course outlines, official syllabi, textbooks and the like. These documents are prepared and approved externally to the classroom or school, usually at the national, state or regional level by education authorities who mandate through public law the minimum breadth and depth of what is to be taught and learned. In turn, political dictates form the basis for curriculum developers, textbook writers and publishers when preparing materials from which schools and teachers make their selection. Curricula, therefore can be conceived at three levels: the nation, the school, the student, where each level can be measured, assessed and compared for degree of overlap and correlation. This model is presented in Figure 1 (Garden, 1987; Travers and Westbury, 1989).

Figure 1

Curriculum types applied in IEA studies

Level	Curricular antecedents	Curricular contexts	Curricular content
System	System features and conditions	Institutional settings	Intended
School or classroom	Community, school and teacher characteristics	School and classroom conditions and processes	Implemented
Student	Student background characteristics	Student behaviours	Attained

At the macro level of the education system (e.g., nation, region), there exists the *intended* curriculum laid down in official syllabi, course outlines, or exist as textbooks which represent shared conceptions by administrators, teachers and parents of what is important. At the meso level -- the school or classroom -- exists the *implemented* curriculum measured by course content, time allocations, instructional strategies, controlled by teachers. Finally, at the micro level of the student, one finds the *attained* curriculum measured by cognitive skills and attitudes of students which results from teaching and instruction of the prescribed curricula. These three aspects of curricula are interlocked and can be measured. National curricula can be assessed by examining national outlines, textbooks, exams, etc. to determine the range of content offered in any grade. Actual classroom curriculum content can be discerned from teachers and student behaviours based on questionnaires which measure what is learned, what is taught, and attitudes toward the teaching-learning process held by students and teachers.

In addition, curriculum antecedents such as the social background of the student's family or school neighbourhood as well as resources possessed by schools can be correlated with curriculum contexts (e.g., institutional setting, instructional processes, and student behaviours) to predict curricular outcomes. Assessment based on this three tier approach allow researchers to study national curricula on different levels. What is more, when the methodology and instruments are used across many nations,

174

the context can be expanded to a regional or international context. Finally, the general model can be used to generate and test a wide range of hypotheses within and between educational systems around the world; providing a powerful means to evaluate national curriculum quality and improvement based on "world class standards".

The Scope of Assessment

Nisbet (1993: 29) points out two uses of assessment: accountability and instructional evaluation. The first use is found among educational authorities wishing to monitor the efficiency of the overall education system and schools within that system. Accountability is a macro level tool. The second use provides feedback on teaching and learning for both teachers and students (o.c. p-30). Instructional use is a micro level tool closely tied to measuring learning outcomes based on instructional processes. This distinction between political and professional responsibility is manifest in these two uses of assessment, and one wonders to what extent these two assessment functions are compatible or reconcilable. In discussing the proposals for educational evaluation in Norway, Granheim and Lundgren (1991) conclude that the two approaches are indeed compatible.

The remainder of this paper presents examples which show international comparative studies do play an important role in the accountability function -- thus providing feedback at the macro and meso levels of educational system in addition to providing insight into assessment strategies and instruments used for instructional assessment purposes.

It is assumed that assessment is used to monitor curriculum context as well as content. This means that, given the purposes and goals of any education system at whatever level, data are collected to make judgments about the status of the system with the purpose to decide on action when necessary to improve schooling. In effect, we assume that educational systems at all levels are, in fact, learning systems amenable to change. The importance of including all three curricular levels stems from the fact that parents and students do have the right to expect quality education -- both up to date facilities and well organised curriculum and instruction. Monitoring the quality of the intended and implemented curricula is the responsibility of the proper education authorities. These authorities do not monitor for the sake of control, but for the sake of improving what student's learn (the attained curriculum), what and how teachers teach (the implemented curriculum), and what the community values (the intended curriculum).

Given the different curricular levels and their different assessment tools, one can be sure assessment will imply different approaches at different levels. For example, assessment questions will be related to:

- -- attained curriculum: student achievement and attitudes measured in international surveys via tests and questionnaires administered to random samples of students;

- -- implemented curriculum: what is actually being taught in the schools (called opportunity to learn in IEA studies), under what conditions (availability of textbooks, trained teachers, instructional processes, equal access by all students, etc.);

- -- intended curriculum: curricular content and objectives (via syllabi, minimum standards, national regulations in the area of teacher qualifications, curriculum content, examination results, etc.).

175

IEA: Mission and Research Process

IEA, the International Association for the Evaluation of Educational Achievement, was founded in the late 1950s as an independent international cooperative of research centres. At present IEA members number about 50 countries -- among them all OECD nations are present. IEA has as its mission the conduct of comparative studies focusing on educational policies and practices in order to enhance learning within and across systems of education (Hayes, 1993). In its studies, IEA does not focus merely on measuring student achievement, but also on the effects of school and home characteristics on learning.

IEA recognises two purposes of international comparative achievement studies: (1) to provide policy makers and educational practitioners with information about the quality of their education system in relation to relevant reference groups of similar nations; and (2) to assist researchers and policy makers in understanding the reasons for observed differences between educational systems. In carrying out studies, IEA researchers strive for two kinds of comparisons. The first consists of straight forward comparisons showing educational influences on international achievement scores or subscores. The second comparison looks at how well a country's intended curriculum (what should be taught) is implemented in the schools and mastered by students. A typical IEA study samples grade levels within three populations: primary, junior secondary and senior secondary. Usually a variety of tests and questionnaires are administered. For example a national questionnaire is administered to leading educators to determine the intended curriculum; a school and teacher questionnaire are administered to school officials and teachers to measure social background, attitudes, and instructional practices held by teachers -- leading to assessment of implemented curriculum; student questionnaires on social background, attitudes and achievement proficiency, all designed to assess the attained curriculum.

Over the years, IEA has conducted many surveys in a variety of school subjects such as mathematics (1966, 1981); science (1974, 1983); English and French as Foreign Languages (1973/4); Civics (1973/4); Writing (1984/5); Reading Literacy (1973/4, 1991). In addition to subject related studies, IEA surveyed Classroom Processes (1982); pre-primary child care (1988, 1992); and Computers in Education (1989, 1992). A major two-subject study is now underway to collect data in 1994 and again in 1998 in Mathematics and Science (TIMSS), while yet another Foreign/Second Language Study is planned for data collection in 1996.

The Impact of IEA Research at the National Level

An important reason why countries participate in IEA studies has to do with letting them review their own educational structures, practices and curricula in light of other educational systems using the same questionnaires. Garden (1987) reports, for example, that in the Second International Mathematics Study (SIMS), junior secondary school students in Sweden and New Zealand scored poorly. In Sweden a task force was set up to find reasons for this poor performance. For example, Husèn (1987) reported that due to concern by policy makers, entry level to teacher training institutes was raised. In New Zealand where mathematics syllabi were already under revision, curriculum writers were specifically instructed to add special emphasis to those subject areas found deficient in the New Zealand SIMS results compared to other OECD nations.

Perhaps the best example of how national policy makers and educators have benefited from international comparisons of achievement performance comes from the USA where analysis of SIMS data provided the Americans with many conclusions which are still having an impact on the way mathematics is organised in American secondary schools (McKnight et al., 1987).

The SIMS study looked at mathematics achievement and curriculum at junior and senior secondary school. At the junior secondary level (eighth grade in the USA), five major topics were included in the international test: arithmetic, algebra, geometry, statistics, and measurement. The senior secondary level examined only specialist mathematics programmes among twelfth grade college-preparatory students. Here, six topics were tested: number systems, sets and relations, algebra, geometry, elementary functions and calculus, probability and statistics. The following three findings are discussed along with their impacts on the mathematics curriculum in the USA.

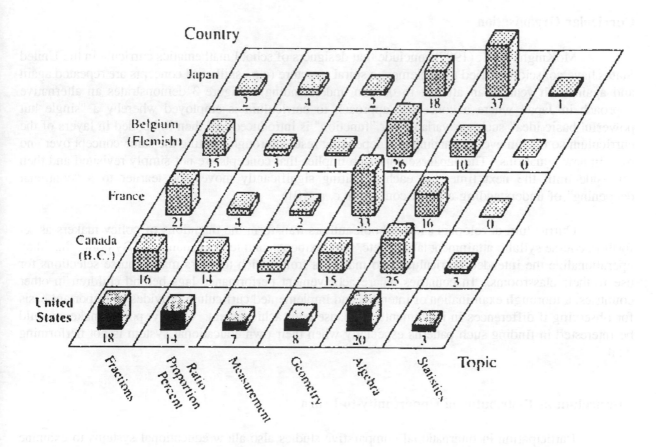

Figure 2

**Intensity of mathematics instruction at junior secondary level
(McKnight *et al.*, 1987)**

Curriculum as Distributor of Content

Figure 2 depicts the intensity of mathematics instruction at the junior secondary level based on teacher reports about percentage of class periods devoted to various mathematics topics (Mcknight et al. 1987). From this analysis, a content characterisation of the mathematics curriculum in 1981 was

177

derived. Given the time spent on fractions, ratio, proportion and percent, American junior students appear to be exposed heavily to arithmetic. By contrast, Japan has an algebra 'driven' curriculum while in France and Belgium (Flemish), the emphasis in 1981 was on geometry. Such data provides information about the implemented curriculum across nations for a given age level and may be useful in redesigning the intended curriculum especially when results show countries employing alternative designs perform better overall and in the case of the United States showed them that they relied too heavily on arithmetic and review without moving children readily into the more abstract subject algebra. The Japanese, by contrast, believe that a strong dose of algebra by age 13 has spill over effects to learning other mathematics topics as witnessed by the strong overall achievement performance of Japanese 13-year-olds (Burstein, 1993).

Curricular Organisation

McKnight *et al.*, (1987) conclude that designers of school mathematics curricula in the United States have consciously tried to implement a spiral structure (e.g., skills and concepts are repeated again and again each year in an attempt to deepen understanding). Figure 3 demonstrates an alternative approach in Japan where a concentric approach to curriculum is employed whereby a "single but powerful basic idea" such as "variable" or "function" is introduced and then imbedded in layers of the curriculum so that an ever-expanding and depending results through meeting the same concept over and over in new situations. The Japanese approach implies that concepts are not simply revisited and then set aside until the next time, but each revisiting significantly moves the learner to a "continual deepening" of understanding a given concept (o.c. p. 101).

Curriculum developers and textbook authors transform the intentions of policy makers as set forth in course syllabi, attainment targets, etc. into textbooks and teacher manuals. By doing this, they operationalize the intended curriculum into materials from which teachers make course selections for use in their classrooms. In countries where achievement performance lags behind children in other countries, a thorough examination of intended and implemented curriculum provides an important basis for observing if differences in implementation cause poor achievement. Clearly, policy makers would be interested in finding such patterns especially when their own educational system is not performing well.

Curriculum as Distributor of Opportunity-to-Learn

Participation in international comparative studies also allow educational systems to examine national data for uniquely national issues using international bench marks. Figure 4 illustrates the way the United States has traditionally employed four distinct types of curricula for grade eight mathematics. It shows that the arithmetic curriculum predominates in the "remedial" and to some extent in the "regular" eighth grade classes, while algebra, geometry and measurement are emphasised in "enriched" and "algebra only" classes.

The large differences by class type in the amount of algebra learned during the school year is clearly a function of teaching time since the algebra classes devote the majority of class time to that subject while remedial and regular classes devote little time. Figure 5 shows the relationship between opportunity to learn (implemented curriculum) and achievement in algebra (the attained curriculum). This kind of data in combination with results found in Figure 4 provide the basis for discussing how differences in the implemented and attained curriculum are affected by opportunity to learn which is just another term for exposure time to specific curricula. Such discussions inevitably lead to curricula improvement and may give rise to changes in the intended curriculum and ultimately, for example, in the allocation of the means to provide low-ability classes with extra opportunities to realise more challenging curriculum coverage, better instruction, and higher achievement scores.

Examples from Other IEA Studies

Other IEA studies report examples of how results from international comparative surveys are used to aid in monitoring the tasks of national, state, regional policy makers and educators. Examples from three IEA studies are reported below: science, reading literacy and computers in education.

Science achievement over time

The IEA Second Science Study (SISS) carried out in the 1980s (c.f., Keeves, 1992a, 1992b, Postlethwaite and Wiley 1992) looked at science achievement among 10, 14, and 17-year-olds in 23 countries world wide. The science data from the 1980s can be compared to science data from the first IEA science survey carried out in 1972. Figure 6, taken from Keeves (1992a, b) displays change over time in 12 selected countries for 10-year-olds. In preparing this chart, Keeves scaled common test items for both 10 and 14-year-olds from two time periods and created international scores linking science achievement in the 1970s and 1980s.

Given changes in science education between 1972 and 1984 (i.e., new technology, ecology issues, integrated sciences, inquiry based science, etc.), it is not easy to maintain identically valid science tests across time. However, among 10 and 14-year-olds around the world much basic science has remained the same. The results displayed in Figure 6 brought home to the Americans that, as in the case of mathematics, there were severe problems with the way science education was organized in primary schools in America. Clearly, curriculum distributes content. As James Coleman (1985) suggested after comparing IEA data for industrialised nations; those countries which appear to teach science intensively from an early age also tend to produce better able students later. According to Coleman, "... the very design of IEA studies, the fact that they cover educational systems that exhibit a greater range of variation than schools found in a single country ever do, makes IEA data a potentially rich source of information on the effects of schooling".

Reading literacy findings

The IEA Reading Literacy Study (Elley, 1992; Postlethwaite and Ross, 1992; Lundberg and Linnäkylä, 1993; Wagemaker, forthcoming) studied the relationship between teaching conditions, teacher characteristics, teaching strategies and student outcomes measured by three reading subscores: narrative, expository and document comprehension. Teaching aims of reading were rated by teachers and classified according to two dimensions and four poles (Lundberg and Linnäkylä, 1993):

teacher-centred skill orientation:

-- improving student reading comprehension;
-- extending student vocabulary;
-- increasing student reading speed;

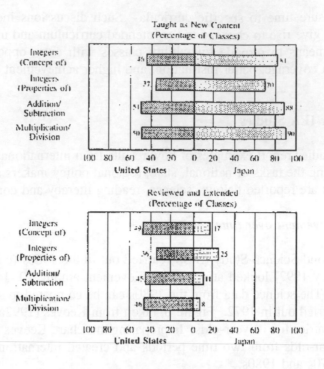

Figure 3: Illustration of spiral and concentric curriculum (from McKnight *et al.*, 1987).

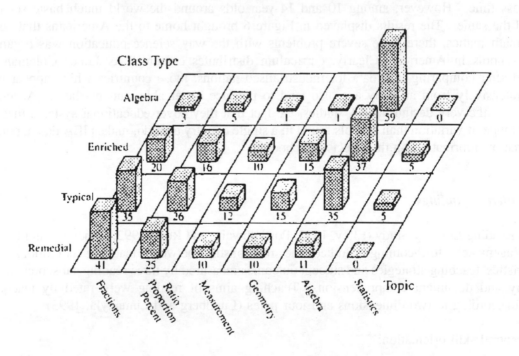

Figure 4: Four different eighth grade mathematics programmes in the USA (McKnight *et al.*, 1987).

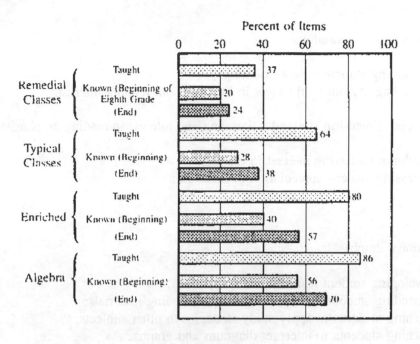

Figure 5: The amount of algebra taught and learned by students in each of four different class types in the USA (McKnight *et al.*, 1987).

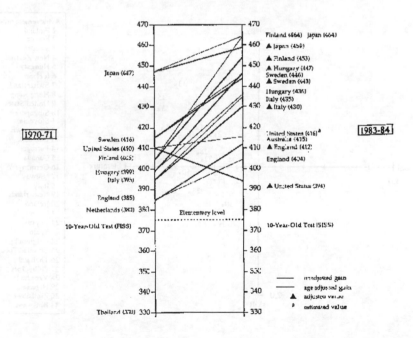

Figure 6: Mean Scale Scores for 10-year-old level, 1970-71 and 1983-84.

181

versus

student-centred orientation:

-- developing student critical thinking;
-- expanding student world view in literature and reading interest.

The second dimension stressed a literature and interest in reading emphasis:

-- developing a lasting interest in reading;
-- increasing student appreciation of literature;

versus

a functional emphasis:

-- developing student research and study skills;
-- expanding student variety and choice of reading materials;
-- teaching students to apply study strategies to other subjects;
-- teaching students to interpret diagrams and graphs.

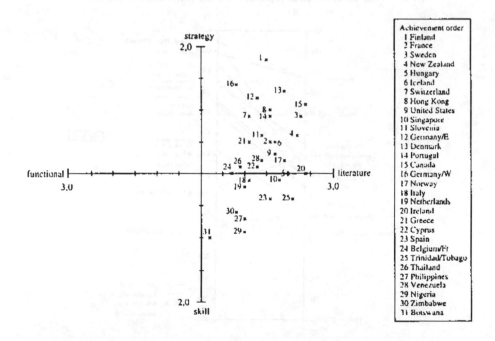

Figure 7:   Two dimensions of aims of reading instruction
(Lundberg and Lynnäkylä, 1993).

Lundberg and Linnäkylä (1993) concluded that the literature orientation was highly valued by teachers in every country perhaps because a large proportion were trained as literature teachers first and reading experts second. They selected the two dimensions orthogonally resulting in Figure 7. It appears that the quadrants where the functional orientation is combined with either strategy orientation or skill orientation are empty -- such combinations being rare or nonexistent at least in the 31 countries examined. It is noteworthy that the quadrant where skill and literature orientation are combined are occupied mostly by low achieving nations. These data may provide educational policy makers and reading experts the opportunity to think carefully about given the present findings in over 30 countries around the world, to decide whether it is still justifiable that no attention be paid to the functional orientation in reading education. Furthermore, reading educators in those countries where skill orientation is still the dominant didactical approach may wonder whether it would be appropriate to change this didactical orientation when formulating an efficient approach to the teaching of reading.

The diffusion of computers throughout schools

The IEA Computers in Education Study (COMPED) looked at the rate computers were disseminated in schools throughout about 20 countries world wide in 1989. A follow up was recently completed in 1992 and trend data will be available shortly. This study so far has revealed an interesting phenomenon with respect to the dissemination and implementation of computer use within schools -- a finding of use to the Dutch government. One of the goals of the stimulation policy of the Dutch government during the 1980s was to encourage the integration of computer use in existing school subjects. In the context of the international comparative study, data were collected about computer use in mathematics, mother tongue, and science as well as information on computer literacy. Figure 8 (Brummelhuis and Plomp, 1992) reveals that in 1989 computers were not much in use in these subject areas among lower secondary schools. However, in 1992, computer use doubled.

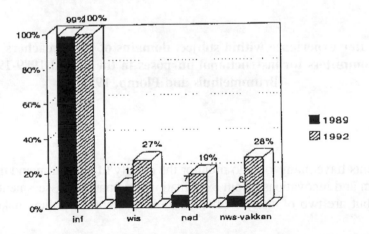

Figure 8: Percentage of junior secondary teachers in computer-using schools in 1989 and 1992, i.e. using computers for instructional purposes (Brummelhuis and Plomp, 1992)

183

The COMPED data show that the growth in computer usage in these three subjects is almost completely attributed to teachers working in a subject matter department where in 1989 no computer was used by any teacher (c.f., Figure 9). One can conclude from these data that the policy goal to broaden computer use in existing subjects has been realised at the school level. But, as Figure 9 shows, at the level of subject matter departments within schools, little increase in the numbers of teachers using computers for instruction has occurred. These IEA data revealed to Dutch school authorities a simple fact: computer use in existing subjects in junior high classrooms is not anchored in the curriculum but rather is a teacher led activity. This kind of information can lead to special measures to stimulate the integration of computers across the school curriculum.

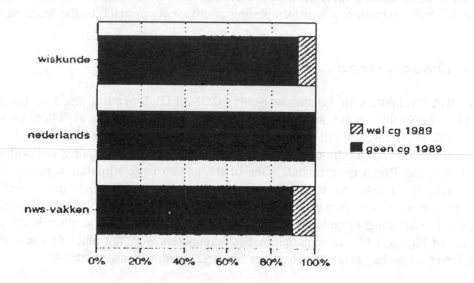

Figure 9: Computer experience within subject domains of those teachers who started using computers for instructional purposes in the period 1989-1992 (Brummelhuis and Plomp, 1992).

Summary

Governments have many tools to monitor the quality of education and thereby focus attention on curriculum reform and innovations. Both examinations and national assessments collect achievement data from students but are two of many evaluation tools available to policy makers.

This paper focused on two aspects of the relationship between curriculum and assessment. First, one can argue that assessment in a curricular context has to encompass more than just student achievement evaluation. By introducing three aspects of curriculum -- the intended, implemented and attained curriculum -- it can be shown that the curriculum is manifested at all three levels of an education system -- national, classroom and individual -- and furthermore can be assessed at each level. Next to this, one can argue that by studying a nation's curriculum in its international context, unique opportunities arise to study the many questions associated to the redesign of a curriculum programme. Using examples of past IEA studies, these points were confirmed. International comparative studies provide opportunities to examine a curriculum system "in situ" within the domain of many alternative systems. Besides this, international surveys also offer the possibility for national options which provide educational authorities unique opportunities to analyze in more detail patterns and organisation of their own educational system. In the present IEA Third International Mathematics and Science Study (TIMSS), many new approaches are being refined and developed, especially in analysing the curriculum of some 60 participating countries world wide as they apply to student success in mathematics and science (c.f., TIMSS, 1992).

References

Brummelhuis, A. ten, & Plomp, Tj. 1992. Resultaten van onderzoek naar computergebruik in het onderwijs (Results of research on educational computer use). The Hague, The Netherlands: Ministry of Education and Sciences. Opstap, 44.

Elley, W. 1992. The IEA Study of Reading Literacy. How in the World do Students Read? Hamburg, Germany: IEA.

Hayes, W.A. (Ed.) 1993. IEA Guidebook: Activities, Institutions and People. IEA: The Hague, The Netherlands.

Keeves, J.P. 1992a. Learning Science in a Changing World: Cross-national Studies of Science Achievement: 1970 to 1984. The Hague, The Netherlands: IEA.

Keeves, J. (Ed.). 1992b. The IEA Study of Science III: Changes in Science Education and Achievement: 1970 to 1984. Oxford, UK: Pergamon Press.

Loxley, W. 1992. How Academic Achievement Surveys Serve School Improvement. Paper presented at the VIIIth World Congress of Comparative Education, Charles University, Prague, Czech Republic.

Loxley, W. 1993. A Comparative Perspective on Functional Literacy Levels. in: Theoretical Issues and Educational Implications. Verhoeven, L. (Ed). Benjamins Publishing: Amsterdam, The Netherlands.

Lundberg, I. & Linnäkylä, P. 1993. The IEA Study of Reading Literacy. Teaching Reading Around the World. The Hague, The Netherlands: IEA.

McKnight, C. *et al.* 1987. The Underachieving Curriculum. Stipes Publishing Company: Champaign, Illinois, USA.

Nisbet, 1993. Curriculum Reform: Assessment in Question. OECD: Paris, France.

Plomp, T. & Loxley, W. 1992. IEA and The Quality of Education in Developing Countries. in: Vedder, P. (ed) Measuring the Quality of Education. Swets and Zeitlinger: Amsterdam, The Netherlands.

Postlethwaite, N. & Ross, K. 1992. The IEA Study of Reading Literacy. Effective Schools in Reading: Implications for Educational Planners. IEA: Hamburg, Germany.

Postlethwaite, N. & Wiley, D. (Eds.) 1992. The IEA Study of Science II: Science Achievement in Twenty-Three Countries. Pergamon Press: Oxford, UK.

Robitaille, D.F. & Garden, R. (Eds.) 1989. The IEA Study of Mathematics II: Contexts and Outcomes of School Mathematics. Oxford, UK: Pergamon Press.

TIMSS. 1992. Project Overview. TIMSS International Coordinating Centre, University of British Columbia: Vancouver B.C., Canada.

Travers, K. & Westbury, I. 1989. The IEA Study of Mathematics I: International Analysis of Mathematics Curricula. Oxford, UK: Pergamon Press.

Wagemaker, H., Taube, K., Kontogiannopoulou-Polydorides, G., Martin, M. (in press). The IEA Reading Literacy Study. Gender Differences in Reading Literacy. Hamburg, Germany: IEA.

V.   THE CURRICULUM FOR THE TWENTY-FIRST CENTURY

Priorities for decision and action

In considering the curriculum for the year 2000 and beyond, we must emphasize that the future is not something that happens but something that is constructed -- constructed on our choices or our failure to choose. Like the past, the future holds unpredictable elements, but it is apparent that we can help to give it shape. That shape depends more on our will and capacity to deal with value issues arising from our social and technological developments than it does on our capacity to predict. Escalating unpredictability need not mean escalating uncertainty. We need to accept that technology only changes possibilities. It is our choices from those possibilities which will build the future. The nature of the major problems which face us show us clearly the nature of those choices. They are not technical but moral choices. They express our beliefs and aspirations about a good society. In this final section, we shall consider the key issues for the 'curriculum of the future', sketching the major problems and possibilities.

As we consider the enormous sweep involved in the social and technological changes in our societies, and as we seek to make a constructive and creative effort to shape the future, what are the priority areas for decisions, studies, actions? That will be the thrust of this section of the paper, picking up the thinking of the earlier sections.

i)   The first requirement is an acceptance of the aim defined, a high quality education and training for all, as a political, social and educational priority.

ii)   The second priority, contingent on the first, is the recognition of the key implications of that commitment for all students. Two aspects will be considered specifically:

-- the reconception of education and schooling, encapsulated in the term life-long learning;
-- the development of the idea of a core curriculum, as a common curriculum, as a required curriculum.

iii) This priority is for a new pedagogy recognising that our previous patterns are not enough for this new challenge and that quite new possibilities exist, in learning opportunities and situations, in the conception of learning. This will be considered under the following aspects:

-- an information society;
-- recognition of broader approaches to the concept of learning;
-- re-valuing teaching;
-- involving the community;
-- involving students.

iv)   This priority relates to the role of assessment and evaluation in the development of quality in education.

A commitment to quality for all

A feature of education for the future will undoubtedly be the expansion of access, to include all students at least for the equivalent of the primary and secondary years. To move beyond slogans and make the statement "a quality education for all" will be the major challenge. In our current education, success in schooling is heavily dependent on social background, with the socially deprived performing more poorly at all stages and with the disparity increasing with time. With the need to extend old areas in the curriculum, to introduce new areas and to reach higher standards of achievement in both, the task of making this slogan a reality is massive. For the sake of equity to individuals and for the sake of cohesion in our society this reality must be achieved. We should not accept the concept of a society with a large and permanent under-class, limited in their opportunities for work, for social participation and for individual fulfilment. There are major possibilities available to us and we will need to pursue these vigorously. The alternative is a deeply divided society where a substantial minority has no access to permanent work and little chance to participate effectively in society. As mentioned before, merely the achievement of higher participation will not in itself guarantee success. This was illustrated by the February 10, 1993 report of the Audit Commission in the United Kingdom. They reported substantial, although unevenly distributed, increases in participation, to 67 per cent of 16 year-olds, and approaching 50 per cent of 17 year-olds. Unfortunately, reported the Commission, about one-third of the students either drop out before completing their courses, or fail to obtain a qualification at the end. The Commission sets this loss in money terms at about £500 million. (Reported in *The Guardian*, February 11, 1993). In terms of individual lives the cost may be higher. The source of the figures is coincidental. Many other countries would report similar occurrences. The reactions of many students to increased periods of schooling are either of boredom or of active hostility. Again, the words of the Minister's Communiqué apply: "more of the same" will not meet the challenges of the 21st Century.

Implications of a commitment to all

Lifelong learning. A major aspect will be a re-consideration of the way we conceive schooling. While it is essential that we increase levels of achievement for all, this does not imply that we are limited to the current conceptions of schooling. Christopher Ball writes on the powerful concept of life-long learning.

"Our hopes of health, wealth and happiness depend on learning -- our own and that of others. Just as the medieval world relied on religion for answers to all important questions, and the modern world has looked to politics for solutions, so in the post-modern world of today and tomorrow it is learning that provides the key to prosperity. In short, the provision of lifelong learning for all is the new agenda for systems of education and training, typically designed in another age on the basis of three false premises: the idea that they should serve only an elite of fast learners; the belief that initial education can not be sufficient; the prejudice that education and training are different in kind. ......The principle of lifelong learning for all inevitably offers a resounding challenge to initial education and the schools. .....In particular the school curriculum is bound to be affected once it is clearly recognised that all pupils are to continue their learning throughout their lives" (Ball, 1993).

For Ball, this concept sees the school curriculum as the first of three linked phases of life-long education, foundation, formation and continuation. Considering it rigorously in this light, introduces new criteria for selection of the school curriculum. Equally importantly, it opens up new pathways by which people can obtain the qualifications they wish. This broadening of education from the narrow concept of schooling will be significant.

The core curriculum. The re-conceptualisation of the curriculum which sees it as a foundation stage for our continued learning, broadens the concept of literacy. The early emphasis on the three R's, reading, writing and arithmetic, was an attempt to define for the period what students *must* know. That concept is still valid but now has a broader range of implications. Literacy, as the capacity to use a particular body of knowledge and of skills, now needs to cover a much wider range of human activities: science, the arts, the humanities, technology, economics, politics, mathematics. What is involved here is the need for a rigorous and continuing cultural analysis which takes our culture from a variety of perspectives, to define a new literacy, a cultural literacy.

Considering these as complementary ways to approach the development task gives a depth to the concept which is absent from a specification of subjects as the sole measure. Richard Pring (1989) spells out a number of similar ways in which a core curriculum can be specified. In whatever way it is approached, some principles apply.

Breadth: Contact with the major areas of learning.
Balance: Appropriate emphasis throughout compulsory schooling to the different areas.
Relevance: Seen by the parents and students as meeting current or future needs.
Focus: Related to abilities and needs of the full range of students.
Coherence: The studies relate to one another.
Continuity: There is a meaningful sequence in development.

Possibilities for a new pedagogy

An information society. The new information technology will open up entirely new possibilities for education and can, potentially, make possible the lifelong learning that has been the preserve of an elite. Access by individuals to multiple sources of information is now possible instantaneously and the modes of delivery will become easier and more open. Individuals can now work together in learning and in production through information technology. As the OECD Programme on Educational Building (PEB) stated in the 1992 Seminar:

"Learning will become a more diverse networked activity for all ages of students and only part of it will take place in permanent community facilities, designed to provide a social and resource focus in the form of a welcoming and technologically democratic architecture" (PEB, 1992).

Thus, education now becomes possible, separate from schools and teachers, in a way open in the past to very few. Of course we must remember that many technologies in the past have been predicted to transform eduction. Since printing developed, no others have done so. We can be at the beginning of a new transformation.

The new technology can be used as a means of control, or an avenue of privileged access. If equity is a major goal of our societies, as it should be, no group should be excluded from access. This will mean that the needs of the disabled and disadvantaged should be given special recognition as the technology can undoubtedly be of major benefit. The same need applies to the economically deprived and to rural and isolated students.

A feature of the new technology is the greater choice of options and methods becoming available to individuals, the so-called "autonomy of learners". This may take place quite rapidly but, however rapid it may be, it offers entirely new possibilities. One responsibility of systems will be to ensure that there are worthwhile options available and another to ensure that the organisation of teaching and learning provides appropriate opportunities. The impact of the new information technology on the curriculum has been very significant in OECD member countries, particularly since the early 1980s. OECD has played a major role through its own programmes in documenting the very diverse and substantial initiatives, which relate not only to new subject-matter to the curriculum but to the introduction of new possibilities and capacities in every area of the curriculum.

Among the many major changes from this technology, the use of buildings for education will need to be reconsidered. Since this may imply quite different use of space for group and individual learning, for library/resource areas, for movement and preparation spaces, building design will demand particular flexibility since the pace of change in this area is rapid.

Recognition of broader approach. The broader approach to the concept of intelligence by writers such as Gardner, mentioned earlier, have great potential in themselves and particularly for the more varied school population. The essential change is the change from valuing only one type of thinking, the convergent thinking involved in book learning, to valuing many different phases of human activity. This can make major changes to teaching and to assessment as we learn to value and encourage the full range of human endeavours.

Revaluing teaching. One of the more difficult aspects of schooling is the reduced status afforded to teachers. Where the teacher was once one of the few educated people in a community, now there are many with high qualifications. Further, the demand for teacher numbers has grown so much with higher participation rates over the years, and smaller classes, that very large numbers of teachers are required. This has often meant lower salaries for teachers, compounding and confirming the lower status. This is not universally true. In Japan, the concept of the teacher as "*sensei*", is one of respect and admiration and this attitude is reflected in teacher salaries. The demand for high quality teachers in the years ahead will not be met unless there is a substantial change in standing. In terms of the social value of teaching, such a revaluation is justified.

Involving community. There will be, of necessity, a stronger link between schools and their communities, if there is to be a significant advance in the quality of schooling. Demographically, this is difficult as much smaller proportions of the community have direct links with school. This will provide a continuing challenge.

Involving students. The success of curriculum reform will depend finally on the extent to which the goals of reform become the goals of students, and the processes of reform are accepted as the appropriate. An unwilling or hostile sector of the school population, even a passive sector, can spell failure.

Assessment, evaluation and quality

Evaluation is one of the major aspects of curriculum and because of its powerful impact on students is potentially a significant influence in curriculum reform, an area where there are notably few powerful influences. There are frequent denigratory references in education to "evaluation-driven curriculum" or, more specifically, "exam-driven curriculum". This becomes a problem when, as is often the case, the examinations or the more general evaluation, are limited or distorting. Our efforts should be directed, not at reducing the influence of evaluation, but at making sure that influence is entirely consistent with the goals and aims of the curriculum. This is not an easy task as many studies have shown the tendency in testing to be restricted to aspects which are easy to assess, such as rote learning. Our evaluation methods are now sufficiently sophisticated to avoid this limitation and make the evaluation, and also the pedagogy, entirely consistent with the statements of purposes.

Respondents to the questionnaire on standards in education indicated, almost universally, a concern for education standards, often a contentious issue. For example, the New Zealand statement identifies the following purposes for specifying achievement standards:

> "-- to diagnose the level of achievement of individuals or groups in relation to the learning objectives;
>
> -- to monitor student competence in a skill or area of learning;
>
> -- to measure the effectiveness of teaching strategies and learning programmes;
>
> -- to plan appropriate improvement or extension work;
>
> -- to monitor individual or group progress throughout schooling;
>
> -- to provide feedback to students and parents on the student's level of learning achievement."

The breadth of these purposes implies that a variety of approaches is required, including school and teacher-based assessment and also assessment which makes it possible to report using national standards.

The dual uses of assessment, as a means of assisting teaching and learning, as a means of process, school and system accountability are not simple alternatives but valid and necessary aspects of the use of information. It will be important for individual teachers and students to make decisions on their own progress. It is equally important for parents that they have meaningful information on their children's progress. It plays a key role in resource decisions at what the New Zealanders call transition points, levels of schooling at which decisions on progress and treatment will be made. At key points in the educational career, standardized results are a guarantee of competence in particular fields, for example vocational qualifications. Paradoxically, the introduction of the open learning concept as a part of life-long education makes it more important that assessment at key stages should be in comparable forms.

These issues, of purposes and of the processes through which purposes are achieved, were the focus of Robert Carneiro's paper and of the panel discussion which comment on that paper.

Paper 17: CURRICULUM FOR THE 21ST CENTURY

Roberto Carneiro

Introduction

The Secretariat's Background Document to the Conference -- CERI/CR(93)1 -- provides an excellent comprehensive discussion of the major issues at stake in this forward looking exercise.

Moreover, the OECD has published to date an impressive set of frontier thinking reports focusing on the same broad matter, summarising relevant studies and enquiries conducted in a vast sample of Member countries.

Thus, it is my belief that at this stage of the Conference, at the concluding session of three intensive working days, there is not much left of radically new or profoundly innovative to be remarked which could add substantively to the pool of thinking so far generated.

Under the circumstances my personal contribution to this Theme will follow the frame of topical issues designed in an open-end fashion and aimed at fostering avenues for discussion.

Grassroots institution development vs. central curriculum reformism

We are witnessing the last laps of an era.

This period covering at least the last 30 years is characterised by *wholesale curriculum reformism*.

Year after year, country after country, system after system, the educational establishment addressed reform as a necessary and mythical thrust.

In a provisional balance and generally speaking, this value loaded approach -- good governance was synonymous of engaging in bold programmes of global educational change -- fell short of all the bright promises at the very outset.

In the one hand, actual outcomes remained far from initial expectations.

In the other, the harsh realities of public finance trimmed down over ambitious targets and cushioned triumphal trumpets.

Finally, political cycles and voluntaristic *diktats* revealed themselves alien to school cycles and to the pulsation of real events down the ladder to the classroom level.

General dissatisfaction with compulsive reformism led to the most frequent interrogations:

"Why is it that the reunion of such tremendous inputs -- human efforts, political will, finance, material resources -- lead to so meagre, frustrating, results?"

"Why is there registered a widespread sense of failure and such an outburst of disappointment after so many dreams and generous ideals were put forward?"

Among several explanations I shall offer two:

a) Systemic reformism is by and large deep-rooted on *supply side strategies* and central approaches: legislation, national expertise, training, deployment of additional resources.

Seldom is curriculum change *a product of effective demand* generated down-up.

b) A typical global curriculum reform requires 5 to 10 years between research, preparation, design, experimentation and final assessment, as well as informing, convincing and mobilising the main actors in the educational scene.

By the time a wholesale conducted reform comes to its conclusion, the environmental conditions have undergone radical transformation and the system laboriously set up is deemed obsolete.

Contemporary change occurs at a faster pace than any global reform implementation can achieve.

There is no easy answer to this paradox.

Nevertheless, I shall risk four propositions to steer future developments:

a) Avoid "stop and go" broad-cycle top-down *reformism* in favour of a dynamic *grassroots curriculum* change strategy.

b) Endorse the combination of flexible strategic goal setting at the conceptual level with a process of *"sustainable" adaptation/innovation* at the executive level.

c) Take into account that a versatile curriculum ensures the bloodstream of the school system and is the main provider of the oxygen to keep it alive.

The directions and flows of this stream require a wise *devolution* of responsibility to meet the temperature of the actual demanders of educational services. Decentralised selective innovation can be more rewarding than mere central reformism.

d) Rather than educational reform, the future will set premiums on the reform of actual educational institutions, that is to say the effective dissemination of an innovative spirit conducive to action rather than institutional reaction.

Network curriculum and school governance

Proper curriculum development is directly dependent upon adequate institution development processes and networking.

Thus, curriculum is never context or organisation-free.

The school culture is a potent local determinant of curriculum effectiveness and learning outcomes.

As in any other private or public organisation there are major institutional conditions seriously influencing the curriculum and school performance.

Among several traditional key factors the positive interplay of modern "intangibles" can single out excellence in a school.

Therefore, a sustainable curriculum momentum is linked to those key requirements of successful *school governance*: vision, leadership, mission assignment, partnership, community cohesion, human competence, institutional pride, self-esteem, value sharing, solidarity, and so forth.

Future competition will rest on such distinctive traits that will draw the line between winners and losers in the educational race.

Moreover, these new *flat school management styles* will call to an end the reminiscences of Taylorism and Fordism prevalent for decades in the pattern of school organisation.

Curriculum development endeavours must address school cultures and intangibles.

By the same token, an adaptive curriculum is hardly the rule in a bureaucratic driven, remotely uniform, school environment.

To the contrary, *market-type mechanisms and soundly competitive environments* can provide the thrust for permanent curriculum improvement.

A development strategy based on alternative choices and curriculum rewards must necessarily put premiums on the readiness to improve and the willingness to adapt.

A curriculum networking appeals to multiple sources and interactions.

From this angle, curriculum design bridges the school and a wealth of other relevant learning environments and facilities (family, media, peers, neighbourhood, municipality or county).

A balanced curriculum refuses a reductionist segmentation between different life patterns in the learners experience. It must seek to enhance the intelligibility and purpose of learning settings whichever they may be and however they may appear.

Core curriculum and life-long learning for all

The challenge of setting a system of life-long learning is not merely that of a proper educational supply.

As important as diverse and widespread supply are the skills of demand development and educational scheduling.

Initial training core curriculums must incorporate the tools to equip individuals with the capacity to conduct a constant assessment of educational needs and to manage the balanced convergence between the personal demand and supply of training.

Only the mastery of such skills can warrant a good administration of human capital and the counteracting of quick depreciation over time.

Life-long equity relies on education as the major catalyst towards individual *empowerment* to cope with change and avoid a huge underclass of social inadaptation and marginalisation.

The notion of core curriculum and national standards must be made compatible with that of *individualised curriculum* and the autonomy of learners.

A purposeful curriculum seeks both a full personal valuation and the provision of tools for universal understanding.

Can infinite human diversity allow a common denominator, a universal language to be shared between all peoples and nations, in other words a common curriculum "corpus" supporting a contemporary educational core across border lines and cultural boundaries?

Is a core curriculum trend a natural manifestation of a shared global village?

If so, there may be room for a *grand curriculum design* open to mutual acceptance, interdependence and tolerance, to cross-cultural fertilisation and to a wise balance between tradition and modernity.

The construction of a New International Order is no longer based on economic models, ideology or political boundaries.

Is there a role for Education and for a core curriculum towards global governance?

Certainly, if one can agree on the essentials of that New International Order: the place of culture, the language of science and technology.

School in the 21st century is caught between these two contradictory lines.

Science and technology tend to *unify*, whereas culture tends to *diversify*.

The school curriculum will have to represent the best balance between both trends, a wise choice in favour of universalism allowing both unity and difference.

Quality education for all, employability and vocational education

The overriding priority attributed to a quality education to all cannot minimise the close relationship between *school and work*.

Wealth-driven demands followed by inexorable patterns of educational massification very frequently lead to a strong socialisation towards general education.

Vocational education is often the residual stream left for the underprivileged and the only alternative to potential school drop-outs.

Very often, the school curriculum stresses this bias.

This dual reality is a most dangerous current.

It can only be reversed if the school curriculum including its core encompasses a minimum threshold *vocational education for all*.

In this respect a curriculum architecture for the 21st century must help form highly adaptive citizens and professionals.

Employability is no longer a function of narrow curriculum contents but the consequence of broad-base curriculum designs.

To this purpose, employability relates to skills allowing a better grip on *transitions* from known structures to unknown environments.

Thus, a modern curriculum should cope with fine-tuning transitions:

a) Minimising trauma inside the school system and between educational cycles.

b) From school to working life.

c) Between working environments and learning opportunities in a life-long education strategy.

A media-friendly curriculum

The gap separating school and mass-media is enormous.

Television is regarded as school's enemy number 1.

In the other extreme, school is regarded by the media as a hopeless case of miscommunication, a sort of museum full of spider webs and engaging in strange archaic procedures.

These contrasting views are difficult to link together. Yet, a quality education for all may never be achieved without an effort to bring to the educational forefront the wide range of information and communication technologies.

Children spend on average 25 per cent more of their time watching television than they spend in the classroom. Television sets, video recorders, radios, and home computers form the most impressive paraphernalia of disseminated instructional opportunities in the modern world.

The spread of the media and the information society constitute a constant threat on the traditional fragmented curriculum, split in bits and pieces, slow to meet the speed and the scope of daily challenges.

To inform is no longer the school's monopoly not even its privilege.

In an open competition the school will necessarily lose out to the mass-media. This is a hopeless cause.

Rivalry is hardly the recommended strategy.

School and media are confronted with the formidable task of seeking strategic alliances to improve the instructional modes and foster the effectiveness of educational programmes.

A *media friendly* curriculum will encompass the full length of *communication skills* and accommodate the wealth of new technologies now available and widely utilised to captivate audiences in a media-dominated society.

A complete recital of these possibilities is unnecessary. Among the most common technologies which remain alien to the majority of classrooms are: illustration and visualisation techniques, ultra-high definition, microscopy, compact and digital discs, computerised graphics, modern design, stimulating sets, use of colour, light and sound, videotext, teletext or teleconferencing, multi-sensory forms or virtual reality processes, data bases, etc..

A media friendly school will also turn to the press, radio or television broadcasts as a fundamental source of learning situations.

Further *media literacy* is a major school challenge.

Time and space are highly disputed commodities in the media. Usually they are the most scarce resource when dealing with fierce competition for clients.

The mass-media deliver instancy and immediateness in a volatile consumption-oriented environment. Under these severe circumstances, cognition and perception are not allowed *critical time* to evolve.

School can provide a wise *time management* and a balanced allocation of this preciously abundant resource in the formal education system to the benefit of unified knowledge, self-fulfilment and purpose.

Education requires strategic time that is unavailable in the media vertigo.
Personal and social development are certainly time consuming. School can provide critical time to build sense and to unveil meaningful patterns where apparently the landscape bears nothing but an aggressive succession of information via "flashes".

If time availability is clearly assimilated as a major curriculum resource then the management of time will become an integral and important message of school education.

Later, in life, *time availability* in an increasingly leisure society and an economy of unemployment will not turn into a major factor of *distress or wastage*. Rather it can be assumed as a most *precious factor of human advancement*.

PANEL DISCUSSIONS

The six panellists followed the presentation by Roberto Carneiro. They were asked to develop a particular aspect of their own choice from the Carneiro paper, as a focal point for further discussion.

1.   Dr John Singh

While pupils and students are clearly the main recipients of education and must be central to its concerns there is an increasing concern to locate provision within the broader context of all of those with an interest either as providers with an involvement in the process of benefit from its outcomes. The interested parties are easy enough to define. One of course is the public at large as represented by government who are major players by virtue of their responsibility for policy and financial provision. Another is parents and other members of local communities as represented by local authorities or governing bodies of institutions who usually take on delegated or devolved responsibilities from government but who can locate provision within local priorities. A third is the range of receiving bodies who look to education to provide them with the means of furthering their commercial and professional concerns and includes business and industry. And then there are the educational institutions themselves whose professional relationships with the pupil and student body give them direct insights into educational need at the individual level.

While the identification of stakeholders is fairly straightforward what is more complex is the extent to which each of these interested parties do or should influence the detail of what is taught and learnt in educational institutions. In the United Kingdom, for example, there is an increasing responsibility taken by central government to ensure that curriculum detail, assessment and institutional quality should meet national requirements while giving more and more responsibility for management of the process at the point of delivery. This is usually the individual institution within the context of school governorship elected by parents; community thus largely being defined within the parent body. However, I am not aware of any serious attempt to define what the relative influence of the various stakeholders might reasonably be to deliver a response to their concerns while at the same time ensuring that the best quality education possible is available to the pupil/student body. This should be a matter for further detailed analysis.

The issue of quality assurance is of course related to the points made above. It raises the issue of institutional and system quality and while including quantifiable input and output data, goes beyond that and raises questions of how more complete judgements of institutions might be made taking account of matters such as value added, the social and cultural development of pupils and other issues which are less amenable to measurement than some aspects of educational provision. There is also the matter of the means by which quality assurance should be undertaken and by whom.

There appears to be a clear trend, particularly but not exclusively, among the English speaking countries to require outcomes known publicly in individual and aggregated form locally and nationally. This reflects a general concern that there should be criteria for judging whether in such an expensive provision as education there is value for money. Alongside this is the concern that in market oriented economies that the consumer should have enough information about individual attainment and institutional quality to enable choice to be made. Of course all evaluation/review/appraisal/inspection systems properly argue that their concern is to identify strengths and weaknesses to bring about improvement both in the quality of the process and the resources made available.

The process of external examination of institutions appears to be developing rapidly ranging from peer review in South Australia through to government contracted teams of independent inspectors in the United Kingdom with many variations in between carrying out quality assurance procedures. It would be useful if the various approaches being currently implemented could be analyzed and compared with a view to identifying the relative effectiveness of different systems but also to explore how the results of institutional and systems inspection and can be undertaken and presented to take account of issues such as value added, social and cultural development with are raised above.

2.   Dr Walo Hutmacher

Rethinking the culture of the school

In the context of the changes in society and education systems that are taking place in all Member countries, several speakers at this conference have emphasised the need for inventing a new culture of the school. They have thus proclaimed the need for a new culture of teaching and learning as human processes, for a new culture of assessment, and for a new conception of knowledge and skills. No doubt one might add to this the need for a new culture of the cultural power or cultural dominance of schools at a time when this is being challenged by the tremendous expansion of a broad array of media which provide new ways of informing and educating the young.

First, I would like to discuss briefly the term culture. If we take an anthropological definition of this concept (although not all participants may agree with this), it seems to me that we can consider the culture of the school as a set of perceptions, beliefs, convictions, practices and techniques that educational practitioners share about school, teaching, learning, assessment, etc. Most of the features of this culture have been inherited from the past, and have been instilled in all of us. This culture, however, is not something that has been taught in any formal sense of the term as part of an official curriculum. Rather it has been absorbed through experience, practice or, as it were, by osmosis or immersion. It is the result of the simple fact of going to school. Experts often point out that in our countries everyone has attended a school, and then usually go on to lament the fact that, because of this, everyone claims to know about education. And the truth is that everyone does know something about it. Aside from specifically cognitive learning, which is set out in the curriculum and which is assessed, the very fact of attending school is educational in itself. Through their experience of schooling, users assimilate a set of perceptions, beliefs, social practices and techniques which are specific to educational institutions. This assimilation is unavoidable, because in each of our lives school is the framework of our daily existence for a number of years. In addition to the long period of immersion within the school culture, two aspects of this process of assimilation tend to ensure that the marks it leaves are particularly profound and long-lasting.

On the one hand, this immersion begins at a very young age (younger and younger, in fact) in each of our lives, at an age when children do not yet have the information and the conceptual tools which will later enable them to distance themselves somewhat from events. The younger they are, the more they tend to consider school as being "always thus", a pre-existing and unchanging world which is beyond question. What I am saying is in no way meant as a criticism; I am simply stating a fact. The perceptions, beliefs and practices which a child encounters at school will be accepted by him as the way things are; he can choose neither his classmates, nor his teacher, nor the teaching methods, nor the disciplinary practices, nor his schedule, nor the subjects to be studied. Whatever the prevailing school culture may be (even the most libertarian one), it is this that the individual child will assimilate, at least during the first six to eight years of school. Admittedly, pupils may feel and even express their likes or dislikes, their acceptance or rejection of the system, but they are in no position to contest it seriously. For one thing, power is overwhelmingly in the hands of adults and, secondly, the children are not yet able to know or imagine alternative school cultures. They will, however, in the meantime have undergone their own individual experience of school and will have assimilated a set of perceptions, beliefs, convictions and practices which will remain deeply rooted in their way of thinking as the permanent foundation for their relationship to school, learning and formal education. This experience will also be the basic yardstick by which they will judge alternative educational theories or practices with which they may later come into contact.

The assimilating of this school culture -- what we could call the informal curriculum, or what English-speaking sociologists call the hidden curriculum -- enables each of us to build an image, a perception of what a school is, of what one does or is supposed to do there as either a pupil or a teacher, of the games that are played there and to what end, of how things are done, etc. In this sense, we can speak of a "theory" of school as a form of "knowledge" retained long after direct involvement in the environment in which one acquired this has ceased. The quotation marks here mean that it is a theory that is not recognised as such. The way it is learned -- whether we term this informal, tacit, implicit or practical -- means that in most respects it is, as Pierre Bourdieu has said, a theory shaped by practice, in action, and one which cannot properly be put into words, but exists primarily in and through praxis (action or judgement). This "practical" type of contact with the outside world governs most of our actions; it is highly efficient from the standpoint of managing our daily life, as it enables us to decide and act "spontaneously" in most situations without the need for lengthy deliberation. The nature of a practical theory is precisely that it seems so "natural", so "automatic" in a world that it makes familiar because we have forgotten the learning processes on which this familiarity is based; it is a familiarity which allows us the luxury of overlooking the fact that what we know we have had to learn. A practical theory is also cut off from conscious thought, and is impervious to the learned arguments or questioning of experts or to formal, logical analysis; often, it will resist even in the face of empirical proof of its fallaciousness.

With respect to the physical world, the natural sciences have taught us to abandon certain subjective impressions in the light of our formalised knowledge, based on theory and/or proven by observation or demonstration. Thus, even if we continue to say that "the sun is going down", our reason accepts as true, in spite of our strong subjective impression, that objectively it is the earth on which we are standing that is turning on its axis. Likewise, regarding schools (and more generally regarding education), each of us has a practical theory, based on our collectively shared practical experience[1]. To the despair of many specialists in the science of education, most people do have just such a practical theory based on a whole set of inherited perceptions, feelings and beliefs.

In this respect, teachers and school administrators are not necessarily any different simply because they have received formal pedagogical training. In many ways, their professional training began much earlier, since their first experience of school also goes back to when they were four or six years old; that was their first contact with the "world" of school, with its specific ways of communicating,

---

[1]

It is possible, in fact, that what we learn simply through our experience of life at school plays a greater role in the cultural integration of our modern societies than what we acquire through all of the specifically cognitive learning processes, at least during our early years at school.

of organising time and space, of managing knowledge or social relations, of teaching, assessing and making judgements. As former pupils, these would-be teachers also necessarily have their own practical theory of the school. From a psychological standpoint, it is likely that, unless the teacher training programme directly addresses the existence of this "theory" among its trainees and its powers of "resistance", it will continue to survive as the main basis for their future conduct in class. We should point out that this way of transmitting the school culture, since it is efficient and economical, is highly desirable when the educational system is in a stable state. Being relatively immune to debate and controversy, the practical theory's survival is virtually assured. However, this means of transmission becomes more problematic when, as is now the case in the late 20th Century, the educational system is in a state of flux and the school culture is likely to have to change even though it is so deeply enmeshed in our individual and collective subconscious.

In certain fields, the school culture is already changing. During the past thirty years, perhaps nothing has changed as greatly in the schools (especially in primary schools) in our countries as certain of the more entrenched attitudes of teachers. I am thinking, for example, of the widespread acceptance of the principles of active pupil-centred pedagogy, the growing belief in a pedagogical approach based on the psychology of child development psychology, the gradual adoption of new procedures based on formative assessment or self-assessment of learning, etc. These ideas were not necessarily new; some of them are even very old. What did change was the extent to which they were accepted by teachers (and by parents, at least by middle class parents), coupled with the feeling that certain methods of teaching and supervision widely practised forty or fifty years ago had become obsolete. Under certain conditions which I cannot go into here, the principle of the perpetuating effect of the practical theory no longer holds true. It should be pointed out, however, that it was only because of great social pressure that this change in attitudes took place, that it took at least a generation to do so, and that the process is not entirely over even now.

The change in the culture of the school has, however, had little impact on the conception of schooling as a formally organised teaching and learning process, structured by a set of institutional rules. The first thing one notices about the prevailing image of education is that schools and educational systems are not really thought of (nor do they think of themselves) as organisations, although in all countries they are large, even very large, collective entities. The second thing is that, in schools, only teachers and administrators consider themselves or are considered by others to be workers (no doubt because they are paid for what they do). Pupils are indeed encouraged to "work", but they are not workers whose working conditions, for example are a concern, as is the case for the professional staff.

Nevertheless, within these "vast enterprises of knowledge" the work is organised, staffed, planned, structured, and co-ordinated. This comparison with business establishments provides a useful contrast which enables us more easily to situate the culture of the school in a present-day perspective. Banks, insurance companies and industrial firms long ago began to change the culture of the workplace. There is a growing trend towards promoting consultation and co-operation among workers, towards focusing on basic goals in the assessment and supervision of staff, towards fostering a culture of human resources, and towards devoting a significant portion of both their financial and human resources to research and technological or organisational innovation. Meanwhile, most of our education systems and schools still function along basically bureaucratic and Taylorian lines. The assessment and supervision of staff is still centred primarily on the observance of rules and regulations; workers are compartmentalised, isolated from one another (everyone works for themselves); teachers and pupils are defined by their role and status; they are considered to be completely interchangeable (this is particularly evident in the way teachers are assigned to pupils); consultation among teachers was long discouraged by an administration fearful of factions or intrigue, and even today, whenever consultation is organised (albeit to a very limited extent) it most often focuses on problems of pupil assessment or selection rather than on overall goals, educational strategies or interdisciplinary co-operation; and lastly, the investment in research and innovation is generally a totally insignificant portion of the overall educational budget.

More concretely, let us consider the way an educational establishment determines the use of time, one of its most important resources. First and foremost, educational schedules are strictly regulated by the clock (the most impersonal way possible). Each day is sliced up into micro-sequences, into class periods, and in between pupils are "zapped" from a mathematics class to a composition class, from history to geography. Regardless of the pupils' level or their ability to keep pace, the work expected of them progresses continuously with the passage of time. This time is added up into weeks, terms or semesters which are then totalled up into years. Often, this time imperative is more important in schools than the achievement of ultimate goals. Whether one is on time, early or late is what really matters. In this respect, schools behave more like an airline worried about keeping to its timetable than like a company training people to master complex skills. The analogy with airlines can be taken a step further since, like them, most schools take only a secondary interest in the overall itinerary of each of its users. Education systems and schools are justifiably concerned with the careers of their teachers, but only in exceptional cases do they attach much importance to the overall itinerary of their pupils (that is to say, over a number of years).

Historically, this method of apportioning time which today is so much an integral part of the school system came into being in the 16th Century. It is now fully five hundred year old, and has become so familiar that no one is really aware of it. Nevertheless, today we understand better the uneven and irregular (and rarely linear) nature of the learning process and of psychological development; we are also better able to measure individual differences in this respect. Considered from this standpoint, therefore, the traditional approach to the organisation of time in schools seems less and less rational. Can the new demand for high quality and effective education for all who go to school be satisfied without rethinking this central component of the school's culture, namely its timetable?

On another level, take the question of the evaluation of the work of teachers. All educational systems and all schools like to define their action in terms of lofty goals, usually however expressed in a rather vague and general manner. But when we examine more specifically the criteria for evaluating and monitoring their teachers (or indeed their pupils), it is clear that the matching of their work to these goals is a somewhat secondary consideration; following rules and regulations, however, is of the utmost importance. It is compliance with guidelines, instructions and official circulars as well as with the curriculum that is strictly enforced and sanctioned if necessary. Education systems and educators have yet to define credible methods for evaluating whether they truly achieve the goals that they describe so eloquently.

The regular and familiar way that schools operate actually corresponds quite closely to the bureaucratic model described by Max Weber. We know that in a bureaucracy any innovation emanating from the grassroots level is considered as a transgression of the rules and something that is best kept hidden. When it cannot be concealed, such innovation often means a head-on conflict with these existing rules. This can easily discourage those who wish to innovate. We should add, in a situation like this, the legitimate expectations of one's superiors and colleagues impose certain loyalties and patterns of behaviour: by and large, teachers feel that their first allegiance is to their institution and to their colleagues, with their users lagging well behind.

There is no denying that there are some very real advantages to this bureaucratic system of organisation. The first of these is that it ensures the smooth, relatively widely accepted and peaceful operation of these vast gatherings of young people we call schools. This system too was invented in the 16th Century and gradually perfected over time. It is, in fact, the historic "solution" to the problem posed by the often conflicting interests and expectations of pupils, parents, teachers, administrators, as well as political and business circles. Furthermore, coupled with certain other aspects of the school culture, it has facilitated the extraordinary expansion of the education system over the last thirty years. In addition, it is perfectly compatible with an education system in which picking out and concentrating on the best students takes precedence over high-quality education for all, and it ensures that a majority of young people are exposed to and gain an experience of bureaucratic methods and respect for rules and standards. During the educational process itself, learning respect for rules is often more important than mastering the subject, and the most gifted students quickly learn that it is important to maintain at least an outward appearance of conformity, and that one can slack off occasionally as long as one "keeps up one's average".

However, precisely because of these socialisation effects, this traditional bureaucratic system and its accompanying school culture also have their drawbacks. They are already perceived as being incompatible with the ambitious goals which we now assign to our education systems, and are likely to seem even more so in the future, assuming that schools take these goals seriously and make a real attempt to achieve them.

In a brief presentation, one has to use a fairly broad brush, and many points we have covered need to be qualified, analyzed in greater depth or explained more fully. But this is not the heart of the matter. The question that strikes me at the close of this conference on the curriculum is whether, when we discuss education for the 21st century, we should continue to focus so single-mindedly on the formal curriculum and programmes, that is, on the traditional elements that shape our education systems. Might we not do better to concentrate our analysis and strategic thinking on the whole set of unchanging elements within the school culture which go to make up the working conditions of teachers and pupils? To rethink and to restructure the way work is organised in schools, to reform the informal curriculum -- that is, the culture of the school -- is a programme for change so fundamental that it might also profoundly alter the way we envisage the formal curriculum.

3.   Mme Chiara Croce Castelletti

I wish to indicate what is, in my opinion, the most important innovative element for schools of the 21st century. The answer is undoubtedly not easy if you consider the school as "a system", since several changes should affect at the same time the different components of the system. It is impossible, for example to think of the curriculum as redefined, leaving out of consideration new methods of teacher training.

And yet I think there is a top priority objective and it is to identify and establish a balance between the requirements of those who have national and system responsibility and those who operate at the school level. I am convinced that the state must have the responsibility of education and that a national curriculum is of fundamental importance in guaranteeing democracy and equity for all, especially in a country where there are different social, economic and cultural circumstances. On the other it is undeniable that in different regions of the country, schools have their specific requirements and therefore they must have some freedom of action.

A balance between the centre and the regions could be built, in my opinion, on a strong relationship between the central Ministry and schools intended as "scientific laboratories" where new models of national interest are tried out. Today, in fact, the education system is often opaque, with insufficient communication and poor quality information between the centre and the regions, the centre and schools.

Yet, schools are not only isolated from the centre, but from each other and there are insufficient means for them to share their perceptions and exchange views on problems and issues of concern. They are close to their communities and have a more immediate sense of social movements, but this knowledge seldom is properly utilised.

This is harmful both for the schools and society at large: therefore we must work so that a new relationship is established between schools.

If problems were shared, the way would be paved towards an overall growth of the school system, (as the linking together of different schools in co-operative projects has well proved) and towards overcoming the division -- often artificial -- between national and local requirements.

The improvement in the *horizontal* and *vertical* communication could also assist the system need for accountability and could lead schools to much greater confidence on appropriate roles to be performed.

4. Dr Ed Bales

The present model of education is preparing students for a society and workplace which no longer exists. The private sector (business) has moved from the industrial model of work to the information age where the strategic resource is knowledge and the energy source is the mind.

Business as the customer of the education system proposes that the three components of the education mission are: preparation of students to be socially responsible in a democratic society, be employable, and have life-long learning skills. While the education system has students for 12-16 years, the business sector has them for 30-40 years.

Many industrial universities are beginning to educate and train the existing workforce. These industrial universities, (e.g. Motorola University) are necessary because the present education system is not providing the skills we now need.

The education system must understand that the changes necessary are systemic and must be addressed in a systemic way. This means that the curriculum, instructional methods and assessment methods must all be integrated because they are the interrelated components of the system.

The private sector has many excellent models of systemic change because business has had to adapt and modify itself in order to survive. These models of change, which are outside the education system, must be utilised by educators to understand the process of change and apply this process to their own system.

If the education system does not rapidly change to address the needs of the next century, most of the education jobs that exist currently will be obsolete by the year 2000. Educators will not survive because some other form of education will be developed by the business sector which needs a radically different workforce in order to continue.

5.   Dr Robert Harris

My first point emphasises the significance of the unemployment problem as we assess the future of education. The existence of long-term structural unemployment, particularly affecting the young, changes dramatically the perspective which young people have today as they complete their schooling. As the representative of BIAC has just stated, unless there are reasonable opportunities for employment, the approach which young people have to education is likely to be a negative one. There is therefore a heavy responsibility on the productive sectors of society. A statement on this matter was included in the joint TUAC/BIAC paper presented to the 1991 Conference of Ministers of education and is included as an annex to the report of that conference. I would again like to draw the attention of participants to this important statement.

Like other panellists, I was asked this morning to focus on one main point. I would like to focus on the question of participation in the process of change.

My initial thought was to emphasise the importance of consultation with education unions in OECD Member countries, which would be natural because I come from the Education International. Education unions in OECD countries are now discussing how to take a more pro-active role in education reform. However, from the preparatory papers for this conference and from the reports presented by the working groups, it is clear that there is a consensus around this table on the need to involve education unions in the development of education policy, in order to ensure the success of those policies, so it is perhaps not necessary for me to dwell any further on this point.

Rather, I would like to speak about the importance of involving not only the education unions but the trade union movement as a whole.

A theme which has been stressed repeatedly throughout this conference is that of the response of education to rapid societal change. Education reform movements have arisen to a large extent because of a perceived need to respond to societal changes, and in particular to economic constraints associated with them. One of the papers made the point that the term "education reform" is somewhat "loaded" and we should rather be speaking about educational change. Whether we use the term reform, or the term change, it is clear there is a dynamic process under way involving interaction between developments in education and developments in society.

That is part of the problem in any attempt to look into the future and to work out how education should prepare for that future.

I am reminded of a process we went through recently in my own organisation, called "strategic planning". Now strategic planning has been pursued in organisations of all kinds in many industrialised countries in recent years, within private companies and government ministries, and yes, within trade unions as well. I must admit that I was sceptical when this was first suggested in the case of our organisation. I thought it might be another one of those passing fads. However, we did find the exercise useful and I think this was so because we placed the emphasis on a process which is best described by analogy with an example from the world of sport.

The particular sport in question is the game of ice-hockey. The puck moves about the ice-hockey field with great speed and often changes direction rapidly in a way which is difficult to anticipate. The all-time highest goal scorer in ice-hockey is a player called Wayne Gretsky. When Gretsky was asked, some time ago, the secret of his success, he replied: "I skate to where the puck will be".

So we found strategic planning to be useful as an exercise by deciding that our collective task was to try to work out how we as an organisation should "skate to where the puck will be".

I submit that this statement sums up the challenge for education. We do not have to move towards a goal which is fixed, but rather to move towards an objective, or objectives which are changing rapidly and in ways which are difficult to anticipate. Education also has to "skate to where the puck will be".

The difficulty of putting this concept into practice is evident. Our only hope of success is to engage all partners in society in a collective, participatory, effort to figure out where the puck is likely to be, and how we should get there.

The only hope of achieving this is to involve all those concerned -- the teachers and the other education employees, through the education unions, the parents and students, civic societies, and the broader community of working people through the representative trade union movement. All the more so, since the trade union movement itself is undergoing major rethink about its role in society.

This participation and involvement should be sought at all levels -- the national level certainly, but also at the level of local communities and educational establishments. If we think of the EC, and to some extent EFTA and NAFTA, it also entails participation in decisions taken at the supra-national level.

Nothing, not even questions of salaries and conditions of employment (and those are important questions) would provide such a boost to the motivation and morale of teachers as the very real sense that they are fully recognised and engaged participants in the process of change.

The participation of teachers in a process which also involves the broader community will not only help to give a sense of direction which is sadly lacking in the education systems of most OECD countries today, but will also help to re-establish the recognition by the community that they so fully merit.

Broadly based participation in the process of change, with the full involvement of the social partners, will help to change the paradigm of debate from one which is determined essentially by economic concerns, to one which involves people and is closer to the realities which they experience.

6. Dr Bi Puranen

Bi Puranen of the Institute for Future Studies in Stockholm gave an innovative presentation in thinking about the curriculum of the future. She stressed the changing sociological dimensions that envelop the surroundings of the school. Firstly, the human life cycle has changed dramatically. Humans live much longer; the period between childbirth and death, humoristically illustrated by a caricature of a female Cro-Magnon, has nearly quadrupled in the last century. This phenomenon has far reaching implications for lifelong learning. Learning does not start at infancy and cease at an early point of adulthood, but continues through adult life. For man to survive in the complex and dynamically changing 21st century, lifelong learning must be cultivated in all members of society at all stages of life. As she emphasised quite fervently, lifelong learning is the survival strategy of the future.

What promotes lifelong learning is a propensity to learn, an aptness to the new and to the unknown. In the western philosophical tradition, the dialectic of change has been pushed forward by the diametrical opposition of opposites; for example, good and bad, master and slave, *sturm* and *drang*. In the Eastern tradition, symbolized by the forces of the *ying* and *yang*, opposites are encrusted in each other; the black is in the white, the white in the black. Society changes less as the result of warring contradictory forces, but vacillates within the realm of grey areas. It is within this grey area that Pi Puranen would wish to contemplate the future. The grey area is the area of the unknown, also symbolized by Ghandi holding a bowl, with the open end facing the sky. It is precisely the openness, the readiness to learn, the adaptability to rapid and unforeseen changes in society that propels humans forward in understanding their role in the future of the world.

A sense of historical continuity and an appreciation for man's physical environment is also an important factor in preparing for the future. She discussed the "Future Scope Programme" where a number of schools in European cites experiment with innovative models of schooling. One such school exists in Poitiers. The computer lab in the school has sand on the floor. Unlike the cold and sterile learning environments of many computer labs, this classroom reminds children of the natural matter that comprises the micro-chips in the computer hardware. Children then are able to reflect on the nature of high technology and the environment from which it originates.

Another factor which is important in building societies of the future is developing in all members of society a sense of genuine participation and belonging to the group, as defined as the nation state and sub-groups within the nation state. People need to feel that their work is of necessity and value, and that there is a sense of collaboration and proximity with other members of society. Another challenge for our societies is to find meaningful work for all citizens rather than repetitious, thoughtless activities estranged from enriching human experiences.

In conclusion, her presentation argues for a re-evaluation of the new in light of the past and present with an sustainable readiness for change, an inclination to adapt to an accept the unknown. Creating learning environments in compulsory schooling through to adult education which are guided by the concept of lifelong learning and take into account dynamic change will be a very valuable vehicle for cultivating survival tactics in the world of unknown futures.

Paper 18

THE OPTIONS TO EMERGE: WHERE DO WE TRAVEL FROM HERE?

Malcolm Skilbeck

This publication on "The Curriculum Re-defined", comes at the end-point of much thought and activity by OECD and its Member countries. It is also a beginning, building on activities which the conference seems to want to continue and initiating new and different activities. The basis for both development and change is here, in the strong interest shown throughout by the Member countries and the very active dialogue on future possibilities, a dialogue in which all participating countries have shared. This active interest demonstrates the relevance to us all of the key items identified by the conference.

The many valuable suggestions for further action are on record, and will be given the careful attention they deserve. The substantial degree of consensus shown in the distribution provides a good basis for future policies and actions. I have included the various issues under seven major headings which we at OECD will use as the basis for further discussion, study and action. The issues are substantial, complex and challenging. It will be necessary, in the consideration we give them, to gauge the extent to which it will be feasible to work on all fronts. Certainly, with the resources at our disposal there is need for a phased programme in the years ahead.

1.   Opportunity for all to learn.

A major implication of the concept of communication, and the commitment to a high quality education and training for all is the opportunity to learn. Our task, and a difficult one, is to make a reality out of that commitment, to identify and overcome barriers to learning. In a society involved in life-long learning, the capacity and the will to continue to learn are the essential requirements for each individual. What are the implications for the design of the school curriculum and for pedagogy? Do we have to consider a variety of types of school organisation? What are the implications for teacher education? How should we use time to achieve this entitlement? How can we make the core curriculum into the best short-term answer for our needs and still subject it to continuing appraisal? In this approach, the commitment to provide a foundation education for life-long learning is taken as fixed. All other aspects of the content, processes and organisation of education thus come under question. In the course of the conference we have addressed these questions and in attempting answers have identified an agenda for further collaborative effort among the Member countries grappling with them in their own national planning.

2.   The human condition.

All our societies experience the stress of major changes, both predictable and unpredictable. Our social conditions provide one set: social order and cohesion; family structures and patterns of operation; work patterns and employment; the economy and the distribution of wealth. Our physical conditions give another set: urbanisation, the green-house effect, the ionosphere, atmospheric pollution, the world's water supplies. Our political situation provides yet another: provision for minorities;

recognition of cultural differences, building a working consensus in a pluralist society; solving long-term problems in systems geared to short-term changes. These are examples only of elements of a context which raises grave doubts about the future. The 'human condition' is not a given, it reflects our responses to change that is pervasive and problematic. Both the curriculum as planned and taught conveys certain kinds of answers to the questions raised. A searching and profound analysis is required if these answers are to provide a basis for adequate learning in the future. In what ways can and should the curriculum respond to these contextual changes?

3. Critical interfaces and transitions.

Our attention at this conference has quite properly been focused on the period of compulsory schooling, or extending it slightly, the so-called K-12 sequence. Yet the reality is profoundly affected by discontinuities within the sequence, and disjunctions outside it.

Within the sequence now extending to 12 or 13 years of education there are transitions which frequently cause major discontinuities for students, discontinuities in content, in style, in organisation, in assumptions, in implicit purposes, in information flow. These may include the early childhood-primary transition, the primary-lower secondary transition, and the lower-upper secondary transition, not to mention the various changes of class within these sub-sequences. Have we found the best ways to arrange the total sequence of experience for students, to provide continuity and coherence in their learning? This is a system developed, piece by piece, over a long period. It is almost certainly not the most effective one as is shown by the incidence of school failure, dropouts, and the mediocre standard of learning achieved by many students, who find the sequence of studies an increasing source of boredom or alienation, compounding rather than helping to resolve such problems as low motivation and weak attention.

Of equal concern are the links with other major institutions or sectors: the home-school link, the school-work interface, the school-further education link. Whether these links worked well in the past is doubtful. What is certain now is that they must be more significant and more constructive in assisting learning. New pathways are needed linking for example, general and vocational education school, further education and work. How can that best be done?

4. Building a research and development base.

The potential importance of research in improving the quality of education for all has been a continuing strand throughout the conference. It was stressed in the activities before-hand and in the background papers for the conference. The paper by Marshall Smith stressed its centrality, both in the options it already suggests, and in the unanswered questions it should seek to resolve. OECD has a potentially valuable role in acting as a communication link, both in focusing on what is currently available and usable from research and in helping to identify the important questions to be answered. The Marshall Smith paper already contributes in both these regards. In relation to the questions many are readily identified as important. A few examples will suffice. What are examples of the most effective pedagogies? Under what conditions? For what purposes? What are the implications for teaching and learning of new types of design and delivery systems? What sorts of benefits and disadvantages accompany different types of school organisation? The transformation of research into pedagogical action remains a difficult task but progress continues to be made. Closer linkages are

209

needed between policy makers, the research community and the schools and CERI has a part to play here.

5.   Decision-making and communication.

Decision-making in the curriculum in a pluralist democratic society is a complex affair. It involves a number of areas of decision: purposes, content, teaching-learning process, organisation, evaluation, development.   It arouses the legitimate concern of many institutions and groups: government, business, the learned community, special interest groups, school decision makers, students, parents, teachers. It requires decisions at a variety of levels: national and sometimes international, regional, local and individual. In the different Member countries different patterns operate with respect to all these dimensions. Some patterns have particular historical bases in different societies. Given that there will almost certainly be diversity, are there particular constellations of decision making processes that have significant advantages? What are the roles of various partners? What is the impact of the changing functions at all levels of governance? How can we develop constructive dialogues between the various potential partners? Again the conference has contributed to the answering of these questions and no one would claim that the matter can satisfactorily rest there not least because of the continuing changes in the roles and relations of the different actions mentioned. Further intensive inquiry and analysis would seem to be of value to Member countries.

6.   Areas of knowledge and experience.

We have recognised in this conference the importance of developing further our understanding of the roles of science, of mathematics, of technology. The project covering this area has developed a valuable approach and will continue its work. In the area of humanities and the arts, our way ahead is less clear but no less important. Our project in that area has raised some important questions and the conference has heard a number of suggestions for further development, both in the schools and in higher education. Both these projects also identified the central, but frequently implicit, role played by values in education and the difficulty many schools and teachers encountered in dealing with contentious issues. It is in some of the wider areas of the curriculum, such as environmental studies, where science and technology and the social sciences, in this case politics and economics, converge.   The new convergences in the curriculum, and the shifting boundaries of areas of knowledge and experience, offer rich possibilities for further study with respect to curriculum implications e.g. integration on which CERI has done valuable if not always well understood work over the years. We are not clear, however, about the meaning of these shifting boundaries and new amalgamations for the school curriculum. There is need to explore more actively the relations between the knowledge domains and the particular rendering of them that we give in the definition of school subjects.

7.   Reconciling assessment for development and assessment for accountability.

We have been very conscious in this conference of the quite different possibilities made available by evaluation, including assessment of students. Three of our papers emphasise different aspects of educational policy and practice which may be supported and strengthened by evaluation. We have also been conscious in the history of education of the contradictions which can arise from inappropriate or conflicting uses of evaluation. There are current examples of this conflict. Yet the conference has expressed clearly and strongly the view that it is not only desirable but necessary to

210

reconcile the possible conflicts, in particular the conflict between the use of evaluation to assist students and teacher towards better learning and its use by others to monitor the broader system and its promises to ensure justice and equity and to use resources to the best effect. Both these approaches can be distorted, with ill-effects. Yet evaluation is such a powerful instrument in education for reform and improvement, that its use in both these roles is worth pursuing. In that pursuit it will be necessary to bring together the diverse interests, in particular those who use or are directly affected by the various approaches to assessment.

Paper 19

SUMMARY COMMENTS

Phillip Hughes, General Rapporteur

Seven Aspects of Curriculum Change: A Basis for Future Action

This conference publication brings together the papers and discussions of the four days in April, set in the context of the material made available to participants for their reflection. The publication cannot convey the breadth and warmth of the social exchange and the individual benefits to result. It can, however, indicate the sense of crisis and challenge, but not only this, of the opportunity which the participants shared together. This brief conclusion seeks to put together the elements held in common by the participants, not as a least common denominator, nor as prescriptions or recipes, but as starting points for action or for further consideration.

-- Our consideration of curriculum change is in a *context of social crisis* -- not just a crisis for schools but for the total fabric of our societies -- government, economy, families, religion, morality. That crisis is severe enough to raise serious questions on the nature of our future.

-- Schools are a *necessary part of the solution*, but only a part. Our purposes in schools must be purposes to which the broader society is committed and which schools seek whole-heartedly to interpret in "the attained curriculum", the actuality of school practice. For this to be possible the various elements of our society must work in partnership and with an understanding of the complex demands made on the different partners. For example, political leaders need to recognise the necessary complexity of the curriculum process and the *long time-scale of educational change* and, even more, of benefits to be derived from educational change. Equally, schools must recognise the contending force of political life and the *need to define and achieve short-term goals*, as inherent parts of our democratic pattern.

-- The concept of a *core curriculum*, is the school's contribution to *life-long learning*, a necessary part of democratic life: "establishing publicly known and acknowledged agreements about the substance of universal schooling, as a necessary part of the democratic condition". It is, if you like, a passport to participation, a life-long equity, the common base on which diversity and choice and individuality can be built. That core curriculum, and particularly its inclusiveness and equity, implies a redefined pedagogy and a constructive use of evaluation: constructive as a means of guideline learning for students and teachers, constructive as a means of providing parents with meaningful information, constructive as a means of helping systems to involve their communities, to ensure equity, to form the use of resources, to recognise and encourage quality. As Dr Carneiro said, this core curriculum is not a finished product but a sustainable adaptation. It is not a final solution but a continuing process, one which is a search for significance and meaning.

-- *As individuals*, we live, identify our needs, develop our purposes, work out our lives in many contexts: as persons, in families, in secular and/or religious communities, in regions, nations, international groupings. Where our needs and circumstances were once defined by the smaller and more intimate settings, they are increasingly shaped by and, in turn, help to shape the wider settings. Employment, peace, culture, the environment are national and international issues. *Internationalism* is not just a context for quaint comparisons, it is the powerful reality of the world we live in. Our exchanges between national groups, at this conference and in the future are not an optional extra but part of an attempt to construct a more caring, more just, more timely a learning society.

-- Our reason for working together towards such a society is not because of an existing consensus, but because of controversy and conflict. Our work is a *continuing search for a consensus* as an unfolding task, the unfinished and unfinishable task of building a curriculum for the future. In building that curriculum we will be involved in making and sharing decisions on purposes, content, style, settings, strategies, evaluations. Those decisions will be made where and by whom? By government, by business and industry, by interest groups, by universities, by schools, by parents. The answer is Yes, all of these, at appropriate levels of appropriate topics. The detail of who, at what level, on what topic needs careful definition, for this is the reality of participation. Within that partnership we have stressed the cultural roles of the teacher and the student, for their interaction gives final shape to the curriculum. It may be that we need to re-emphasise the role of the teacher: not so much the teacher as social worker, the teacher as counsellor, not even the teacher as facilitator or curriculum designer, but the teacher as teacher. There has been a tendency to down-grade the importance of that role yet it is vital, bringing a deep and continuing commitment to learning and personal development. Dr Puranen spoke of the Japanese concept of the teacher as "*sensei*", a figure of respect. This is a concept which our societies need to encourage now, for the crucial role of individual teachers is something to which each of us as individuals can attest.

-- We should not underestimate the *magnitude of the task of curriculum reform*. The school's part of the social contract is to create a high quality education and training for all. This is something more achieved before. We should neither underestimate nor shirk the task, but recognise that the alternative, a bitterly divided and unjust society, is not acceptable.

-- We should not underestimate *what can be achieved by a society* which recognises an urgent need and is prepared to recognise and welcome the talents of all its members, returning to be bound by past prejudices and exclusions. Such a society can bring the energy, intensity, ingenuity and caring which it has focused on sport or war to this peaceful, constructive task, a curriculum re-defined, a curriculum for the 21st century.

Bibliography

ABBOTT-CHAPMAN, HUGHES and WYLD (1991), *Improving Access of Disadvantaged Youth to Higher Education*, Department of Employment, Education and Training, Canberra.

ATKIN, Myron (1993), *CERI/OECD Project on Innovations in Science, Mathematics and Technology Education.* OECD, Paris.

AUSTRALIAN EDUCATION COUNCIL (AEC) (1989), The *Hobart Declaration*, AEC, Melbourne.

BALL, Christopher (1993), *Lifelong Learning and the Curriculum.* Paper for OECD Project.

BLACKBURN, Jean (1991), Public Schooling and the Democratic Commitment. *Education Quarterly*, No. 1.

BONO, Edward de (1973), *CoRT 1: Teachers' Handbook*, Pergamon Press, Oxford.

BOOMER, Garth (1992), The Advent of Standards in Australian Education. *Curriculum Perspectives*, Vol. 12, No. 1, April 1992.

BRENNAN, Séamus, Minister for Education, Ireland (1992), *Education for a Changing World.* Green Paper, Stationery Office, Dublin.

CAMPBELL and McMENIMAN (1992), New Horizons in Education, No. 87, December 1992.

CARMICHAEL, L. (1990), Quoted in Schools Council, 1990. *Australia's Teachers: An Agenda for the Next Decade,* AGPS, Canberra.

CDC (1980), *Core Curriculum for Australian Schools: What it is and Why it is Needed.* Curriculum Development Centre, Canberra.

CERI (1992), *Schools and Businesses: A New Partnership*, OECD, Paris.

CHALL, Jeanne S. et al. (1982), *Families and Literacy.* Final Report to the National Institute of Education, Washington, D.C.

DEBRAY, Rosine (1991), Reviving Thought Processes, in OECD, 1991.

ECKERSLEY, Richard (1990), *Casualties of Change.* Commission for the Future, Melbourne.

EIKEN, Odd (1992), *Keynote Address at OECD International Conference on Educational Co-operation*, Hiroshima, Japan.

FINN, Brian (1991), Chester, *Young People's Participation in Post-Compulsory Education and Training.* Report of the AEC Review Committee, AGPS, Canberra.

GAGNON, Paul (1982). Reported in *Wingspread Conference*, December 1982, Cambridge, Mass.

GARDNER, Howard (1983), *Frames of Mind*, Basic Books, New York.

HILL, Brian (1992), Setting Educational Goals for the Future. *New Horizons in Education*, No. 87, December 1992.

KENNEDY, Kerry (1991), *Towards a National Curriculum in Australia: Policy Developments as a Prescription for Action*, Paper at ACEA 1991 Conference.

MAYER (1992), *Employment-Related Key Competencies for Post-Compulsory Education and Training*, Mayer Committee, Melbourne.

MINISTERE DE L'EDUCATION NATIONALE (1989), *Educational Evaluation and Reform Strategies: National Policies and Strategies*, OECD, Paris.

MOON, Robert (1993), *CERI/OECD Project on Humanities and Arts in the Curriculum*, OECD, Paris.

MOSER, Sir Claus (1990), *Our Need for An Informed Society*. Presidential Address, The British Association for the Advancement of Science, Swansea, August 1990.

NEW ZEALAND MINISTRY OF EDUCATION (1993), *The New Zealand Curriculum Framework*. Learning Media, Ministry of Education, Wellington.

NISBET, John (Ed.) (1993), *Assessment and Curriculum Reform*, OECD, Paris.

OECD (1989), *Japan, Survey of Trends in Curriculum Reform*, OECD, Paris.

OECD Review (1991), OECD Review of National Policies for Education on the Netherlands.

OECD (1991), *Learning to Think: Thinking to Learn*, Pergamon Press, London.

OECD (1992), *OECD Economic Outlook*, December 1992, OECD, Paris.

OECD, Programme on Educational Building, 1992. *New Technology and the Impact on Educational Building*, OECD, Paris.

OECD (1992a), *High Quality Education and Training for All*, OECD, Paris.

OECD (1993), *Main Economic Indicators*, January 1993, OECD, Paris.

OKAMOTO, Kaoru (1992), *Education of the Rising Sun*. Ministry of Education, Science and Culture (Monbusho), Tokyo.

OSLER, Sir William (1913), Examinations, examiners and examinees, *Lancet*, 1913.

PATTEN, John (1993), Britain Opts in to a Better Kind of School, The Sunday Times, 31 January 1993.

POSTMAN, N. (1983), *Engaging Students in the Great Conversation*, Phi Delta Kappan, N.Y.

PRING, Richard (1989). *The New Curriculum*. Cassell, London.

RAIZEN, Senta (1991), *Learning and Work: The Research Base*. Paper for US Department of Education and OECD Seminar, March 1991, Phoenix, Arizona.

RAVITCH, DIANNE and FINN, Chester, (1990), *What Do Our Seventeen-Year-Olds Know?*, National Assessment of Educational Progress, Washington, D.C.

SHANKER, Albert (1990), *The End of the Traditional Model of Schooling*, Phi Delta Kappan, January 1949.

SKILBECK, Malcolm (1982), *A Core Curriculum for the Common School*. Inaugural Lecture, Institute of Education, University of London.

SKILBECK, Malcolm (1990), *Curriculum Reform: An Overview of Trends*, OECD, Paris.

SPAIN, (1990), *The White Paper for the Reform of Education Systems*. Ministry of Education and Science, English Version, Madrid.

SWEDISH MINISTRY OF EDUCATION AND SCIENCE (1992), *A school for Life: Report of the Commission on the Curriculum*. Stockholm, 1992.

US DEPARTMENT OF EDUCATION (1992), *World Class Standards for American Education*, OERI, Washington D.C.

US OFFICE OF EDUCATION, Washington (1991), *America 2000, an Educational Strategy*.

WALLIN, Eric (1993), *Lifelong Learning and Its Consequences for Upper Secondary Curriculum Planning*. Paper for OECD Project on Lifelong Learning.

WATKINS, Peter (1991), *From Secret Garden to Public Allotment: The Introduction of the National Curriculum in England*. Victorian Ministry of Education and Training, Melbourne, April 1991.

LIST OF PARTICIPANTS

CHAIRMAN

Sir Claus MOSER
Warden
Warden's Lodgings
Wadham College
Oxford OX1 3PN
United Kingdom

AUSTRALIA

Ms Fran HINTON
Assistant Secretary
Schools and Curriculum Policy Branch
Department of Employment, Education and Training
Canberra,
A.C.T.

Mrs Barbara JAMESON
Executive Oficer
ACTRAC
P.O. Box 1281
Frankston
Victoria 3199

Dr Lloyd LOGAN
Faculty of Education
University of Queensland
St. Lucia, Queensland

Ms Susic PASCOE
Co-ordinating Chairperson,
Policy Catholic Education Office
P.O. Box 146
East Melbourne 3002

AUSTRIA

Professor Werner LENZ
Institut für Erziehungswissenschaften
Attemgasse 8
9010 Graz

Mr Klaus SCHEDLER
Institut für Bildungsforschung der Wirtschaft
Rainergasse 38
1050 Vienna

Dr Christian DORNINGER
BmUK abt.22
Federal Chancellery
Vienna

Dr Karl PARISOT
Universität Salzburg
Hellbrunnerstr.34
5020 Salzburg

Mag. Richard STOCKHAMMER
BmUK, ABT.1/5
Federal Chancellery
Minoritenplatz 5
1014 Vienna

BELGIUM

Ms Rita DUNON
Service "Développement de l'enseignement"
Ministère de l'Enseignement
(Communauté flamande)
Rijksadministratief Centrum
Arcadengebouw
Handelskaai 7
1000 Bruxelles

Mme Valerie PIRON
Ministry of Education
Bld Puchico 19
1010 Bruxelles

Monsieur Martial LELEUX
Ministry of Education
Bld Puchico 19
1010 Bruxelles

CANADA

Mrs Robin SYNE
Director
Curriculum Division
Ministry of Education
British Columbia
201-633 Courtney Street
Victoria
British Columbia

CZECH REPUBLIC

Mr Josef NAGY
Ministry of Education
Youth and Sport
Department of Universities
Karmelitska 8
Prague 11812

DENMARK

Mr Ole BREINHOLDT
Statsseminarium
Vejlevej 2
DK 7300 Jelling
Copenhagen

FINLAND

Mr Pentti TAKALA
Director
National Board of Education
Hakaniemenkatu 2
00530 Helsinki

Dr Yrjö YRJÖNSUURI
Counsellor of Education
National Board of Education
Hakaniemenkatu 2
00530 Helsinki

FRANCE

Monsieur Philippe REYMOND
Ministère de l'Education Nationale
Direction des Affaires Internationales
173, Boulevard St. Germain
75006 Paris

Madame Monique CLAUDE
Principal
Collège Raymond Queneau
66, boulevard Saint-Marcel
75005 Paris

Monsieur Roger F. GAUTHIER
Sous Directeur, Direction des Ecoles
Ministère de l'Education Nationale
107, rue de Grenelle,
75007 Paris

Monsieur GUERIN
Sous Directeur à la Direction des Ecoles
Ministère de l'Education Nationale
107, rue de Grenelle,
75007 Paris

GERMANY

Herrn Regierungsdirektor SCHEIBENGRUBER
Staatsinstitut für Schulpädagogik und Bildungsforschung
8000 Munich 81
Arabellastr.1

GREECE

Mrs A. KOSTAKI
Pedagogical Institute
Messogion 396
Agia Paraskeui 15-341
Athens

HUNGARY

Mr Zoltan BATHORY
National Institute for Public Education,
1051 Budapest

IRELAND

Mr Patrick BOLAND
Senior Inspector
Department of Education Offices
1a South Mall
Cork

ITALY

Madame Chiara CASTELLETTI CROCE
Inspectrice du Ministère de l'Instruction Publique
Via Tuscolana 69
00182 Rome

Mr Orazio NICEFORO
Proviseur et membre du Conseil d'Administration du C.E.D.E.
Villa Falconieri
00044 Frascati

JAPAN

Mr Takashi YAMAGIWA
Chief School Inspector,
Elementary and Secondary Education Bureau
Ministry of Education, Science and Culture,
3-2-2 Kasumigaseki,
Chiyoda-ku, Tokyo

Mr Yoshihiro KIZAWA
Deputy Director
Elementary School Division
Elementary and Secondary Education Bureau,
Ministry of Education,
Science and Culture
3-2-2 Kasumigaseki,
Chiyodaku,
Tokyo

Mr Toshikazu ISHINO
Permanent Delegation to OECD
11, avenue Hoche,
75008 Paris

THE NETHERLANDS   Drs Jenne van der VELDE
National Institute for Curriculum Development (SLO)
Boulvard 1945 3
P.O. Box 2041
7511 AA Enschede

Drs Melis MELISSEN
Ministry of Education
Department for Secondary Education
Station 813, room E 203
P.O. Box 25000
2700 LZ Zoetermeer

NEW ZEALAND   Mr James IRVING
Policy division
Ministry of Education
P.O. Box 1666
Wellington

NORWAY   Mrs Torbjorg JAEGER
Head of Division
Ministry of Education, Research and Church Affairs
Akersgt. 42
Postbox 8119 Dep
0032 Oslo 1

221

Mrs Edel HAUKELAND
County Director of Schools
Ministry of Education, Research and Church Affairs
Akersgt. 42
Postbox 8119 Dep
0032 Oslo 1

PORTUGAL
Mme Brigitte THUDICHUM
Direction General des Enseignements Basiques et Secondaires
Av. 24 de Julho 140
Lisbon

SPAIN
Mr Jesus DOMINGUEZ
Ministry of Education and Science
Service d'Innovation de la Direction Général de Programmes
Expérimentaux du Ministère de l'Education et de la Science
Calle General Oraa, 55
28006 Madrid

SWEDEN
Ms Berit HÖRNQUIST
Head of Section,
National Agency for Education,
106 20 Stockholm

Mr Mats BJÖRNSSON
Head of Section,
National Agency for Education
106-20 Stockholm

SWITZERLAND
M. Jean-Pierre MEYLAN
Secrétariat CDIP, division de l'enseignement post-obligatoire, de
la recherche et de la planification
Sulgeneckstrasse 70
3005 Berne

TURKEY
Professor Ayse KIRAN
Hacettepe Universitesi
Egitim Fakültesi
Ankara

Mr Izzet CEZIK
MEB Talin ve Terbiye Kurulus
Ankara 212 6530

UNITED KINGDOM

HMI Mr John SINGH
OFSTED
Department for Education
Elizabeth House
York Road
London SE1 7PH

Mr M.B. BAKER
Assistant Secretary
Department of Education
Sanctuary Buildings
Great Smith Street
Westminster
London SW1P 3BT

Mr John HAMER
OFSTED
Turret House
1 Jenner Road
Guildford
Surrey GU1 3PH

Mr Neil STRAKER
OFSTED
Warwick House
Grantham Road
Newcastle-upon-Tyne NE2 1SW

Dr Roger AUSTIN
Faculty of Education
University of Ulster
Coleraine
County Londonderry BT 52 1FA

Mr Chris WOODHEAD
Chief Executive
National Curriculum Council
Albien Wharf
25 Skeldergate
York YO1 2XL

Mr WARDLE
Department for Education
Room 4.34
Sanctuary Buildings
Great Snith Street
London SW1P 3BT

HMI Mrs M. MACFARLANE
Scottish Office Education Department
Room 4/110
New St. Andrew's House
Edinburgh EH1 3TG

U.S.A.

Dr Marshall SMITH
Advisor to the Secretary
U.S. Department of Education
400 Maryland Avenue S.W.
Washington D.C. 20202

Dr Joseph CONATY
Acting Director
Officer of Research
U.S. Department of Education
555 New Jersey Avenue, NW
Washington, D.C. 20208
N.W. Washington D.C. 20208-5570

Mr Sam McKEE
International and Territorial Services Staff
U.S. Department of Education
400 Maryland Avenue S.W.
Washington D.C. 20202

Mr Richard NANCE
Howard-Winneshiek Community School District
1000 Schroder Drive
Cresco,
Iowa

C.C.E./E.C.C.

Mme A. FRACCHIA
Expert à la Task Force Ressources Humaines,
Education Commission des Communautés Européennes
200 rue de la Loi
1049 Bruxelles
Belgium

BIAC

Mr Edward W. BALES
Vice Chairman of the BIAC
Committee on Education, Director of Education, External Systems
Motorola University
Motorola Inc.
1303 E. Algonquin Road
Schaumburg, Illinois 60196

224

Mr Jan EDGREN
Swedish Employers' Confederation
S-103 30 Stockholm
Sweden

TUAC Mr Andreas BOTSCH
TUAC
Assistant to the General Secretary
26 avenue de la Grande-Armée
75017 Paris
France

Mr Robert HARRIS
Executive Director
Education International
5 avenue du Moulin
1110 Morges
Switzerland

UNESCO Mr Colin N. POWER
Assistant director general for education
7 place de Fontenoy
75007 Paris
France

Mr Hans-Wolf RISSOM
Chief
Co-ordination and Evaluation Unit, Education Sector
7 place de Fontenoy
75007 Paris
France

Mrs Leslie LIMAGE
Education Sector
7 place de Fontenoy
75007 Paris
France

COUNCIL OF EUROPE Monsieur Jean Pierre TITZ
Administrateur
Section de l'enseignement scolaire et extrascolaire
BPUSIR6 Strasbourg Cedex 67006
France

EXPERTS

Professor J. Myron ATKIN
School of Education
Stanford University
STANFORD
California 94305
U.S.A.

Professor Paul J. BLACK,
Centre for Educational Studies
King's College London
University of London
Cornwall House Annex
Waterloo Road
London SE1 8TX
U.K.

Professor Eric BOLTON
Institute of Education
University of London
20 Bedford Way
London WC1 HOAL
U.K.

Dr Roberto CARNEIRO
President TV1
TV IND. s.a.
Edificio Altego
Rua 3, 6to piso
Sala 609
Braco de Prata
1900 Lisboa
Portugal

Professor Didier DACUNHA-CASTELLE
Directeur
Conseil National des Programmes
Ministère de l'Education Nationale et de la Culture
131 rue du Bac
75007 Paris
France

Professor Judith CHAPMAN
Department of Education
The University of Western Australia
Nedlands, Perth
Western Australia 6009

Dr Peter HÜBNER
Senatsverwaltung für Schule
Berufsbildung und Sport
Bredtschneider str. 5-8
1000 Berlin 19
Germany

Professor Walo HUTMACHER
Directeur
Service de la recherche sociologique
Département de l'instruction publique
8 rue du 31 décembre
1207 Geneve
Switzerland

Professor Robert MOON
Professor of Education
The Open University
Walton Hall
Milton Keynes MK7 6AA
U.K.

Professor John NISBET
Department of Education
King's College
University of Aberdeen
Aberdeen AB9 2UB
U.K.

Professor T. PLOMP
University of Twente
Faculty of Educational Science and Technology
P.O.Box 217
7500 AE Enschede
Netherlands

Dr Bi PURANEN
Co-Director
The Swedish Institute for Future Studies
Box 6799, S-113 85 Stockholm
Sweden

Professor Helen SIMONS
School of Education
University of Southampton
Highfield
Southampton S09 5NH
U.K.

Professor Claude THÉLOT
Directeur de l'Evaluation et de la Prospective
Ministère de l'Education Nationale
110 rue de Grenelle
75007 Paris
France

Professor Birgitte TUFTE
The Royal Danish School of Educational Studies
Centre of Mass Communication Research and Media Education
Emdrupvej 101
2400 Copenhagen
Denmark

OBSERVERS

Professor David ASPIN
Faculty of Education
Monash University
Melbourne
Australia

Mr J.M. BEDNALL
The Hutchins School
Sandy Bay
Tasmania, 7005
Australia

Dr Patricia BROADFOOT
School of Education
University of Bristol
35 Berkeley Square
Bristol BS8 1JA
U.K.

Mr T. HORIO
Faculty of Education
The University of Tokyo
Hongo 7-3-1
Bunkyo-Ku 113
Japan

Mr Jack KEATING
Visiting Scholar
The Institute for Education
20 Bedford Way
London

Ms. MCGHIE
S.C.C.C.
Gardyne Road
Boroughly Ferry
Scotland
U.K.

Mr D.S. MCNEILL
St. Michael's Collegiate School
218 Macquarie Street,
Hobart 7000 P.O. Box 215
Sandy Bay,
Tasmania 7005
Australia

Professor David SKILTON
University of Wales
College of Cardiff
P.O. Box 94
Cardiff CF1 3XB
U.K.

Dr STUART
SCCC
Gardyne Road
Boroughty Ferry
Scotland

Professor Margaret SUTHERLAND
46 The Scores
St. Andrews
Fife
U.K.

Mrs Evangeline STEFANAKIS
Harvard Institute of International Development
Longfellow Hall
Cambridge, Mass. 02138
U.S.A.

Ms Penelope WESTON
National Foundation for Educational
Research in England and Wales
The Mere, Upton Park
Slough, Berks S11 2DQ
U.K.

Ms Jennifer WILLIAMS
Executive Director
British American Arts Association
116 Commercial Street
London E1 6NF
U.K.

OECD SECRETARIAT

Mr Pierre VINDE
Deputy Secretary-General

Mr Thomas J. ALEXANDER
Director, Education, Employment, Labour and Social Affairs and
Director of CERI

Mr Malcolm SKILBECK
Deputy Director for Education

Mr David THOMAS
Counsellor

Mr Phillip HUGHES
Consultant

Miss Christina PANOTIS
Consultant

MAIN SALES OUTLETS OF OECD PUBLICATIONS
PRINCIPAUX POINTS DE VENTE DES PUBLICATIONS DE L'OCDE

ARGENTINA – ARGENTINE
Carlos Hirsch S.R.L.
Galería Güemes, Florida 165, 4° Piso
1333 Buenos Aires   Tel. (1) 331.1787 y 331.2391
                                   Telefax: (1) 331.1787

AUSTRALIA – AUSTRALIE
D.A. Information Services
648 Whitehorse Road, P.O.B 163
Mitcham, Victoria 3132   Tel. (03) 873.4411
                              Telefax: (03) 873.5679

AUSTRIA – AUTRICHE
Gerold & Co.
Graben 31
Wien I   Tel. (0222) 533.50.14

BELGIUM – BELGIQUE
Jean De Lannoy
Avenue du Roi 202
B-1060 Bruxelles   Tel. (02) 538.51.69/538.08.41
                           Telefax: (02) 538.08.41

CANADA
Renouf Publishing Company Ltd.
1294 Algoma Road
Ottawa, ON K1B 3W8   Tel. (613) 741.4333
                             Telefax: (613) 741.5439
Stores:
61 Sparks Street
Ottawa, ON K1P 5R1   Tel. (613) 238.8985
211 Yonge Street
Toronto, ON M5B 1M4   Tel. (416) 363.3171
                             Telefax: (416)363.59.63

Les Éditions La Liberté Inc.
3020 Chemin Sainte-Foy
Sainte-Foy, PQ G1X 3V6   Tel. (418) 658.3763
                             Telefax: (418) 658.3763

Federal Publications Inc.
165 University Avenue, Suite 701
Toronto, ON M5H 3B8   Tel. (416) 860.1611
                             Telefax: (416) 860.1608

Les Publications Fédérales
1185 Université
Montréal, QC H3B 3A7   Tel. (514) 954.1633
                             Telefax : (514) 954.1635

CHINA – CHINE
China National Publications Import
Export Corporation (CNPIEC)
16 Gongti E. Road, Chaoyang District
P.O. Box 88 or 50
Beijing 100704 PR   Tel. (01) 506.6688
                             Telefax: (01) 506.3101

DENMARK – DANEMARK
Munksgaard Book and Subscription Service
35, Nørre Søgade, P.O. Box 2148
DK-1016 København K   Tel. (33) 12.85.70
                             Telefax: (33) 12.93.87

FINLAND – FINLANDE
Akateeminen Kirjakauppa
Keskuskatu 1, P.O. Box 128
00100 Helsinki
Subscription Services/Agence d'abonnements :
P.O. Box 23
00371 Helsinki   Tel. (358 0) 12141
                             Telefax: (358 0) 121.4450

FRANCE
OECD/OCDE
Mail Orders/Commandes par correspondance:
2, rue André-Pascal
75775 Paris Cedex 16   Tel. (33-1) 45.24.82.00
                             Telefax: (33-1) 49.10.42.76
                               Telex: 640048 OCDE

OECD Bookshop/Librairie de l'OCDE :
33, rue Octave-Feuillet
75016 Paris   Tel. (33-1) 45.24.81.67
                                  (33-1) 45.24.81.81

Documentation Française
29, quai Voltaire
75007 Paris   Tel. 40.15.70.00

Gibert Jeune (Droit-Économie)
6, place Saint-Michel
75006 Paris   Tel. 43.25.91.19

Librairie du Commerce International
10, avenue d'Iéna
75016 Paris   Tel. 40.73.34.60

Librairie Dunod
Université Paris-Dauphine
Place du Maréchal de Lattre de Tassigny
75016 Paris   Tel. (1) 44.05.40.13

Librairie Lavoisier
11, rue Lavoisier
75008 Paris   Tel. 42.65.39.95

Librairie L.G.D.J. - Montchrestien
20, rue Soufflot
75005 Paris   Tel. 46.33.89.85

Librairie des Sciences Politiques
30, rue Saint-Guillaume
75007 Paris   Tel. 45.48.36.02

P.U.F.
49, boulevard Saint-Michel
75005 Paris   Tel. 43.25.83.40

Librairie de l'Université
12a, rue Nazareth
13100 Aix-en-Provence   Tel. (16) 42.26.18.08

Documentation Française
165, rue Garibaldi
69003 Lyon   Tel. (16) 78.63.32.23

Librairie Decitre
29, place Bellecour
69002 Lyon   Tel. (16) 72.40.54.54

GERMANY – ALLEMAGNE
OECD Publications and Information Centre
August-Bebel-Allee 6
D-53175 Bonn   Tel. (0228) 959.120
                             Telefax: (0228) 959.12.17

GREECE – GRÈCE
Librairie Kauffmann
Mavrokordatou 9
106 78 Athens   Tel. (01) 32.55.321
                             Telefax: (01) 36.33.967

HONG-KONG
Swindon Book Co. Ltd.
13–15 Lock Road
Kowloon, Hong Kong   Tel. 366.80.31
                             Telefax: 739.49.75

HUNGARY – HONGRIE
Euro Info Service
Margitsziget, Európa Ház
1138 Budapest   Tel. (1) 111.62.16
                             Telefax : (1) 111.60.61

ICELAND – ISLANDE
Mál Mog Menning
Laugavegi 18, Pósthólf 392
121 Reykjavik   Tel. 162.35.23

INDIA – INDE
Oxford Book and Stationery Co.
Scindia House
New Delhi 110001   Tel.(11) 331.5896/5308
                             Telefax: (11) 332.5993
17 Park Street
Calcutta 700016   Tel. 240832

INDONESIA – INDONÉSIE
Pdii-Lipi
P.O. Box 269/JKSMG/88
Jakarta 12790   Tel. 583467
                             Telex: 62 875

IRELAND – IRLANDE
TDC Publishers – Library Suppliers
12 North Frederick Street
Dublin 1   Tel. (01) 874.48.35
                             Telefax: (01) 874.84.16

ISRAEL
Praedicta
5 Shatner Street
P.O. Box 34030
Jerusalem 91430   Tel. (2) 52.84.90/1/2
                             Telefax: (2) 52.84.93

ITALY – ITALIE
Libreria Commissionaria Sansoni
Via Duca di Calabria 1/1
50125 Firenze   Tel. (055) 64.54.15
                             Telefax: (055) 64.12.57
Via Bartolini 29
20155 Milano   Tel. (02) 36.50.83
Editrice e Libreria Herder
Piazza Montecitorio 120
00186 Roma   Tel. 679.46.28
                             Telefax: 678.47.51
Libreria Hoepli
Via Hoepli 5
20121 Milano   Tel. (02) 86.54.46
                             Telefax: (02) 805.28.86
Libreria Scientifica
Dott. Lucio de Biasio 'Aeiou'
Via Coronelli, 6
20146 Milano   Tel. (02) 48.95.45.52
                             Telefax: (02) 48.95.45.48

JAPAN – JAPON
OECD Publications and Information Centre
Landic Akasaka Building
2-3-4 Akasaka, Minato-ku
Tokyo 107   Tel. (81.3) 3586.2016
                             Telefax: (81.3) 3584.7929

KOREA – CORÉE
Kyobo Book Centre Co. Ltd.
P.O. Box 1658, Kwang Hwa Moon
Seoul   Tel. 730.78.91
                             Telefax: 735.00.30

MALAYSIA – MALAISIE
Co-operative Bookshop Ltd.
University of Malaya
P.O. Box 1127, Jalan Pantai Baru
59700 Kuala Lumpur
Malaysia   Tel. 756.5000/756.5425
                             Telefax: 757.3661

MEXICO – MEXIQUE
Revistas y Periodicos Internacionales S.A. de C.V.
Florencia 57 - 1004
Mexico, D.F. 06600   Tel. 207.81.00
                             Telefax : 208.39.79

NETHERLANDS – PAYS-BAS
SDU Uitgeverij Plantijnstraat
Externe Fondsen
Postbus 20014
2500 EA's-Gravenhage   Tel. (070) 37.89.880
Voor bestellingen: Telefax: (070) 34.75.778

NEW ZEALAND
NOUVELLE-ZÉLANDE
Legislation Services
P.O. Box 12418
Thorndon, Wellington   Tel. (04) 496.5652
                             Telefax: (04) 496.5698

OECD PUBLICATIONS, 2 rue André-Pascal, 75775 PARIS CEDEX 16
PRINTED IN FRANCE
(96 94 06 1) ISBN 92-64-14183-9 - No. 47339 1994